The Streets *of* St. Louis

William B. and Marcella C. Magnan

Copyright © 1994 and 1996 by William B. Magnan

All rights reserved. No part of this book may be reproduced in any form or by any electronic or mechanical means, including information storage and retrieval systems without permission in writing from the author, except by a reviewer, who may quote brief passages in review.

Printed in the United States of America

Second Edition

Library of Congress Cataloging-in-Publication Data
Magnan, William B.

Streets of St. Louis by
William B. Magnan and Marcella C. Magnan

ISBN 0-9638816-2-0

1. St. Louis, Missouri-History
2. History-St. Louis, Missouri

Library of Congress number: Pending

Edited and read by: Jeffrey Fister, Jay Nies, Anna Ross and Frances Hurd Stadler

Table of Contents

Dedication
Author's Notes
Acknowledgments

PART I: HISTORY OF ST. LOUIS STREET NAMES ~ 9

Chapter 1	EARLY HISTORY	10
Chapter 2	ST. LOUIS AND STATEHOOD	17
Chapter 3	EARLY ARRIVALS	24
Chapter 4	GROWTH AS A CITY	34
Chapter 5	TRAGEDY AND RECOVERY	40
Chapter 6	REBUILDING AND IMMIGRANTS	44
Chapter 7	NORTH ST. LOUIS	50
Chapter 8	SOUTH ST. LOUIS	55
Chapter 9	COMPTON HEIGHTS - SHAW - RUSSELL	64
Chapter 10	SOUTHWEST ST. LOUIS	74
Chapter 11	WEST END, COUNTY AND OUTSTATE	80
Chapter 12	DUELS AND PARKS	91
Chapter 13	MISCELLANEOUS INFORMATION	98
Chapter 14	CHURCHES	103
Chapter 15	HISTORICAL TABLES	106

PART II: APPENDICES ~ 111

Appendix I	STATES	112
Appendix II	GOVERNORS AND MAYORS	116
Appendix III	ST. LOUIS PUBLIC SCHOOLS	143
Appendix IV	STREETS AND ZIP CODES	174
Appendix V	MISCELLANEOUS VIGNETTES	176
Appendix VI	BIBLIOGRAPHY AND SOURCES	184

PART III: INDEX OF STREET NAMES ~ 188

This book is dedicated
to the memory of:

Alois D. Schaefer

*A fellow Letter Carrier
who was my friend,
sometimes mentor,
and my St. Louis big brother.*

"I'll meet you at the regular place, Al."

and

Cecilia M. Wesselny

*Our Loving Mother
Caring Grandmother of our Children
Proud Great-Grandmother of their Children*

*You will always be with us in our hearts,
as we try to live what you taught us.*

Author's Notes

The information contained in this book was gathered over many years, for my own information and pleasure.

I was born and raised in Kalamazoo, Michigan. I joined the Navy in World War II and was sent to St. Louis to attend school. I met a special girl while stationed in St. Louis; we corresponded while I was overseas, and when the war ended I came back to the States. We married and stayed in St. Louis. I've always considered myself a "War Groom."

Many other veterans were also looking for work when I was discharged, so finding the right job was not an easy task. I took a temporary job with the post office until I could get one in the field I wanted. It became a case of "I wanted what I found," and nearly 34 years later I retired from the post office.

My wife Marcella, on the other hand, stayed home and raised our family. We were blessed with seven children, five boys and two girls. There is a 16-year span from the oldest to the youngest, and Marcella often said she felt like her mental capacity was stuck in pre-school and primary grades for 24 years. After the children were grown, she returned to the business world for 10 wonderful years. When she retired, she took writing courses for her own pleasure through OASIS, and Elderhostels; I gravitated to history classes. In retrospect, it seems that we were guided in many decisions of our life.

As a stranger to St. Louis, so to speak, I was fascinated with the eclectic mixture of street names. Many cities have numbered streets — a Main Street, streets named Broadway, Grand, Elm, etc. The names of St. Louis streets sounded unique to me. I wanted to know why some neighborhoods seemed to have "clustered" street names while other neighborhood street names didn't seem to have any underlying connection. All the years I worked in the postal service, I gathered information about St. Louis from many sources, to save it for my retirement years when I would have more time to thoroughly pursue the subject.

I do not consider myself a historian; I am just interested in history and I enjoy reading. After I retired, I seriously started reading books about the history of St. Louis and took notes about interesting facts from most of them. I was intrigued to discover how many lives and families are interwoven in the street names. In the course of this discovery, I spent many hours in libraries and at the Missouri Historical Society, studying maps from different time periods and trying to satisfy my insatiable curiosity.

The information I gathered was so interesting and exciting that I shared some of it with a walking group I joined at Stupp Memorial Garden in Tower Grove Park. One member suggested I give a talk to the group as a whole, instead of just telling one or two walking partners of the day. She both publicized the fact that I would talk on this subject and made all the arrangements.

I was amazed when 50 people arrived. I have given hundreds of talks since that first one, usually to AARP and other Senior, church and civic groups, and those attending always wanted more. They asked for a book to permit them to share the information with family and friends who had been unable to attend, and also to be able to refresh their own memories at a later date. I still get numerous requests for the book I never intended to write.

Marcella and I started putting the information into book form and discussed the possibility of publishing it with several people. Reactions varied from positive to negative, with dire warnings about the involvement of massive expenditures of time and money. I had plenty of time but no money. We were very discouraged.

After several disappointing experiences with publishers, we finally have a book we are proud of. We included some stories that are not about St. Louis streets; they are about Missouri, St. Louis and the people who resided there, along with a few other vignettes that we found interesting and wanted to share with you.

We hope you enjoy the product of our efforts.

Acknowledgments

After working on this project for a number of years, I must acknowledge my appreciation to many people; some for their actions, some I had the pleasure of meeting. Some I only know their names but I enjoy the facts learned as a result of their efforts.

My wife Marcella who always worked with me, who typed and retyped my talks as I learned new facts, corrected my spelling and punctuation, rephrased thoughts at times, and helped check and edit the manuscript over and over. She patiently sits through many, many presentations, serving as my timekeeper and loving critic. She has always encouraged and helped me in everything I have done. Any success I may attain is due to her supportive presence and assistance.

Although my parents have been dead for many years. I am still aware of the influence of their early training.

The Sisters of St. Joseph who took this shy, skinny, stubborn, confused, redheaded boy, and inspired him to learn during his twelve years under their tutelage at St. Augustine School in Kalamazoo, Michigan. Using patience, love and care, they infused a curiosity, a perception for facts, and a thirst for knowledge which I still have. I will never forget them.

Our seven children, who really didn't like to accompany us to Soulard Market every Saturday, but had to come so that they wouldn't miss any part of the stories I told while we waited for Mom to do the shopping. They continue to impress and assist me, and periodically boost my ego.

Innumerable librarians, archivists, and historical enthusiasts, far too numerous to mention by name; they all deserve my thanks for their courteous reception and assistance. Marilyn Ferrario, a librarian at the Kingshighway Branch Library, my primary source, was particularly helpful. She delved into many records to locate older books for my research; at times she found information in some books I didn't know existed.

Other people loaned me books that are out of circulation, which contained information I would not have had access to. Other friends recommended an origin or resource, contributed advice and supplied encouragement. After a presentation, people still often give me information about a street or streets that were part of their family history. I would never have discovered these facts without their kindness in sharing them with me.

I am also deeply grateful to any others who helped me, and who have enriched my life over the years by their presence.

I have been as accurate as humanly possible in gathering this information. I accepted all information, as disclosed to me, in good faith. If mistakes were made, please forgive these errors; they were not intentional and are certainly without malice.

Part I

History of St. Louis Street Names

Chapter 1

Early History

When I drive south of Chippewa on Macklind Avenue and see the streets named Sutherland, Lansdowne, Nottingham and Devonshire, I sometimes smile and remember the first day I carried mail in St. Louis. The supervisor of Gardner Station Post Office assigned me to help the letter carrier on Route 931. "You will be working in the heart of the South St. Louis Dutch," he said. "Go out the front door, take a Chippewa Bus east, get off at Kingshighway, transfer to a Southampton street car going south, ride to the end of the line at Macklind and Devonshire, walk one block north and start delivering the mail on Lansdowne Avenue."

I came from Michigan, accustomed to Holland Dutch names, and none of those sounded like Dutch names to me. I wondered why streets with English names would be "in the heart of South St. Louis Dutch." I soon learned that the "Dutch" of South St. Louis referred to German heritage. It was quite a long while before I discovered the English connection.

I was a substitute letter carrier for six years, and worked at many different postal stations around the city. In some neighborhoods I could see a general theme for the names of streets, but I could not understand the reason for the eclectic assortment of names in other areas. I learned that St. Louis grew by absorbing small communities; some were ethnic in nature and the street names reflected that. Names of other streets honored early explorers, settlers, land owners, surveyors and developers of the city. Many other streets were named for Europeans who helped the Colonies in the Revolutionary War. As I continued to read and study early maps, I began to understand the reason behind the placement of the varied assortment of names.

I'd like to give a brief history of the area, to start my story.

We all know Christopher Columbus has a part in the history of our country because of his explorations in 1492. Columbus is honored by a statue in Tower Grove Park in South St. Louis.

Forty-nine years later, in 1541, another European, a Spaniard named Hernando De Soto, explored the Mississippi River. He named the river "Rio del Espiritu Santo," meaning River of the Holy Spirit.

One hundred thirty-two years after De Soto, records show that two French explorers, Louis Jolliet and a Jesuit missionary Father Jacques Marquette, came down the Mississippi River from Canada in 1673. They were exploring the "Ne-Tongo," the Sioux name for "Big River." Jolliet and Marquette traveled as far as the Arkansas River before returning to Canada. The Sioux name for the Missouri River is "Ne-Shodse," meaning "Muddy River"; Ne-Osho means Main River, Ne-Ska means White River and Ne-Braska means Flat River.

The Algonquin Indians called it the "Mississippi." Their word for big is "missi," their word for river is "sippi," and their word for boat is "souri"; thus "Big Boat," because only large canoes could navigate the swift and rough waters of the Missouri River. "Mer" means "ugly," and "amec," means fish; Meramec therefore means "ugly fish," which must be a reference to the catfish. The wide range of the Algonquin language is shown by the Merrimack River in Massachusetts and a Mississippi River near Ottawa, Canada. "Gan" means lake, Missigan (Michigan) means "Big Lake." The Algonquins' also had a word for anything with a bad smell. A strong odor hung heavy in the air where a river emptied into Lake Michigan; the water was covered with decaying wild onions. The city founded there still carries the Algonquin name for bad smell — "Chicago."

Nine years after Jolliet and Marquette, Frenchmen Robert Cavelier Sieur De La Salle and Henri De Tonty left Canada to explore the Mississippi River. They reached the Gulf of Mexico on April 9, 1682 and claimed the entire valley for France. It is estimated that this territory covered 1,245,000 square miles. (see Chapter 15, Page 107) They named this land Louisiana, for King Louis XIV of France.

Sixteen years later, in 1703, Catholic missionaries established an Indian mission on a small river located a few miles south of the junction of the Missouri and the Mississippi rivers. This mission did not survive because the Indians moved from the west to the east side of the Mississippi River. The name the Indians gave this small river is still used; in English it would be "River of the Fathers," but the French name is "River Des Peres."

At the end of the French and Indian War, the Mississippi Valley, which until this time had been claimed by France, was divided by the Treaty of Paris signed on February 10, 1763. The English acquired everything east of the river; the French kept the land on the west side of the river, which they secretly transferred to Spain.

Pierre Laclede left New Orleans in 1763 with his young companion Auguste Chouteau and 28 men, and founded what is now St. Louis on February 15, 1764. Although Laclede knew that the territory east of the Mississippi River belonged to England, he did not know that the territory west of the river belonged to Spain. He believed he was establishing a fur trading post on French soil. He named St. Louis after King Louis IX of France. A statue of this king, dressed in full armor and mounted on a horse, now stands in front of the Art Museum in Forest Park. It was often used as the symbol of the city of St. Louis before the Arch was built in 1965.

Although Chouteau was only 13 when St. Louis was established, the men respected him because he could read and write. Also, Laclede had entrusted him with many responsibilities on the journey. Many years after Chouteau's death, his weather-worn tombstone in Calvary Cemetery was replaced and the year of his birth was changed from 1750 to 1740. This new inscription added 10 years to his age when he first arrived in St. Louis. If he had been 23 when he arrived with Laclede, his mother would have been 7 years old when he was born!

Auguste Chouteau's mother, Madame Marie Therese Chouteau, is buried on the Pierre Chouteau family plot in Calvary Cemetery. Madame Chouteau was born in 1733 and died on August 14, 1814; Auguste Chouteau was born on September 17, 1750, and died on February 24, 1825.

Charles Gratiot and Gabriel Cerré, French merchants and traders, were living in Illinois. Gratiot had been a prisoner of the English during the French and Indian War when Ottawa Indian Chief Pontiac rescued him. Both Gratiot and Cerré moved across the river to the Village of St. Louis. Soon more French inhabitants living east of the river moved to Laclede's village, including the French commandant Louis St. Ange de Bellerive and the soldiers under his command. Bellerive served as governor until the Spanish sent a replacement on May 20, 1770. Life in the village did not change; the French soldiers simply changed from French to Spanish uniforms, and everyone continued to speak French.

Seven Spanish governors served in the Louisiana Territory. Although the village remained under the jurisdiction of Spain for 36 years, Spain never tried to colonize the territory. One important item the Spanish introduced to the settlers was the silver dollar. Previously, the settlers and trappers had used a barter system. The silver dollar was the only "hard" or real money in this fur trading post, so it was cut into eight pieces or bits worth 12 and a half cents each. We still call a quarter of a dollar "two bits." Some people were so expert, they could get nine bits out of a dollar without being detected!

By 1799 the population had increased to 500. The majority was predominantly men; this figure included 150 Black and Indian slaves. Records from the Old Cathedral, from May 1772 to June 1775, show there were 107 baptisms, 72 deaths and only four marriages in that period. Even without the gentle, stabilizing presence of women, it was not a violent village; only one murder occurred from the founding in 1764 until the Louisiana Purchase in 1803. Very few of the inhabitants had any formal education.

There is record of an attack on St. Louis by Indians friendly to the British on May 26, 1780. These Indians, largely from the Saux, Fox, and Winnebago tribes, crossed the river where Bremen Street (McKinley Bridge) is now located. The attack was planned by the British commandant Patrick Sinclair. He reported the Indians returned with 43 scalps; others said 33 St. Louisans were killed, while some accounts list 21 casualties. Whatever the number, a community that only had a total population of less than 500 considered it a heavy loss. Two of the Frenchmen killed in the attack were Jean Cardinal and Francis Hebert. (see Appendix V "A" p. 176.)

After this attack in the fall of 1780, a nine-foot-high log stockade was constructed from what is now Lombard to Delmar streets between Third and Fourth. Fort San Carlos, a tower, was erected at what is now Fourth and Walnut. Blockhouses were built at what is now Third and Lombard, Broadway and Poplar, Third and Vine, and between the levee and Morgan Street. Their purpose was to help protect the village from another surprise Indian attack.

At the end of the Revolutionary War in 1783, due to the exploits of George Rogers Clark (1752-1818), Virginia was able to claim all the territory from the Alleghenies to the Mississippi and extend its border to the Mississippi River. Gabriel Cerré helped Clark's expedition get its necessary supplies and equipment when Clark and 200 men from Virginia captured Kaskaskia and Cahokia, Illinois, and Vincennes, Indiana, from the British. What we now know as Illinois became part of Virginia. This territory was included in what became known as the Northwest Territory in 1784. Slavery was forbidden in this territory.

The United States was called the Confederation of States (1783-1789) when the Northwest Territory was first formed. The Constitution of the United States became effective on March 4, 1789. George Washington was inaugurated as the first President of the United States on April 30, 1789, with only 11 states forming the Union. North Carolina did not ratify the Constitution until November 21, 1789, and Rhode Island officially joined the Union on May 29, 1790. (see Chapter 15, Page 106) The Bill of

Rights took effect on September 25, 1789. Founded in 1764, St. Louis is 25 years older than the United States.

While Louisiana was under Spanish control, the Mississippi River was often closed to the American colonists. Spain returned the territory west of the Mississippi to France in 1800. When Thomas Jefferson became president, he wanted to keep the Mississippi River open for use by the American people, and persuaded Congress to negotiate with France to buy New Orleans for $2 million. Robert R. Livingston, the American Minister to France, was involved in negotiations for months.

Unexpectedly, France offered the United States the entire Louisiana Territory. When Jefferson heard this, he fumed, "We will not need Louisiana for colonization for a thousand years. We could not protect it if we got it, we only want New Orleans." France replied with a "take-it-or-leave-it" offer — "the entire Louisiana Territory or nothing." James Monroe went to France as a special envoy; he and Livingston wisely signed the papers transferring the Louisiana Territory to the United States on April 30, 1803. The news surprised Jefferson; he felt the signing was "an act beyond the Constitution." (see Appendix V "B" p. 176.) Many congressmen also considered the treaty "clearly unconstitutional. It will destroy the sectional balance of the nation and the republican form of government would break down, if attempted on so large a scale." Jefferson sent the treaty to Congress on October 17, 1803; it was approved two weeks later. The actual transfer of ownership was completed at New Orleans on December 20, 1803. The Louisiana Territory was the first territory acquired by the United States. The United States received the title to this fantastic land which it did not want, from a country that did not own it, and paid for it with money it did not have!

It was one of the best land deals of all time. The Louisiana Territory consisted of 899,579 square miles. It was four times larger than the country of France (which is 212,659 square miles). This acquisition more than doubled the size of the United States, from 820,680 to 1,720,259 square miles. It cost $11,250,000, or $13.58 a square mile, less than three cents an acre. Fifteen states were formed from this territory. (see Chapter 15, Page 107)

March 8, 1804, was the last day the Spanish flag flew over the 40-year-old village of "St. Louis of the Illinois," in the Louisiana Territory. Almost the entire population of 925 stood and silently watched as the Spanish flag was lowered and the French flag raised, to show Spain's return of the territory to France. This was the last time a French flag was to fly over a French possession in North America. The Stars and Stripes of the United States replaced the French flag on March 10, 1804, designating the beginning of the great American western expansion.

The first American flag raised over St. Louis was the 15-star, 15-stripe flag; the same flag that would be carried by U.S. Marines into Tripoli on April 27, 1805. It was the same flag that flew over Fort McHenry on September 13, 1814, and inspired Francis Scott Key to write *The Star-Spangled Banner*; and the same flag that would be used by Gen. Andrew Jackson in the historic Battle of New Orleans on January 8, 1815. This flag was used for 48 years; second in length of usage to the 48-star flag.

American Capt. Amos Stoddard became the governor of the Louisiana Territory, which was part of the Indiana Territory until 1805. Meriwether Lewis and William Clark (1770-1838), the younger brother of George Rogers Clark, left to explore the Louisiana Territory on May 14, 1804, traveling on orders from President Jefferson.

All the men mentioned above, who were so involved in the history of our country and especially this area of the country, have streets named after them in St. Louis. There are two streets named for the River Des Peres, and a public school is named Des Peres; Laclede, Stoddard, Lewis and Clark have counties in Missouri named for them. Clark, Stoddard and Laclede have public schools named for them. A county is also named for George F. "Pegleg" Shannon, who accompanied Lewis and Clark.

Although I think the story of the Lewis and Clark expedition is very interesting, I have included just one segment. Forty-five men left St. Louis on May 14, 1804 for this expedition. After traveling 1,600 miles, they established Fort Mandan (where the Knife and Missouri rivers meet) in January 1805. There they hired a French Canadian named Toussaint Charbonneau for a guide; his young, pregnant, Indian wife Sacajawea ("Bird Woman") accompanied him. She was from the Shoshone or Snake tribe, but had been captured and adopted by an Eastern tribe. Clark called her "Janey." Her baby boy was born in February 1805, and given the name John Baptiste. Clark nicknamed the boy "Pomp."

This young Indian mother and child were an unexpected blessing for the expedition. Other tribes of Indians knew the mission must be a peaceful one, because a war party would never travel with a woman and child. Their boats almost foundered during a storm, and Sacajawea was quick enough to save the scientific instruments and books. She also served as interpreter with some Indians, and found interpreters for communication with other tribes. Lewis thought she was one of the most valuable persons on the expedition.

Sacajawea became ill on June 13, 1805, and Lewis was able to use his medical skills to help her.

The group could not travel by water after August 15, 1805. While beaching the boats, they were suddenly aware of a large party of Indians approaching on horseback. Readying their weapons for what looked like a helpless stand, they were astonished to hear Sacajawea cry out and run toward the Indians. The chief of the War Party was Shoshone Chief Cameahwait, her brother. The atmosphere suddenly changed and the Indians welcomed them, took them to their village, gave them horses and pack animals and replenished their dwindling supplies. Chief Cameahwait also sent "Toby," a member of his tribe, to accompany and guide them through the mountains. Because of Sacajawea and Toby, the expedition experienced a safe journey through the territories of the Western tribes.

On November 7, 1805, they reached the Pacific Ocean and camped there for the winter. The trip back was started on March 23, 1806. The animals were returned to Chief Cameahwait's tribe, and they retrieved the boats for the journey down river. Sacajawea's sister had died, leaving a son named Basil. Sacajawea adopted her nephew and it was never mentioned that he was not her own child (as was the custom of the tribe). They arrived in St. Louis on September 23, 1806 — two years, four months and nine days after they left, and over 7,700 miles of travel. "Pomp" was brought to St. Louis by Clark to receive an education. It is believed "Pomp" died on his way to the gold fields of Montana in 1866. Monuments were erected to Sacajawea by Portland, Oregon; Bismarck, North Dakota; and the state of Wyoming.

It has been said that the Lewis and Clark expedition was more daring than our putting a man on the moon. It cost the U.S. government $38,722.75. It was a large amount for that period, but it also was one of the most important and successful events in our early American history.

It might surprise you to learn that the life expectancy for a male at that time was 40 years. Pierre Laclede died at age 54 in 1778, the same year that George Rogers Clark captured Kaskaskia from the British. A statue of Laclede has a prominent place in front of St. Louis City Hall. La Salle died at 44, a bronze plaque on the base of the Columbus statue in Tower Grove Park commemorates him. De Soto died at 42, Marquette at 38, and Meriwether Lewis at 35. These men all implemented, attempted and completed many exploits in the short period of time that they lived. There were exceptions, of course; two I might mention are Henry Shaw, who died at the age of 89, and Daniel Boone, who was 86 when he died.

Chapter 2: St. Louis and Statehood

To travel in this era, one had to use rivers for first streets; there was no other choice. Rivers were sometimes the only (and certainly the most cost-efficient) means for travel and shipping freight. The cost of transporting a ton of goods 30 miles inland by land equaled the cost of transporting the same goods across the Atlantic Ocean.

Except for a few trails and village lanes created by people walking on them, roads hardly existed. A Missouri law was passed in 1822 that stated, "All trees and branches must be cleared from roads, and no stump higher than 10 inches may be left in the road." These stumps were major hazards for wagons and buggies. The roads were difficult to use in dry weather and virtually impassable in wet weather. One traveler remarked, "It is a fairly decent road if the mud does not quite go over your boot tops when you are sitting in the saddle." Winter and snow were considered a blessing because roads were trampled by pooling oxen teams, and sledges and sluice were used to haul heavy timber.

"Three Notch Road," which ran from Ste. Genevieve to Mine La Motte, is acknowledged as the oldest road in Missouri. Its name resulted from the custom of notching trees along the way to identify the road, a process also known as "tracing" a road. Many early roads were called traces. The Natchez Trace, more than 500 miles long, runs from Natchez, Mississippi, almost to Columbia, Tennessee.

"Kingshighway" was the name of the second oldest road in Missouri; it ran from St. Louis to New Madrid. The French called it "Rue Royale," and the Spanish, "El Camino Reale." After 1850, part of this route became Telegraph Road because an early telegraph line was installed along it. Today Highway 61 follows the same route, more or less.

St. Louis remained a small French town for almost 50 years. In 1812, a market containing 12 stalls opened on Rue de la Place; rent for each stall was $10 a year. The Americans started calling Rue de la Place "the street where the market is," which evolved to Market Street. It is still called Market Street, making it the oldest street in the city with the original "American" name.

The streets in early St. Louis were very narrow, presumably just one cart wide. Still, they were the only major open spaces in the city. Washington Avenue was an exception because of the foresight of Jeremiah Connor who arrived in St. Louis in 1805. Territorial Governor Wilkinson appointed Connor the third Sheriff of St. Louis in September 1806, a post he held until November 1810. By 1818, Connor owned two arpents of land from what is now Third Street to Jefferson, between Judge Lucas' and Maj. William Christy's land. An arpent was a unit of measure that was 1.5 miles in length and 380 feet wide. Connor laid out an area 80 feet wide through the center of his land and the length of his property. He gave it to the city with the request that the street be named Washington Avenue, after George Washington. Connor retained ownership of a 150-foot strip on either side of Washington Avenue, convinced that this would be a main artery of the city and its value would greatly increase. Unfortunately, Connor died on September 23, 1823, at age 50, before he could develop his land. Washington is the second oldest named street in use in St. Louis. The width of Washington Avenue was one of the factors considered for the location of Eads Bridge 75 years later.

Missouri became a territory separate from the Louisiana Territory on June 4, 1812, when James Madison was president. Missouri Territory included what are now the states of Missouri, Arkansas, Iowa, Minnesota, Oklahoma, North and South Dakota, Nebraska, Montana, Kansas, Colorado and Wyoming. It was the sixth territory admitted to the Union.

The Louisiana Territory, once known as Orlean Territory, encountered problems when it applied for admittance into the Union. The northeastern states resisted sharing space with people whose appearance, language and cultural practices were unfamiliar to them. Josiah Quincy of Massachusetts stated, "Citizens of the Territory of Louisiana are inhabitants from a foreign country. ... They never have been, and never will be, citizens of the United States. The political rights of the original United States will be trampled under foot by these foreigners." Louisiana was admitted as a state in 1811. The northeastern states decided that if they couldn't prevent admission of more western states, they would devise rigid conditions which must be met before admission was granted. If the territories would not accept these conditions, the northeastern states would not have a problem. When Vermont became a state in 1791, no mention of "foreigners" was heard.

Missouri applied for admission to the Union as a state in 1818, but the same northern states again blocked admittance. One reason used to justify their action was Missouri's status as a slave state. This was the first time slavery was openly discussed in Congress. Most Americans did not approve of slavery; they only differed about the manner of solving the problem. Most Southerners (and President Lincoln) preferred a gradual emancipation, but radical Northerners wanted immediate emancipation. No other slave state was located as far north as Missouri, which is both farther north than Kansas, a free state, and farther south than Virginia, a slave state.

Missouri had the least amount of slaves in the slave-holding states. Missouri had fewer blacks — with 17,000 free blacks and slaves — than some free northern states such as New York with 39,000, Pennsylvania with 30,000, or New Jersey with 20,000. A survey held in 1790 in Yonkers, New York, showed that 15 percent of the city's population were slaves, even though New York was not a slave state. (see Appendix V "C" p. 176) In 1850, the percentage of slaves in St. Louis was 3 percent; by 1860, the number had fallen to 1 percent.

Slavery was not the foundation of Missouri's social and economic structure; slavery's impact on Missouri was more emotional than economics. At this time, two-thirds of all the slaves in Missouri lived within 20 miles of the Missouri River in an area still known as "Little Dixie," where Southerners from Virginia, Kentucky, Tennessee and North Carolina had settled. Most of the slaves in the rest of the state were domestic servants.

Many do not realize that the Mason-Dixon line, surveyed by British astronomers Charles Mason and Jeremiah Dixon between 1763 and 1767, was drawn to settle the dispute between Maryland and Pennsylvania over the location of their common border. (see Appendix V "D" p. 176) In later years, the Mason-Dixon line was used to designate the separation of the slave states and the free states. Many people have forgotten that Maryland was a slave state.

Missouri's size, its central location on the two largest rivers in the country and its potential wealth were just a few of the reasons the northern states feared Missouri's entrance into the Union. They were concerned that any one of these reasons could give Missouri a commanding position in the Union. The eastern states would not willingly allow the states west of them to usurp their political power and prestige.

Missouri's application was turned down and Illinois was accepted as the 21st state in 1818. At this time, the population of Missouri was greater than that of Illinois. Shawneetown Bank, the first bank chartered by the Illinois Territorial Legislature in 1816, rejected a loan application from a

Chicago investment group in the 1830s because they said, "Chicago would not amount to anything."

Missouri was rejected again in 1819. Alabama, a slave state located east of the Mississippi River, was accepted as the 22nd state that year. Neither the "foreign" problem nor slavery was mentioned. Alabama did not have the choice central location of Missouri and covered a smaller area.

Congress then attempted to tell Missouri how to write its constitution to be eligible for admission. Missouri was cognizant that Congress was stepping outside of its authority, and fully aware of the unjust treatment the territory was receiving by Congressional attempts to restrict the Missouri Constitution (which closely resembled the constitution of Kentucky). With help from Henry Clay of Kentucky and passage of the Missouri Compromise, Missouri was finally accepted into the Union as a slave state on March 2, 1820, when James Monroe was president. The Missouri Compromise provided that no territory north of "36 degrees-30 minutes," the established southern border of Missouri, could become slave territory.

John Hardeman Walker, who lived at the southeastern extremity of Missouri, asked Congress to include all 1,100 square miles of his property (located between the Mississippi and St. Francois rivers, as far south as the 36th parallel) in the state. His request was granted and that is how Missouri got the "Boot Heel." Walker founded Caruthersville in 1857.

I find it interesting that 15 years after acceptance of Missouri as a state, when the U.S. government moved the Iowa, Sac, Fox and other smaller tribes of Indians from the Platte region, they gave this land to the state of Missouri. The Platte area covered 3,420 square miles; three times larger than state of Rhode Island. Missouri is the only state that increased in size after admittance to the Union. Andrew, Atchison, Buchanan, Holt, Nodaway and Platte counties were formed from this "gift." (see Appendix V "E" p. 177) The Platte region, north of the slavery line as delineated in the Missouri Compromise, was free territory prior to the accession but was given to a slave state. The senators who dealt with this annexation knew that it violated the Missouri Compromise, but no one felt the need for a confrontation.

Maine, which had been part of Massachusetts, was the free state accepted in 1820. Slave states and free states remained equal at 12 each until Texas, the last slave state, entered the Union in 1845. Slave-free states remained in balance until 1848 when California, Minnesota and Oregon entered the Union, resulting in 18 free, and 15 slave states. Before the start of the Civil War, Kansas also entered as a free state, making the total 19 free and 15 slave states. Eleven slave states seceded from the Union to form the Confederate States. Four slave states — Maryland, Delaware, Kentucky and Missouri — did not leave the Union.

On July 14, 1820, Missouri adopted its first state constitution.

William Clark, who had been appointed governor of the Missouri Territory by President Monroe, had his salary stopped on September 1, 1820, upon formation of Missouri as a state. By September, two senators and a representative had been elected. They arrived in Washington, D.C., but Congress refused to seat them; they were paid but were not acknowledged as voting members of Congress. The recorded date Missouri became a state and formally accepted in the Union is August 10, 1821. The Great Seal of the state of Missouri bears the year 1820, because that is the year Missouri began to function as a state. After Missouri's first attempt to enter the Union, it was four years before the elected representatives were recognized and seated. Missouri was the 13th state to enter the Union after Washington became president. (see Appendix III p. 143)

Conversely, the electoral votes Indiana cast for James Monroe in November 1816 were counted with the rest of the votes in February 1817. Yet Indiana wasn't admitted as a state by Congress until December 1816.

Missouri's first senator, David Barton, was born in North Carolina on December 13, 1783. He moved to St. Louis in 1812, and was chosen senator without opposition. The Legislature deadlocked on the choice for the second senator, so Barton was allowed to choose someone. He selected Thomas Hart Benton, who was also from North Carolina. David Barton died September 28, 1837, at age 54. There is a Barton Street in St. Louis.

Barton apparently made a wise choice because Thomas Hart Benton remained in the Senate for 30 years. There are three streets in St. Louis named for Benton: Benton Place, Benton Street and Benton Terrace. A public school, a city in Missouri and a park also bear his name.

John Scott, Missouri's first House representative, has a downtown street named for him. The Scott Street, near Barnes Hospital, is named for Gen. Winfield Scott of the Union army.

Missouri remained the largest state for 24 years until Texas joined the Union in December 1845. Missouri is still 10,000 square miles larger than any of the 26 states east of the Mississippi River. (see Appendix III p. 143)

St. Louis had a population of 5,000 in 1818; by 1860, the population had increased to more than 160,000. Missouri grew seven times faster than the nation as a whole.

Five New England states (New Hampshire, Vermont, Rhode Island, Connecticut, and New Jersey) increased their population from 1820 to

1860 by 831,949. Missouri's population from 1820 to 1860 increased by 1,115,426; a substantially larger increase than the total of these five states. When Missouri became a state, it ranked 23rd out of 24 states in population; by 1860, Missouri ranked eighth out of 33 states. As the New England states predicted, Missouri gained a commanding position in the Union. Missouri once had 16 representatives in Congress, and St. Louis was the fourth largest city in the nation for 50 years. It was the largest city west of the Mississippi for 150 years.

The city of St. Louis and Missouri were unable to maintain this rapid growth. The Civil War had a particularly disastrous effect on Missouri. River traffic came to a halt throughout the four years of the Civil War, causing St. Louis to lose its southern, eastern and foreign markets. During the winter of 1865-1866, after the end of the war, steamboats were docked and idle for over a mile on the river front. Business was so bad that the "Forwarding Merchants" diminished by 50 percent; from 109 in 1859 to 52 in 1864. The U.S. government imposed a 5 percent tariff on all goods shipped to or through St. Louis, making it a more costly port.

In 1850, St. Louis had a population of 77,860; 2,656 slaves were included in that number. Ten years later the population had more than doubled to 160,000; 100,000 of this number consisted mainly of immigrants from Germany and Ireland. The number of slaves had decreased to 1,542. While some slaves had been sold, many were given their freedom. French slave holders honored the custom of freeing the slaves when the owner died. Freed slaves were often given the family name and property as well. If some of the slaves were old, ill or infirm, the family of the slave owner would care for them. Slaves were also buried on family plots.

St. Louis lost its position as mid-America's leading metropolis when the railroad replaced the river as the method of trade.

In 1850, there was talk of using trains for primary transportation but many were against it. They said, "It isn't fittin' that a person should rush over the countryside at the speed of 15 miles per hour!" Between 1862-1871, the builders of the railroads were given 174 million acres of land by the federal government (an amount equal to the total area of the New England states, plus New York, Pennsylvania and Ohio). Pre-war shipping moved products north and south on the rivers; post-war shipping now moved products east and west on the railroads. A slogan started in Chicago said, "Rivers run where nature pleases; railroads run where man pleases." It took two weeks to travel by boat from New York to Chicago in 1840; it took two days traveling by train in 1860. (see Appendix V "F" p. 177) Commerce moved from the Upper Mississippi Valley to Chicago — the home of the railroads where no tariff was charged. Most of this business did not return to St. Louis when the war ended.

The Southern states experienced total defeat politically, economically and socially. They were so impoverished after the Civil War that they were unable to purchase goods from anyone. "In the South, the Civil War is used as 'A.D.' is everywhere else — they date from it," wrote Samuel Clemens in 1882.

Missouri is located precisely in the center of the country and borders eight states: Iowa, Illinois, Kentucky, Nebraska, Kansas, Arkansas, Oklahoma and Tennessee. It lies two states from the Canadian border (Iowa and Wisconsin) and two states from the Gulf of Mexico (Arkansas and Louisiana). It is five states from the Atlantic Ocean (Illinois, Indiana, Ohio, Pennsylvania, and New York) and five states from the Pacific Ocean (Kansas, Oklahoma, Colorado, Nevada, and California). Missouri was the 24th state to enter the Union. Even in alphabetical order Missouri is in the center, ranking 25th in the list of 50. On the East Coast, they say people from St. Louis are from the West; on the West Coast, they say St. Louisans are from the East. In Wisconsin; they say a St. Louisan is a Southerner; citizens from Louisiana would call him a Yankee. The population of Missouri is 50 percent urban and 50 percent rural.

Missouri is also the only state in which two of the 12 Federal Reserve Banks of the United States are found. Results from the 1990 Census showed that Missouri, which once ranked eighth, was now 15th in population and 18th in area. The state which once had 16 representatives now only had nine. St. Louis, formerly the fourth largest city in the United States, was now ranked 43rd in population.

Today, on a smaller scale, Missouri represents the entire United States. The percentage of the popular vote cast in Missouri is almost identical to the percentage of the nation. Since 1904, Missouri has voted for the victor of every presidential election (except for 1956 when it chose Adlai Stevenson over Eisenhower). Only seven states have a greater percent of population over age 65 than Missouri; only two states west of the Mississippi (California and Texas) have larger populations than Missouri. In many respects, Missouri is a "bellwether" state.

Chapter 3

Early Arrivals

In 1818 St. Louis had the French nickname of "The Post of Pain Court," which translated to "short of bread." Few traditional families were in St. Louis at this time; the population still consisted mainly of hunters, trappers and traders, so the nickname was fitting. The men did very little cooking, and certainly didn't try baking bread. A few cultivated the land and grew vegetables out of necessity, but most of the residents in St. Louis bought their agricultural products from other villages. Carondelet, which had the nickname "Vide Poche," or "empty pockets," was the principal supplier of fruits and vegetables to St. Louis residents.

Daniel Page arrived in St. Louis at this time and opened a grocery store and bakery. He traveled around the city daily with a push cart selling bread; he was a very honest man. It wasn't difficult for him to cross the city in a day. The boundaries of the city were formed by: present-day Franklin Avenue on the north, Third Street on the west, and the present-day Poplar Street Bridge on the south. John Mullanphy gave Page $400, and told him never to refuse bread to anyone who could not afford to pay for it. Mullanphy stipulated that Page was not to reveal the source of these funds; whenever the money was depleted, he would provide more. With the generosity of Mullanphy, everyone soon knew that "Page" was the name of the man who gave bread to the poor. He was elected the second mayor of St. Louis, built a flour mill, and became a respected and wealthy man.

To give you an idea of the generosity of John Mullanphy, when he gave hundreds of dollars to Page so that the poor would have bread, most men earned $1 a week or less; the average rent for a small house was $20 for one year, a servant girl's salary was $5 a year. The Erie Canal (begun in 1817 and completed in 1825) is 363 miles long, 40 feet wide and four feet deep, with 84 locks, for a total lift of 689 feet. Erie Canal diggers received 37 cents for working a 12-hour day. In the New England mills, female needle workers were paid 14 cents for a 12-hour day. In 1838, when Abraham Lincoln was postmaster of the New Salem Post Office in Illinois, his salary was $50 a year.

Years later, Page opened a bank with his son-in-law, Henry D. Bacon. It is recorded that the stockholders of the Ohio and Mississippi railroads found it necessary to sue Page and Bacon for fraud and conflict of interest. The evidence seemed to suggest they were guilty. They hired a young Illinois lawyer named Abraham Lincoln to represent them. Lincoln argued the law, asking for dismissal on a technicality. Although they lost the case, Lincoln's expert pleading on their behalf saved Page and Bacon "a large sum of money." Page Boulevard is named for Daniel Page, and Bacon Street in North St. Louis is named for Henry D. Bacon. A street in North St. Louis and a public school are both named for Abraham Lincoln.

In 1818, Lincoln County, Missouri, was named for Benjamin Lincoln, a general in the American Revolution and the first secretary of war under the Confederation of States. Major Christopher Clark from Winchester, Virginia, settled in Missouri in 1801. When the time came to select a name for the county, Clark said, "I was born in Lincoln County, North Carolina; I lived for many years in Lincoln County, Kentucky; I wish to live my remaining years and die in Lincoln County, Missouri." In addition to Missouri, four other states have counties named for Benjamin Lincoln. (See Appendix V "U" p. 182)

THE MULLANPHYS

John Mullanphy (born in 1758) arrived in St. Louis in 1804. He ran a book store, and purchased land for an inexpensive price when it was available in the Florissant, Bridgeton, Hazelwood and St. Charles areas. In addition, he also owned more than 90 parcels of land in the city when he died in 1833. Mullanphy Street is named for him.

Mullanphy bought large amounts of cotton to sell in Europe, but he had to store it in New Orleans due to the War of 1812. According to records, these cotton bales were used for "breastworks" by Andrew Jackson's men in the historic Battle of New Orleans. Mullanphy complained to Jackson about his cotton being used for this purpose; Jackson handed him a rifle and told him if he was worried about his cotton, he should help protect it. Mullanphy did. When the battle ended, the cotton was returned to Mullanphy, and the government paid him for using it. He removed the debris from the bales and shipped it to England, along with other cotton he had purchased for a low price. Mullanphy realized a substantial profit from this shipment.

The Sisters of Charity arrived in St. Louis on November 5, 1828. They started the first hospital west of the Mississippi in John Mullanphy's house, which was called "St. Louis Mullanphy Hospital." The street on which Mullanphy built a home for the Sisters of Charity is given the name Convent Street. The order moved to another location in July 1874, but Convent Street still remains near downtown St. Louis. Mullanphy also built four houses for rental property to provide an income for the nuns.

Mullanphy gave the Ladies of the Sacred Heart 20 arpents of land in Carondelet, along with a 999-year lease. But he requested a promise that they would educate 20 orphans each year as compensation for it. When they moved, the Ladies of the Sacred Heart applied for and received a decree in Circuit Court, which changed the obligation to include any new property ever acquired by them. They continue to fulfill this commitment.

Mullanphy and his wife had 15 children; only seven daughters and one son, Bryan, survived their father. Bryan was as generous as his father, but Mullanphy believed his son was living foolishly, so he cut Bryan out of his will. However, Bryan's seven sisters gave him a full share by dividing the inheritance eight ways.

A story is told about Bryan Mullanphy walking in the city early one morning, when he met a woman with a cow. He asked her where she was going so early in the day, and she replied that she was recently widowed, had a young son to support and must sell her only cow to pay the rent on her house. Mullanphy said, "I am so lucky, I was looking for a cow to buy." He paid her the price she was asking, but then told her he had a problem — he didn't have a place to keep the cow nor did he have any use for the milk. He asked if she would take care of his cow and dispose of the milk. He would, of course, pay her for this service. The woman was happy to be able to be of service to him, and Mullanphy continued to pay her for taking care of his cow.

Bryan Mullanphy also owned several furnished homes. He asked poor families to live in them, and paid them for taking care of his property. When their lives were more stable and they could provide for themselves, they moved out. He would then find other families to move into the houses "to take care of them for him." In his lifetime, Mullanphy became mayor of St. Louis, a federal judge, one of the founders of the St. Vincent de Paul Society in the United States and founder of the Traveler's Aid Society.

As his father had provided for the Sisters of Charity and the Ladies of the Sacred Heart, Bryan Mullanphy provided for the Traveler's Aid Society. He left a fortune in investments and property to this organization when he died. The Traveler's Aid Society is still in existence in downtown St. Louis. Mullanphy's bequest continues to furnish the organization today with an annual budget of $60,000. Mullanphy died in 1851 at age

42; he never married. A public school is named for him.

A brief look at the seven daughters of John Mullanphy and his wife illustrates a rich history of St. Louis families and descendants:

Mary Mullanphy married Gen. William S. Harney. Their descendants are the De Thury, De Noue, De Este, De Menou, De Montivault, De Sevin, Beauregard, Bassetts and Whittemore families.

Octavia Mullanphy married twice — Dennis Delaney and Henry Boyce. Their descendants are the Lindsay, Taylor and Franciscus families.

Catherine Mullanphy married Maj. Richard Graham. Their descendants are the Frost, Fordyce, Hirschberg, Molesworth, Vernon, Hope, Murray and Blacker families.

Ellen Mullanphy died while studying for religious life.

Eliza Mullanphy married James Clemens Jr. Their descendants are the Clymer, Cates, Clarke and von Versen families.

Jane Mullanphy married Charles Chambers. Their descendants are the Hudson, Tilton, Hardaway, Cates, Smith, Larkin, Desloge, LaMotte, Loker, Chittenden, Thomas, Coppinger, Spaulding, Brown, Thatcher, Feustman, Hunt, Beale, Oliver, Lewis, Campbell and Boland families.

Ann Mullanphy married Thomas Biddle, a paymaster at Jefferson Barracks. Representative Spencer Darwin Pettis (1802-1831) wrote an article about Biddle's brother, which infuriated Thomas Biddle very much. He went to the hotel where Pettis was staying and horse-whipped him while he was still in bed. Pettis was indignant about this action. The rules of society decreed that gentlemen fought duels with other gentlemen; they caned or horsewhipped those considered their "inferior," or had them arrested. Pettis was humiliated and challenged Biddle to a duel; since Biddle was nearsighted, he set the rule of pistols at five paces. On August 27, 1831, they met on Bloody Island (see Appendix V "G" p. 177), in full view of most of the citizens of the city who were gathered to watch; both men were killed. There is a Biddle Street in St. Louis. We do not have a street named Pettis, but Missouri has a county named Pettis. William. H. Ashley took the place of Pettis in Congress, and there is a street named for William Ashley.

Ann Mullanphy Biddle offered her house for the Visitation Sisters' use after the flood at Kaskaskia on June 26, 1844. She gave land and funds for St. Joseph Catholic Church, land and funds to the Daughters of Charity to build an orphanage for girls, and land and funds to build St. Patrick Catholic Church. The Clerics of St. Viator stayed at her home from 1842 to 1843.

Eliza Mullanphy married John James Clemens Jr., a cousin of Samuel

Clemens (Mark Twain)[1].

Their daughter, Alice, married Baron Maxmilian von Versen of the German army in the 1850s. Many streets were named after the Mullanphy descendants, including von Versen. During World War I, all the von Versen property was confiscated by the government because of anti-German sentiments. St. Louis changed the name of von Versen Street to Enright, for one of the first St. Louis soldiers killed in World War I. Other street names changed around this time were:

Kaiser to Gresham   Wiesenhan to Bonita
Berlin to Pershing   Hasburger to Cecil Place
Brunswick to January   Helvetia to Stolle.

THE CHOUTEAUS

Auguste Chouteau was born on September 26, 1750, and came to St. Louis with Pierre Laclede. He married Marie Therese Cerré on July 27, 1786; he was 36, she was 16. Auguste Chouteau died February 24, 1829, at the age of 79; Marie Therese Cerré Chouteau died August 14, 1842, at the age of 72. Their descendants are the Dyer, Clark, Winthrop, Barlow, Dillon, Randolph, Paul, Ham, De Breuil, Beckwith, Ulriei, Bogy, Foy, Mellier, Taylor and Smith families.

Pierre Chouteau married Pelagie Kiersereau and Brigitte Saucier. Their descendants are the Sanford, Lawnin, Maffitt, Walsh, Bates, Chambers, Geraghty, Sawyer, Henshaw, Johnson, DeMenil, Cortambert, Watson, Priest, Berthold, Ewing, Peugnet, Kerr, Taylor and Wilson families.

Pelagie Chouteau married Sylvester Labaddie. Their descendants are the Pratte, Honey, Little and Sarpy families.

Marie Louise Chouteau married Joseph M. Papin. Their descendants are the Ledic, Deaver, Wilcox, Masure, Chenie, Pratte, Gourd, Carriere, Roy, Chauvin, Duchouquette, Dupre, Genestelle, Schofield, Norcum, Wilkinson, Atchinson, Hirschberg, Tracy and Greer families.

Victoire Chouteau married Charles Gratiot. Their descendants are the Cabanne, Edwards, Hempstead, Sarpy, Berthold, Kingsbury, DeGiverville, Waterman, De Mun, Walsh, Chenie, Barnes and Smith families.

Many of the names of Chouteau descendants are familiar because of the streets named after them. There is also a public school named Chouteau.

Ann Lucas, daughter of Jean Baptiste Lucas, married Capt. Theodore

---

[1] Capt. Isaiah Sellers was the first to write using the name "Mark Twain." He enjoyed the distinction of having never lost a steamboat in 40 years on the Mississippi River.

Hunt on June 23, 1814; he was 26, she was 17. They occupied a house on Gravois Road until 1820, when it was sold to Frederick Dent. Dent's son, also named Frederick, was stationed in the Army at Jefferson Barracks. Young Frederick invited a lieutenant who had been his roommate at West Point to visit his family. Frederick's sister, Julia, and the roommate fell in love. The couple was married in the Dent city home (at Fourth and Cerre) upon the lieutenant's return from the Mexican War.

Frederick Dent's former roommate (and Julia Dent's husband) was Ulysses S. Grant. After the Civil War, Grant purchased the 1,000-acre Dent estate, but was forced to mortgage the property. It was later purchased by Luther H. Conn, a St. Louis real estate agent, who sold the west portion to August A. Busch. The east tract, with the home called Whitehaven, was sold to another real estate agent, Albert Wenzlick. Whitehaven is now under the care of the U.S. Park Service.

Capt. Theodore Hunt died January 21, 1832, at the age of 50. After a respectable mourning period, Ann married his cousin, Wilson Price Hunt, on April 20, 1836; he was 54, she was 39. President Monroe appointed Wilson Hunt as postmaster of St. Louis the same year. Ann's father gave them a parcel of land for her dowry. This land is known as Normandy, after Normandy, France, from where the Lucas family originated. That is where you will also find Lucas and Hunt Road. Julia Dent Drive is in 63123, Grant Place is in 63116, Grant Drive is in 63107. A statue of Ulysses S. Grant stands in front of the St. Louis City Hall. St. Louis also has a public school named for Grant.

Ann Lucas Hunt gave land at 10th and St. Charles for St. Francis Xavier Church, land for a girls' school at Third and Gratiot, land for Our Lady of Victories Church at 17th and Chestnut, land for the Convent of the Good Shepherd and the Loretto Sisters at Pine and Jefferson, and land for St. Ann's Church in Normandy. Wilson P. Hunt died in 1842 at age 60; Ann died April 12, 1879, when she was 82.

Joseph Victor Garnier arrived in St. Louis in 1804. He was a justice of the peace, a notary, and the first clerk of the Circuit Court. He married Marie, daughter of Charles Sanguinette. Their only daughter, Harriet, married John Hogan, a postmaster. There is a street named Garnier, and another named Hogan.

Gabriel Dodier was one of the earliest inhabitants of St. Louis; Dodier Street in North St. Louis is named for him. His son Rene sold some of their property at what is now Grand and Gravois to Charles Sanguinette and his wife Marie, the daughter of Dr. Andre August Conde. Years later, Sanguinette gave this land to his daughter Adele, who was married to a storekeeper from France. They lived on the land for many years before selling it to South Side National Bank, which still conducts business at that location. The street behind the bank is named Tholozan for Adele's husband, John Eli Tholozan.

It was learned that 232 people owed money to Dr. Andre Conde when he died. Considering the size of the population of St. Louis at that time, a large portion of it was indebted to him. One of the streets named for Conde was changed to Montgomery for Revolutionary War Gen. Richard Montgomery, killed in the Quebec campaign. There is still a Conde Street by O'Fallon Park.

Peter Lindell came to St. Louis in 1811 when he was 25. He boarded with a fur trader named Manuel Lisa, and started a dry goods business. Lindell remained a bachelor all his life. The street between his land and his brother Jessie's land was called Lindell Lane; it is now called North Grand. Lindell Boulevard was the name of the street that ran down the center of Peter Lindell's property. Peter Lindell named a street McCombs for his sister; this has been changed to Theresa. He named another street Baker for his other sister; it is now West Pine. He named Sarah Street for his niece Sarah Coleman; Boyle for a Methodist minister, Rev. Joseph Boyle; and Maryland for the home state of the Lindells.

Spring Avenue of today was named for a large spring on the Lindell property. On its course east to the river, the spring passed under a natural limestone bridge near present-day 23rd and Palm streets. The road that ran over this spring was appropriately called Natural Bridge Road. The name of the stream was Rocky Branch Creek, and the eastern part ran along what we now call Branch Street in North St. Louis.

After John O'Fallon (1791-1865) was wounded in the Battle of Tippecanoe in 1811, his uncle William Clark invited him to come to St. Louis to recuperate. O'Fallon became the first president of the Missouri Pacific, the Baltimore & Ohio and the Wabash railroads, and became a very wealthy man. He was also a very generous man. His estate, now O'Fallon Park, was acquired by the city. He gave land east of his estate to St. Louis University, which was a college at the time. This land was called College Hill, and the street bordering it was named College Avenue, in anticipation of the college to be built there. St. Louis University did not build the college there; they sold the land, and later built the college at what is now Grand and Lindell. O'Fallon also gave land to Washington University, and a street in that area is called University Street. It is near the area where Sportsman's Park was once located. Washington University did not build on that property either; they moved west of Forest Park.

O'Fallon was very proud of his son-in-law, Dr. Charles Pope, and built Pope Medical College and O'Fallon Poly Technical School for him.

Both became part of Washington University Medical School. In 1854, O'Fallon gave 60 acres west of Grand and north of Natural Bridge to the city for Fairgrounds Park.

His benevolence didn't stop there; he gave millions of dollars to various charities. Some of Bellefontaine and Calvary cemeteries include land that once was O'Fallon property. He was so highly regarded by the people in St. Louis that all business was suspended on the day of his funeral. (I could not find a record of this ever occurring again.) Robert Campbell and Henry Shaw were two of his pallbearers. Streets named by and for him, and his family are: O'Fallon, Mary, Alice, Adelaide, Algernon, Rosalie, Clarence, Pope, Emily, Holly, Red Bud, Barrett, Sophia, Bailey, Ruth, Peck, Athlone, Carrie, Pamela, and Keber. Harris and Carter were named for sons-in-law. St. Louis already had a street named O'Fallon, so the name of the street near O'Fallon Park was changed to Warne for Marinus W. Warne, a manufacturer and banker. Sophia was changed to Red Bud, Ruth to Fair and Pamela to Harris. There are public schools named for both O'Fallon and Pope.

Dr. John Gano Bryan owned property east of the O'Fallon estate. He named streets Bryan, John and Gano for himself; Evaline for his wife; Emily and Maria for daughters; Guy for a son; and Obear for Josia O'Bear, his son-in-law. Bryan has been changed to Prairie, Evaline to 20th Street, Guy to Blair (for Francis P. Blair) and Maria to Carter (after one of O'Fallon's sons-in-law). Bryan Hill public school was named for Dr. Bryan. There is also a public school named for Blair.

Hempstead was named for Edward Hempstead, a banker and one of the founders of the Board of Education. He was influential in getting common grounds for the public schools, and a public school is named for him. Hempstead's daughter Mary, who spoke English, very little French and no Spanish, married Manuel Lisa in 1818. Lisa spoke Spanish, a little French, but no English. Lisa was born in 1772 in New Orleans. He arrived in St. Louis in the late 1790s and became a partner in the fur trading business with Charles Sanguinette, Gregoire Sarpy and Francois Benoist. Lisa was known as "Mr. Manuel," and Mary Hempstead Lisa was called "Aunt Manuel." Mr. Manuel also had an Omaha Indian wife named Mitain and two half-Indian children. He left $4,000 for their care when he died in 1820. Lisa Street, once named after Manuel Lisa, was changed to O'Fallon for John O'Fallon.

Jacques Clamorgan arrived in St. Louis in 1784. He never married but fathered four children by three African-American women. The children's names were: St. Eutrope, Appoline (called Pauline), Cyprian Martial and Maximin. Clamorgan died on November 11, 1814, and gave his children his name, his property and their freedom.

St. Eutrope was born April 30, 1799, and married Pelagie Aillotte on April 20, 1820; Eutrope died in 1822. His widow Pelagie married Louis Rutgers on February 2, 1826; they had one daughter named Antoinette. Rutgers died in February 1847. Arend Rutgers had given Louis land in the Soulard area. His widow Pelagie was considered a major landholder, and she rented her property and buildings to businesses. Her wealth was estimated at more than $500,000 in the 1840s. By comparison, Henry Shaw retired in 1839 with $250,000; an amount he considered "enough wealth for anyone." The widow had twice as much money as Henry Shaw.

Antoinette Rutgers was born on November 21, 1838. She married James P. Thomas on February 12, 1868, at St. Vincent de Paul Church; she died in 1897 and was buried from the same church. James P. Thomas died in 1913. They are both buried in Calvary Cemetery.

Appoline, known as Pauline Clamorgan, was born on February 7, 1803. She never married, but had seven children by Elias T. Langham, a white man. Her children's names were Cyprian Leon, Henry, Louis, Charles, Louisa, Pelagie Julia and Cyprian. Pauline died on May 1, 1830. Her property and home were at what is now known as Laclede's Landing. Clamorgan Alley was named for her.

Pauline's son Henry was born in 1823. He became a barber and opened a shop on Fourth and Pine. In 1859, Henry moved to the southwest corner of Chippewa and Iowa; he lived, worked and died there on March 9, 1883.

Jacques Clamorgan acquired the rights to 38,111 acres of U.S. territory. The children of Pauline were his only heirs. On June 7, 1858, Congress confirmed that the acreage in Kansas belonged to them, and the Clamorgan family moved to Kansas.

Besides Clamorgan Alley, some other streets named after African-Americans are: Dr. Martin Luther King, formerly Easton Avenue; Dick Gregory Place was Wagoner Place; Redd Fox Lane was North Spring; Annie Malone Drive was Goode; Billups Avenue was Pendleton; Samuel Shepard Avenue was Lucas; James "Cool Papa" Bell was Dickson; Harriet Tubman Lane; Rev. T.E. Huntley was Ewing; and Archie Moore Street is in 63121.

The "Ville," located in what is now the area between Martin Luther King Drive, St. Louis Avenue, Sarah and Taylor streets, was once the estate of Charles Elleards, a horticulturist. It was first known as "Elleardsville." There is a public school named Elleardsville. Early in the 1900s, African-Americans comprised nearly 90 percent of the residents of the "Ville." Names of other well-known African Americans in the "Ville" include:

The Annie Malone Children and Family Service Center, named for Annie Malone, the first self-made female millionaire in the nation.

Homer G. Phillips Hospital, which was named in honor of the lawyer who was killed on his way to work, has been closed.

Simmons Elementary School was the first African-American institution in the "Ville." It was first known as "Elleardsville School for Colored Children." The school was renamed for Dr. William J. Simmons, a Baptist clergyman.

Sumner High School, named for U.S. Sen. Charles Sumner, who in 1861 became the first prominent politician to call for full emancipation.

Tandy Community Center, named for Civil War hero Charlton H. Tandy.

Turner School, named for Charles Henry Turner, a teacher at Sumner High School.

The "Ville" was a bustling, progressive area, known as "the cradle of Black culture." The area started to change when the Fair Housing Act of 1954 was approved by Congress. The doctors, lawyers, teachers and other middle-class families who were leaders of the neighborhood found what they considered "better" housing elsewhere. When they moved, businesses followed. What was once the home of nearly 11,000 people now accommodates about 3,000. Boarded-up, vacant, commercial buildings, as well as single- and four- family flats, stand next to littered lots. The remaining residents are hoping for a return to the glory days of the "Ville." It will take a lot of hard work, and a lot of help.

Chapter 4
Growth as a City

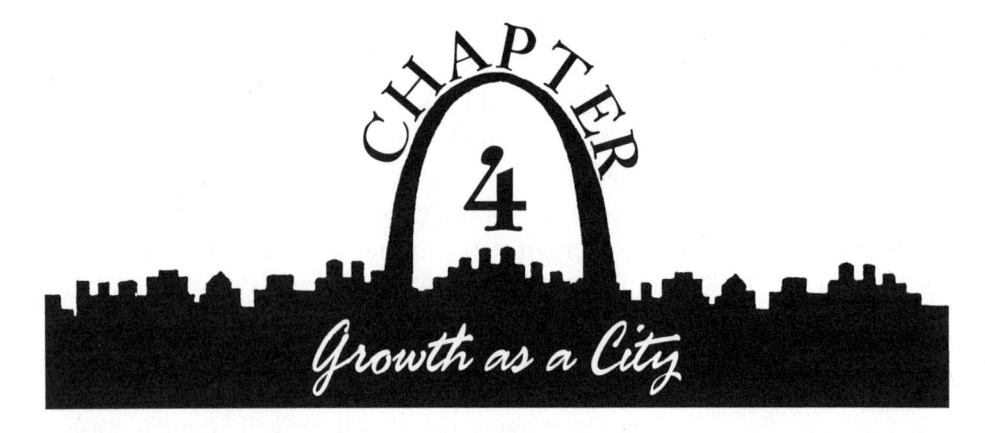

The city limits were extended "all the way out to Seventh Street" when St. Louis finally became a city in 1822. Even though the population exceeded 5,000 at this time, very few buildings were built west of Third Street.

St. Louis had become very important to the shipping industry because larger vessels could not travel north of St. Louis due to the "Chain of Rocks" rapids in the river. Merchandise was unloaded and stored in warehouses by Draymen and employees of the Forwarding Merchants. The merchandise was loaded onto smaller vessels, and the shipment went on to its destination. Many warehouses were built at this time. A canal has been cut to bypass the Chain of Rocks, eliminating the need for the warehouses and the storage.

An army barracks was established in 1826 on 1,700 acres purchased from Carondelet for $5. (By way of comparison, Forest Park is 1,300 acres.) Fort San Carlos at Fourth and Walnut, and Fort Bellefontaine on the Missouri River, were then closed. The new camp was named Adams Barracks, for President John Quincy Adams. The name was soon changed to Jefferson Barracks when Thomas Jefferson died on July 4, 1826. There are more than 40 streets, parks, etc., in Missouri named for Thomas Jefferson, including Jefferson Avenue in St. Louis and Jefferson County. St. Louis also has a public school named for him. The state of Colorado was originally incorporated under the name Jefferson.

In 1826, after French street names had been used for 62 years, the city passed an ordinance adopting the Philadelphia system of naming streets. Numbers were used for the north-south streets, and the east-west streets were given names of trees (except for Market Street). There were 12 streets north and 12 streets south of Market Street named for trees. Seventh Street was the western boundary of the city; the northern boundary was where Biddle Street is. The southern boundary was where the creek that formed Chouteau's Mill Pond entered the Mississippi River, approximately where the Poplar Street Bridge now stands.

Grand Rue	became	First or Main.
Rue de Eglise	became	Second or Church Street.
Rue de Grange	became	Third or Barn Street.
Rue de la Tour	became	Walnut Street.
Rue de la Place	became	Market Street.
Rue Missouri	became	Chestnut Street.
Rue Quicapou	became	Pine Street.

The "tree" streets going from south to north were:

Sycamore was Labadie, now La Salle	Chestnut
Hazel now Papin	Pine
Lombard	Olive
Mulberry now Gratiot	Locust
Cedar	Vine now St. Charles
Plum now Cerre	Laurel now Washington
Poplar	Prune was Christy, Green and now Lucas
Almond now Valentine	Oak, some now Morgan and the rest Delmar
Spruce	
Myrtle now Clark	Cherry now Franklin
Elm	Hickory was Wash, now Cole
Walnut	Pear now Carr
"Market"	Willow now Biddle.

I questioned a librarian at the Main Library about a tree named "Prune"; she said that prune is French for plum. Prune Street was changed to Christy some years later, then it became Green. It is now Lucas.

A U.S. arsenal was built one mile south of the city limits in 1827, on land formerly owned by Arend Rutgers; Rutger Street is in this area. The street bordering the north side was called Arsenal, the street on the south side was called Wall or Government Street, and the street in front of the Arsenal was called Gate Street. Gate Street was soon changed to Withnell for businessman and brewery owner John Withnell.[2] Wall or Government Street was changed to Utah when many of the east-west streets of South St. Louis were named for Indians or rivers. Arsenal Street is still there.

---

[2] John Withnell donated the land on Meramec for St. Anthony Church.

St. Louis did not expand west for some time because the ground was swampy and contained many sink holes. People didn't see a need to expand because most of the activity occurred along the river bank, as it did in most river cities. When J.B.C. Lucas decided to build a 'country home' away from the congested city, everyone said "it was an imprudent thing for him to do; he should not take his family, which included a 14-year-old girl, so far away from the protection of the town. The Indians might carry her off while he was attending to business in town." His country home was built at what is now Seventh and Market streets, in the downtown area.

In 1831, when the city limits were extended to 18th Street, there were still very few buildings past Third Street. William Glasgow married Sarah Mitchell that year, and they built a house on Fourth Street between Market and Walnut. Mrs. Glasgow's friends "expressed regret that it would not be convenient to visit her in such a distant suburban dwelling." Glasgow Street is in North St. Louis.

Dr. William Beaumont moved to his country estate in 1849, but soon moved back to the city. It was too far away and took too long to travel back and forth every day. His estate was where Beaumont Street is today, one block west of Jefferson.

St. Louis was 94 years old when Henry Shaw built his townhouse at Seventh and Locust in 1858.

Lafayette Park, established in 1836, was one of the first city parks. Thornton Grimsley had a great deal to do with acquiring Lafayette Park for the city. His efforts were called "Grimsley's Folly" for many years, and conservative citizens denounced him for two reasons; namely, because 36 acres was too large and the land was too far away from the people. Chouteau's Pond lay between the city and the park, and one had to travel around it to get to the park. Many thought it was a waste of the taxpayers' money. John Darby was mayor of St. Louis then, so the park was also disparagingly called "Darby's Big Gulley."

Lafayette Park and the street bordering the south side of it were named for the Marquis Marie Joseph Paul Yves Roch Gilbert du Motier de Lafayette (1754-1834), a French military leader and statesman. He sympathized with the American Colonies and encouraged France to offer financial and military aid to America. He offered his services to Washington and was commissioned a major general in the Continental army. He was wounded at the Battle of Brandywine; he still fought at Monmouth and in the Virginia campaign, which ended with the surrender of Cornwallis. Congress voted to give him a gift of $200,000 and a large tract of land. A public school in St. Louis bears his name. (see Appendix V "H" p. 178)

The street bordering the north side of the park was simply called Park Avenue. West Park Avenue, south of Forest Park, is an extension of Park Avenue by Lafayette Park.

A statue of Thomas Hart Benton is in Lafayette Park, along with a statue of George Washington that William J. Hubbard brought to St. Louis in 1860. Hubbard was led to believe the city would pay $10,000 for it, and he stored it for nine years waiting to be paid. He became seriously ill, so he signed a 90-day note for $1,500 to pay his bills. He borrowed this money from Erastus Wells (for whom Wellston and Wells Avenue are named), Henry Blow (Blow Avenue in South St. Louis) and Dr. M.M. Pallen, using the statue for collateral. His health worsened, and he was not able to meet the note when it was due. The note holders took possession of the statue and eventually sold it to the city for $5,000. Hubbard had died by this time, so they deducted what he owed them and sent the balance of the money to his widow.

An iron fence was installed around the entire park in 1869 at a cost of more than $50,000. Some of the most affluent and famous people in the city moved to the Lafayette Park area and built magnificent homes around the perimeter of the park. A few early residents of the area were Archibald Gamble; Charles Gibson; William Maurice; Stephen D. Barlow, president of the Iron Mountain Railroad; Montgomery Blair who served in Lincoln's Cabinet (Blair House in Washington, D.C., is named for him); Mayor James S. Thomas; D.C. Jaccard; and Jacob Arthur Christopher.

On July 13, 1869, Montgomery Blair sold two lots on Benton Place, each 25 feet wide (No. 43-44) for $20,000 to Mrs. Cynthia Desloge, the widow of Firmin Desloge. This transaction occurred when most workers earned $125 a year. What was Firmin Desloge Hospital is now called St. Louis University Hospital.

Other streets around Lafayette Park are:
Kennett, after Mayor Luther Kennett.
Nicholson Place, after David Nicholson, a liquor dealer.
Simpson Place, after William Simpson, an iron manufacturer.
Benton Place, after Sen. Thomas Hart Benton.

Confederate Capt. Edward Bredell Jr., who was an only son, was killed at the battle of Fredericksburg during the Civil War. His parents brought their son's body home and buried it in their flower garden in the back yard of their home on Lafayette. In 1871, the body was moved to Bellefontaine Cemetery. Lafayette Park Presbyterian Church, built in 1881 at the corner of Missouri and Albion, installed a large memorial window in the north wall of the auditorium at the request of his parents to honor his memory.

Other Europeans who helped America during the Revolutionary War and have streets named after them are:

Baron Johann De Kalb (1721-1780) from Germany. He came to America with Lafayette and served under General Washington. He was wounded in the Battle of Camden, New Jersey, in August 1780 against General Cornwallis, and De Kalb and his troops were forced to retreat. De Kalb was captured by the British and died three days later. We have a county named for De Kalb.

Casimir Pulaski (1748-1779) came from Poland. Pulaski met Benjamin Franklin in France and was persuaded to join the fight for the Colonies. As a general with Washington's troops, he fought with Gen. Benjamin Lincoln. Pulaski was mortally wounded at the Battle of Savannah, Georgia, on October 9, 1779. A county in Missouri is also named for him.

Thaddeus Kosciusko (1746-1817) was from Poland. After he completed his studies in France, Kosciusko came to America in 1776 to serve in the Revolutionary Army as an aide to General Washington. In 1783, in recognition of his services, he was granted American citizenship, a pension and property. In 1784 he returned to Poland to lead a revolt; he became a dictator. Kosciusko was eventually defeated, wounded and held a prisoner in Russia until 1796. The remainder of his life was spent trying to persuade the Russian emperor to grant Poland independence.

Baron Friedrich Wilhelm Ludolf Gerhard Augustin von Steuben (1730-1794) came from Prussia. He arrived in Portsmouth, New Hampshire, in 1778, and offered his services to General Washington. Washington immediately recognized von Steuben's intellect, talent and skills and appointed him inspector general. Von Steuben prepared a "Manual of Tactics" for the Army, improved discipline and organized an efficient staff. His manual was used by West Point for many years, and his expertise turned Washington's rag-tag Valley Forge army into a cohesive, well-trained fighting unit. Von Steuben's proficiency in training soldiers was largely responsible for the defeat of Cornwallis and the capture of Yorktown which ended the war. In appreciation, Congress voted him an annual pension of $2,400; he was also given a land grant in New York, and lived there until his death in 1794. That area is known as Steuben Township, near Utica, New York. Steubenville, Ohio, was named for him in 1797. Von Steuben is the only European officer who helped the Colonies in the Revolutionary War that does not have a street in St. Louis named in his memory. There is a statue of him in Tower Grove Park.

A problem was encountered when the city expanded and took in the Soulard area, once called "Frenchtown," in 1841. Lafayette Street extended into the Soulard area on Soulard Street, and the street south of Soulard was Lafayette Street. For better flow, the city eventually reversed the names of the two streets in the Soulard area. Lafayette now runs past Soulard Market, and Soulard Street is one block south of the Market.

Julia Cerré Soulard, wife of Antoine Soulard, gave the city land for Soulard Market. A sign on the market building attests that it has been used as a market since 1779. Julia Soulard gave land and funds to build St. Vincent de Paul Catholic Church in 1844; it is one of the oldest churches in the city. The Old Cathederal, built in 1831, is the oldest church still being used in the city.

Henry Clay owned 220 acres of land on which he named a street for himself, and Ashland and Lexington streets for cities in Kentucky. In 1846 he sold the land for $100 an acre; in 1859 it sold for $2,000 an acre. St. Louis has a public school named for Clay, and a public school named Ashland for Clay's home in Kentucky. Missouri also has a county named for Henry Clay.

Chapter 5
Tragedy and Recovery

St. Louis experienced a flood in the spring of 1849, followed by a cholera epidemic, with the inevitable conclusion of death for one-tenth of the population. It is difficult for us to imagine the condition of public health at that time; antiseptics and sanitation were unknown and infant mortality was very high. Parents considered themselves fortunate if they could raise half of their offspring to adulthood. As previously mentioned, John Mullanphy and his wife had 15 children, yet only eight of them lived to maturity.

Panic monopolized the hearts and minds of all the inhabitants of St. Louis; they were desperate to stop this epidemic. Doctors decided eating root vegetables must be causing the spread of the disease and convinced the City Council to pass an ordinance prohibiting the sale of these vegetables within the city limits. This opinion proved to be incorrect because the number of deaths continued to spiral to an average of 65 per day for 100 days. (The population of the city was 64,000 at the time.)

"Dead" wagons traveled around the city every night to remove the bodies of those who had died that day. Fearing for their lives, no St. Louisan wanted to drive these wagons, so convicts were asked to drive them. As an incentive, any prisoner who drove the wagons would have his sentence reduced. I did not find data suggesting that any convicts died of cholera from driving these wagons. Three Sisters of St. Joseph, two Sisters of Charity, one Visitation Sister and six Religious of the Sacred Heart died caring for the cholera victims. The German St. Vincent Orphan Home was started at this time to provide a home and loving care for the children of cholera victims.

Henry Blow and Roswell Field, both residents of St. Louis, were able to move far, far away from St. Louis during the cholera epidemic. They moved to Carondelet. Many others tried to escape the city but were not as successful. Carondelet passed Ordinance No. 86 which was supposed to "prevent the introduction, into the town of Carondelet, nonresidents who are suffering under contagious or infectious diseases." This ordinance forbade anyone with cholera to enter the town limits unless they could prove they were inhabitants of Carondelet. A $100 fine was imposed on anyone bringing an infected non-resident into the town. Men were drafted for a police force to post guards 24 hours a day against infected individuals entering the city. Carondelet remained a healthy community.

All cemeteries in the city were closed; Bellefontaine and Calvary cemeteries were established after the cholera epidemic. Bodies from all the small churchyard cemeteries were reburied in the new outlying cemeteries. The "Hempstead Farm," purchased from Luther Kennett, along with some of John O'Fallon's property, were included in Bellefontaine Cemetery. Some trustees at the time of incorporation were John F. Darby, Henry Kayser, James E. Yeatman, James Harrison, Charles S. Rannells, Philander Salisbury, William Bennett and William M. McPherson. The city has streets named for all of these men.

Chouteau's Mill Pond, which covered about 1,000 acres, also was suspected as a cause of the cholera epidemic. This pond extended from Fourth Street to west of Vandeventer from Laclede to Chouteau. The city purchased the pond for $400 and drained it. It was a spring-fed pond and these springs still exist. Here are the sites of some of them:

Rock Spring, just west of Vandeventer and Market.

Hammond's Spring at Vandeventer and Lindell.

Two Lucas Springs, one under the Public Library at 13th and Olive, and one under the former site of the Title Insurance Corporation Building at Eighth and Chestnut streets.

One under the Old Post Office on Eighth and Olive.

One under the Main Post Office at 18th and Market.

One under the Missouri Pacific Building at 210 N. 13th Street.

McRee's Spring was in the area called McRee City, and the train station was called McRee Station. This area is now called Tower Grove, due to the influence of Henry Shaw. The pond in the Japanese Garden of Shaw's Garden is the outlet for McRee's Spring.

The Old Post Office, the Main Post Office, the Main Library, the Missouri Pacific Building and other downtown buildings have pumps discharging spring water into the city sewers 24 hours a day.

After Chouteau's Pond was drained, that area became known as the Mill Creek Valley. In the 1920s, the land the city had paid $400 for was now valued at $25 million. The newly arriving railroads made use of this land, as did heavy industry. This resulted in separation of the football-shaped city into two nearly equal parts. Division in St. Louis is not so much by city-county, as it is by north and south.

With the flood and the cholera epidemic, city officials tried to be optimistic. They told everyone to keep smiling, things could be worse. Everyone kept smiling and, sure enough, things got worse. On May 17, 1849, the steamboat *White Cloud* caught fire and burned loose from its moorings north of town. It drifted downstream and ignited one boat after another, until 28 burning steamboats lit the river front. The flaming boats caught the merchandise stored on the levee on fire; then the flames leaped to the nearby buildings, and soon most of the buildings in St. Louis were burning. Before the fire was brought under control, the 28 steamboats and 15 square blocks of St. Louis were destroyed.

Volunteer fire fighters trying to control the blaze used a well-known method at that time: they brought gunpowder from the Arsenal to blow up buildings in the path of the fire. Capt. Thomas B. Targee died when the keg of gunpowder he was carrying into a building exploded prematurely. He was one of three volunteer firefighters who lost their lives that day. Targee Street, located where the Kiel Center now stands, was named for him. (see Appendix V "I" p. 178)

In 1853, Cincinnati became the first city to establish a paid fire department. St. Louis did not mobilize a paid fire department until 1856. Union Electric gave the St. Louis Fire Department a fire boat in July 1992. The department named it *White Cloud* after the steamboat from the 1849 fire.

Three hundred people lost their lives in the great Chicago fire on October 8, 1871. On that same day Peshtigo, Wisconsin, also had a fire, with the loss of 1,500 lives. Which of these fires do you know about? Eastern money and money from the federal government flowed into Chicago to help rebuild that city. St. Louis burned down 22 years before Chicago on May 17, 1849, but no financial resources ever arrived to help St. Louis rebuild.

James B. Eads and the men hired to build the bridge across the Mississippi were aware of the St. Louis fire. Before work could be started on the pilings for the bridge in the 1870s, the fragmented debris of the burned steamboats had to be removed.

The average length of usage for a steamboat was four years. From 1834 to 1852, 27 steamboats sank on the Mississippi, with the loss of 1,000 lives; 54 boats sank between 1852 and 1870, resulting in the additional loss of 3,000 lives.[3]

---

[3] More lives were lost from sinking steamboats than from the Indian Wars in the West.

The only buildings in downtown St. Louis built before the devastating year of 1849 (and still standing) are the Old Cathedral and the Old Courthouse. The Old Cathedral dates from 1831, when the United States consisted of 24 states. It is the third structure built on the original land set aside by Laclede for a church, when he founded St. Louis. That land was never used for any other purpose.

The Old Courthouse dates from 1839. It was built on open ground donated by Jean Baptiste Lucas and Auguste Chouteau on the condition that it be used forever as the site of the courthouse for the county. A 10-foot square near the northwest corner of the Old Courthouse lot contained a framework of stocks which was known as the "Jailers Daughter." Prisoners were placed in them. If whipping was the sentence, the public whipping post was next to the stocks, ready for use.

To give you an example of justice in early St. Louis, on June 29, 1809, at Long's Mill in Bonhomme Township, St. Louis County, John Long Jr. shot and killed his stepfather, George Gordon. He was found guilty at the trial on August 21, 1809, and hanged September 15, three weeks after his trial.

In 1930 the new Civil Courts building opened, replacing the Old Courthouse. The very top of the building was designed as a replica of King Mausolus' tomb built in 352 B.C., one of the original "Seven Wonders of the World."[4].

The heirs of Chouteau and Lucas sued the city for the return of the Old Courthouse property, claiming the new courthouse represented a breech of the original agreement. The claim was denied by the U.S. Supreme Court, and the parties reached a compromise. In 1940, St. Louis gave the Old Courthouse to the U.S. government to be used as a historic museum. It is maintained now by the National Park Service. The Old Courthouse remains a hallmark of St. Louis history.

---

[4] The word "mausoleum" originated from this tomb.

Chapter 6
Rebuilding and Immigrants

After the devastation of the flood, the cholera epidemic and the fire, St. Louis needed to rebuild. The city was able to achieve this without any outside financial help. We are fortunate that officials directing the rebuilding wisely prepared for the future by providing wider streets that were better able to handle the growing traffic flow.

The rebuilding effort was mutually advantageous for the city of St. Louis and the German and Irish immigrants arriving at this time. German architects, carpenters, stonemasons and bricklayers had the skills; Irish immigrants had stamina for the manual labor. Together they supplied the work force to rebuild St. Louis.

The citizens in America before 1840 consisted, for the most part, of what came to be known as W.A.S.P.s (White Anglo-Saxon Protestants). British Protestants from England, Scotland and Northern Ireland brought their anti-Catholic, anti-Irish sentiments with them.

Like so much of St. Louis' history, this immigration of the Irish resulted from the work of bold European explorers of earlier centuries. In the 1500s, high in the mountains of Peru, Indians raised potatoes. Spanish explorers took the potato back to Spain. Europeans had never seen or heard of the root vegetable before now, but it grew very well and became Ireland's most important crop. If the Spanish had never gone to Peru and found the potato, the Irish may never have come to America and to St. Louis.

Centuries before, Britain imposed penal laws that allowed little more than physical survival for the Irish. They were not allowed a formal education or to learn a trade. One in eight Irish deaths in the late 1840s resulted from starvation because of the failure of the potato crop. Deaths and emigration caused the population of Ireland to fall from eight million to four million.

In the early days of St. Louis, the Irish had hard lives. They were triple outsiders: Irish, Catholic and poor. The Irish who came to St. Louis were predominantly young (two-thirds were between 15 and 29 years old), half-starved, uneducated and unskilled. They were held in low esteem and shunned by other inhabitants. There was not only discrimination in employment but also ridicule; "they all look alike," was a comment. Both "lace curtain" and "shanty" Irish were lumped together and considered filthy, ignorant, bad tempered, lazy, worthless, and "given to drink." They were excluded from jobs and attending school. "NINA" — No Irish Need Apply — signs were placed in most store windows, and the Irish were completely ignored in social circles. They faced a terrible pressure to give up their unique ethnic way of life.

For 40 years, a great distinction was made between "the deserving and the undeserving poor," and sympathy was non-existent for most of the newly arriving Irish-Catholic immigrants. Many of them studied for the priesthood and joined religious orders of the Catholic Church in St. Louis, as well as in many other cities. Irish clergy were in the majority for many years and exerted great influence in the Catholic Church, both in St. Louis and the rest of the United States. Some found work as dock hands, laborers and domestic help. The Irish believed in mutual self-help and took care of their own. At the bottom of the social order, they were in constant competition for jobs with recently freed blacks and slaves.

Companies usually hired Irishmen for dangerous or dirty work. A good slave was worth about $1,700. For dangerous jobs, employers preferred to hire an Irishman whose wages were often less than $1 a week. There was no use risking the life of a valuable slave on a dangerous project when an Irish worker could do it.

With the abundant supply of available cheap labor, it was the perfect time to either sell slaves or free them. Over 500,000 slaves were "sold down the river" by their owners in the border states between 1840 and 1860, creating that phrase. The price received for a slave would buy the services of a free common laborer, usually Irish, for many years — without having to furnish board, shelter, clothing and medical care. Ulysses S. Grant freed his slaves in 1859, Frank Blair freed his in 1858 and Henry Shaw sold his slaves in 1857. Irish labor built the rock wall around Shaw's Garden and did much of the work in Tower Grove Park.

The "Know-Nothings" were for "freedom, temperance, Protestantism," and against "slavery, rum and Romanism." Horace Greeley said, "It is liquor which fills so many Catholic homes with discord and violence." Gangs of so-called "Native Americans" would prowl the streets, mocking and taunting the Irish to start brawls and riots. The gangs were dispersed only after the damage was done, usually to Irish taverns and homes and the Irish were on their way to jail in the "paddy wagon." The offenders knew that their assaults on the "lower orders" were supported through a silent mandate. These attacks focused on Irish-Catholics and other occupants of downtown and the levee areas. The riots were as much anti-Catholic as they were anti-immigrant.

The Irish immigrants were not treated any better in other cities. Thirty Irish homes were burned and 16 men were killed in Philadelphia. Four Irishmen were killed In New Orleans, 17 in Baltimore and 22 in Louisville. In Clinton and Southbridge, Massachusetts; Newark, New Jersey; and New York City, mobs burned Catholic churches. In Ellsworth, Maine, a Catholic priest was tarred and feathered. The Sisters of Charity in Providence, Rhode Island, were assaulted, and the Irish bishop was arrested and jailed.

By 1850, the Irish made up 44 percent of the immigrant population in St. Louis; however, 85 percent of those admitted to hospitals were Irish. Fourteen years was the average life span of an Irish immigrant living in slums or ghettos. These living quarters had a wide variety of descriptive names:

Clabber Alley — bounded by north Eighth, north Seventh, Wash (now Cole) and Carr streets. It was notorious for its squalid shacks and crowded tenement houses. It was so named because the people lived on "clabber," or sour cottage cheese. They dumped the sour milk left from making clabber into the gutters.

Poverty Pocket — a self-explanatory title.

Wild Cat Chute — an alley running north and south from Carr to Biddle between Fifth and Sixth where steamboat deckhands and roustabouts lived. The alley was often visited by unsavory characters who could get rid of worthless money known as "wild cat" money, which gave the alley its name.

Castle Thunder — had tenement houses on another alley running north and south from Carr to Biddle, between Seventh and Eighth streets.

Battle Row — a row of dilapidated buildings which extended from Fifth to Sixth on Green Street. It is now Lucas.

Kerry Patch — bounded by Biddle, 17th street, Mullanphy and 20th streets.

The citizens of St. Louis believed all of these areas were occupied by a "notoriously bad class of people; one entered these regions at risk of life and limb." Until 1908, 13,233 people lived in the area from Seventh to 14th and Lucas to Washington. No laws regulated their living conditions; two rooms often housed 16 people. No one could bathe since a hydrant in the yard was the only water supply. Children's clothes were sewn on them in the winter; only the visible parts of the body could be washed. This was all the school authorities required for the children to attend school. Only one in six homes had indoor plumbing, even in the best neighborhoods.

Between 1907 and 1930, six major bath houses opened in St. Louis, as well as several smaller ones. The major ones were located at Soulard Market; on 10th street between Carr and Biddle; on 23rd Street and O'Fallon; on Lucas and Garrison; at 1120 St. Louis Avenue; and one at Hickory and Ewing, which was known as the "Buder Bath." That building is still used as a recreation center. These bath houses supplied more than 500,000 showers a year and were open 16 hours a day, every day.

It was not until after World War II that facilities for bathing became more available in private homes. Older buildings were razed and replaced by new homes with inside plumbing. However, some of the bath houses were used until the 1950s. Sigel School, at 2050 Allen Ave., furnished showers to the neighborhood until the late 1970s. The Census of 1990 showed that the city of St. Louis still had 2,227 homes lacking complete indoor plumbing such as hot and cold water, flush toilet and a bathtub or shower.

The "Buder Bath" was made possible through the efforts of Susan R. Buder, a remarkable businesswoman. She and her family also provided continuing funds for Buder Library and Buder School in the city of St. Louis. The Buder Building stood at Seventh and Market from 1903 to 1984, and Buder Park is in St. Louis County. Buder Court is in 63074.

The city passed an ordinance prohibiting building frame buildings in the city after much of it was destroyed by fire. Because bricks were needed, 27 clay mines opened in the area almost overnight. The Irish men were ready, willing and capable of working in the mines. They also worked on railroad road gangs in St. Louis and other large cities. The Irish worked on the railroad gangs from Chicago to the West, while Chinese employees built the railroads from California to the East[5].

Irishmen also found work on the newly formed police and fire departments in St. Louis and in other large cities. Irish women were hired for domestic work, often to replace slaves that had been sold or recently freed.

Many of the immigrants had heard stories of the grandeur to be found in the United States. One of the classic tales was that "the streets in America were paved with gold." When one immigrant observed the

---

[5] When tracks were being laid through the mountains, the Chinese were assigned to plant the dynamite. Sometimes the dynamite exploded before the person could get out of the way, hence the saying, "He doesn't have a Chinaman's chance."

reality of the situation, he expressed his feelings in this manner:
1. The streets were not paved in gold.
2. The streets were not paved.
3. He had to help pave them.

The Germans came to the United States in solid family groups or in groups from the same locality, fleeing political persecution. They settled in the "German triangle" of cities: Cincinnati, Milwaukee and St. Louis. A good example of this was described in the *St. Louis Post-Dispatch* in August 1992:

"A retired contractor from Missouri went to Germany in 1987 searching for his roots. Someone remarked about the unique dialect he was speaking, and mentioned that Germans in a nearby town spoke in the same dialect. Upon arrival, he discovered that his grandfather left from this town with a group in the 1800s. They lost contact with their relatives in Germany, and became known as the "Lost Rhinelanders." This low-German dialect survives among the older generation in both the United States and Germany, although it is dying out in both localities. It seems incredible that this rare dialect has been preserved for five generations."

Unlike most immigrants, the Germans who came to St. Louis brought substantial financial resources with them. In addition to the skilled tradesmen mentioned earlier, many professional people came — doctors, lawyers, musicians and, of course, brewmasters. The Germans not only brought a new spirit to the city, as had the Irish, they also brought their culture. They too suffered from prejudiced bigotry, particularly in the area of municipal and state employment. Another problem they experienced was difficulty in understanding and speaking the language.

On election day, gangs would gather at polling places and refuse to let the Germans vote. The gangs of so-called "Native Americans" told the German people, "If you don't like it, go back to the Faderland." The gangs maintained they were just protecting the purity of the ballot box. Statistics from St. Louis riots of August 7-9, 1854, show that 10 men were killed, 33 wounded and 93 buildings damaged. Edward Bates, who later became Lincoln's attorney general, organized 700 armed citizens to bring order to the city. The state Legislature passed a bill authorizing St. Louis officials to close saloons during emergencies, and provided for policemen to be placed at all the polls on election days. We still live with some of these regulations.

Nine German newspapers existed in St. Louis by 1860. Classes were conducted exclusively in German in 38 private schools. William Torrey Harris, whose educational philosophy shaped the course of public education nationwide, recommended public schools as the best means for assimilating the immigrants into American society. Some schools introduced German language instruction to entice neighborhood Germans to attend. By 1854, five public schools taught German; 19 years later, 50 percent of the children in public schools received all or part of their education speaking German. Over 5,000 non-German students were receiving instruction in the language by 1880. For 23 years, this language program helped build an appreciation of German culture.

Suddenly it was firmly opposed by other ethnic groups and teaching the German language was eliminated from public schools in 1888. Private and parochial schools continued to teach German for many more years, and German was still taught in special Saturday classes in the public schools. A public school in St. Louis is named for Harris.

Although Germans comprised a large portion of the population of St. Louis, the first German mayor, Henry Overstolz, was not elected until 1876.

Chapter 7

North St. Louis

North St. Louis was incorporated on June 29, 1816. It was founded by Majors William Christy, Tom Wright, and Col. William Chambers. Christy arrived in St. Louis in 1804; Wright married one of Christy's daughters. North St. Louis' location in the city had the Mississippi on the east, what is now 12th Street on the west, Madison Street on the south and Montgomery Street on the north. The streets Madison, Monroe, Clinton, Benton, Warren, Montgomery and Market were named by Christy; Market is now North Market. North St. Louis was annexed by St. Louis in 1841.

The first cable cars were installed in 1886 on Locust, Olive, Easton, Broadway and Fourth streets in St. Louis, many years after electricity was in use in other major cities. Conservative St. Louisans voted against it, "because overhead wires would kill trees and so much electricity in the air would cause sickness." When cable cars were finally introduced, a speed limit of six miles an hour was established. Just 10 years later, 90 percent of the population of St. Louis lived within three blocks of a streetcar line. No other large city had as many people living as close to the service.

The city assimilated many incorporated towns and villages that already had complete street schemes. St. Louis' annexations caused problems, conflicts and confusion, especially with the street names. The offsets in the north and south streets, west of 11th Street and north of Locust, reveal an interesting story about knowledge of the size of a city block. Each property owner gave a different answer to the question "How long is a block?" J.B.C. Lucas said 338 feet; Christy and Carr said 376 feet; Mullanphy and Cass said 270 feet. The new streets in the Labeaume and Union additions were 500 feet each. Jeremiah Connor, who gave Washington Avenue from Third to Jefferson to the city, didn't want any streets to cross Washington Avenue. The streets that now cross it had to be opened by condemnation.

Because there were duplications of street names in the towns and villages and St. Louis, some changes were necessary after these communities became part of St. Louis. Bates in North St. Louis, named after Gov. Frederick Bates, was changed to Dickson for Charles K. Dickson, a real estate developer. There is still a Bates Street in South St. Louis, and a Bates Public School.

Smith Street, named for William Smith, a mill operator, was changed to Columbia after Christopher Columbus; it was later changed to Cass Avenue. A street named Columbia is in South St. Louis, and there is also a Columbia public school. Webster, named for Daniel Webster, was changed to Tyler for the daughter of William Chambers, Mary Lawrence Tyler. We still have a street named for Webster in 63106. A public school, Webster College and the city of Webster Groves were all named for Daniel Webster.

Harrison was named for James Harrison (1803-1870), a merchant who owned a railroad and iron mill. He was one of the wealthiest men in St. Louis in the 1860s. Harrison was heartbroken over the division of his family and other families during the Civil War. Near the war's end, he approached President Lincoln and revealed he had many friends among the Confederate forces. He offered to help reunite the country. Lincoln was interested in his ideas, and issued a special pass to enable Harrison to cross battle lines and meet with members of the Confederate government.

Harrison returned with his report as Lincoln was leaving the White House. The President, eager to hear the results of Harrison's mission, asked him to return for a breakfast meeting the next morning. The President apologized for the delay, and explained that he was taking Mrs. Lincoln to Ford's Theater to see *Our American Cousin*. The date was April 14, 1865.

There are Harrison Streets in Kirkwood, Florissant, Ferguson and Brentwood. Harrison Street in St. Louis was changed to Tyler Street, named after the man who was probably the best known vice president, "Tippecanoe and Tyler Too." Tyler was the first man to succeed to the highest office after the death of a president. Tyler Street is now Branch Street. (see Appendix V "J" p. 179)

Schiller was named for Johann Christoph Friedrich von Schiller, one of the two most important figures in German literature (Goethe is the other one). A statue of Schiller is in the park between 14th and 15th streets, directly across from Kiel Opera House on Market Street. There is a Schiller Place in South St. Louis, but it was named for a different Schiller.

There was a street in North St. Louis named Goethe; it has since been changed to Calvary. A street between the cemeteries had been named

Bellefontaine Avenue, and this was also changed to Calvary. Goethe Street in South St. Louis is named for the aforementioned German Renaissance man.

Cannan, Elias and Jordan streets are all that remain from the early 1900s when Orthodox Jews settled in Baden. They also named streets Isaiah and Sinai; Sinai became Newby. By 1914, the Jews moved back into the city to be closer to their work. Baden, originally called Germantown, was named for a city in Germany by the town's first postmaster, Frederic Kraft. A public school named Baden still exists.

Mound Street's name reminds us of the large Indian mound once located there. About 25 mounds once existed west of the Mississippi; the largest one was near what is now the intersection of Broadway and Mound streets. In French it was "La Grange de Terre"; translated this means, "The Barn of the Earth." This mound was leveled in 1867. There is a public school named Mound.

Lee Avenue in North St. Louis was not named for Gen. Robert E. Lee but for a man named Patrick Lee, who married Constance Conde (one of the daughters of Dr. Conde). Arlington Public School and Arlington Avenue are named for General Lee's home in Virginia.

Thrush, Plover, Wren, Robin and Oriole were named for birds by Clara Bircher, the wife of Dr. Rudolph Bircher. She named the streets Durant, Claxton, Prange, Thekla, Ruskin, Davison, and Gilmore. She also named Alcott for Louisa May Alcott, and Emerson for Ralph Waldo Emerson. Emma was for her sister; Lillian for her mother. Dr. Bircher was called the "leech" doctor because he used them in his practice. The Bircher farm extended from Natural Bridge on the south to Florissant on the north, and from Kingshighway on the east to Goodfellow on the west. The area was called Walnut Park, after a large grove of walnut trees located there. A public school was also named Walnut Park.

Partridge and Thatcher streets were not named for birds as one might think but for George Partridge, a wholesale grocer who did not handle liquor, and for George Thatcher, a landowner.

John Goodfellow, Emanuel Hodiamont and Hamilton Rowan Gamble lived on land they owned in that area; these men have streets named for them. Three streets are named for Gamble, the provisional governor of Missouri during the Civil War. There is also a public school named for Gamble.

Erastus Wells built his home on acreage he bought from the Kienlen family. When a train station was built nearby, it was given the name Wellston Station. The city took its name from the train depot. Isabella is named for the wife of Wells. Their son, Rolla, was mayor of St. Louis during the 1904 Louisiana Purchase Exposition World's Fair.

Humboldt Avenue was named for Baron Alexander von Humboldt, a German scientist who became one of the most admired and respected men of the 19th century. More places around the world are named for him than for any other scientist. As a pioneer in the study of plant geography and climatology, he was considered the founder of modern geography. He had an inquisitive mind, and not only studied nature but was also well-versed in geology, biology, chemistry, physics, botany, political science, mining and metallurgy. One of his major accomplishments was establishing international cooperation in the organization and publication of scientific works. He was the first to record isothermal lines (lines that connect points that have the same temperature). The cool ocean current in the Pacific Ocean that flows northward along the west coast of South America is called the Humbolt Current. Tower Grove Park contains a statue of Humbolt. There is also a public school named for him.

William Clark was appointed governor of the Missouri Territory, and served in that position until Missouri became a state in 1820. He was defeated in the gubernatorial election by Alexander McNair. Clark was then appointed superintendent of Indian Affairs. Large groups of Indians often came to St. Louis to consult with Clark. While they were here, they stayed on his land, near what is now Union and Natural Bridge. These councils were held in a wooded area called "Council Grove." A street by that name is still in the area. At one of these councils, the government proposed to send the Indians to the Indian Territory (Oklahoma). The Indians sent scouts to the area. On their return, the scouts declared they did not want to go because the water was bad. The government insisted that the Indians move, so the Osage Indians were forced to move to Oklahoma. The polluted water turned out to be oil. This tribe of Indians still receives a handsome income from the land they were once forced to occupy. William Clark has a public school named for him.

Jefferson Kearny Clark, one of William's sons, built a home near that area and called it Minoma; the name the Indians gave the land because of the "Sweet Waters," or springs, in the area. He married Mary Susan Glasgow, and his brother, George Rogers Hancock Clark, married Eleanor Glasgow, Mary Susan's sister. Jefferson Kearny Clark's half-brother, Meriwether Lewis Clark (1809-1881), lived with them at the country estate. Meriwether served in the state Legislature, and was an engineer for the city of St. Louis. He was a major in the Confederate army during the Civil War. Theodore Dowler, who owned land nearby, called the spring on his property "Kenwood." Minoma, Theodore, Dowler and Kenwood streets are in this area. Area residents such as David Goodfellow, L.C.

Nelson, Charles Semple, David R. Francis and William H. Glasgow are remembered with streets named for them. Goodfellow and Glasgow are also the names of schools.

Charles, another son of William Clark, planted several fine pine trees on his front lawn, and appropriately called his home "Pine Lawn." When the train station was built near his property, it was given the name of "Pine Lawn Station." The city took its name from the train station.

The first postmaster of St. Louis was Rufus Easton. Easton Avenue existed in St. Louis for a long time, but it is now known as Dr. Martin Luther King Drive. Easton's daughter Mary married Major Sibley; they founded Lindenwood College. Alton, Illinois, is named for Easton's son, Alton.

Chapter 8
South St. Louis

The east-west streets in South St. Louis were named for Indians or rivers, or both:

Delaware	Potomac	Meramec	Cherokee
Pontiac	Miami	Chariton	Gasconade
Shenandoah	Winnebago	Osceola	Rappahanock
Susquehanna	Chippewa	Itaska	Utah
Juniata	Keokuk	Neosho	Cahokia
Wyoming	Osage	Dakota	Kansas
Powhatan	Wacousta	Hiawatha	Accomac

Delaware Indians were members of the Algonquin tribe.

Pontiac was a chief of the Ottawa Indians. When France surrendered to the British in 1763, they lost the area east of the Mississippi. Chief Pontiac led an uprising against the English (known as "Pontiac's War" in history books) that lasted until 1766.[6] Three years after the war ended, Pontiac came to visit his St. Louis friends St. Ange de Bellerive, Charles Gratiot and Gabriel Cerré. Pontiac decided while in St. Louis to visit other friends in Illinois. He was warned that he would not be safe, but he adamantly insisted. He was killed by the Illinois Indians in April 1769, and his body was brought back to St. Louis. Chief Pontiac was buried with full military honors, near what would now be Fourth and Walnut streets.

To avenge the death of Pontiac, the Ottawa and Chippewa Indians hunted the Illinois Indians, persistently following them through the state and finally cornering them on a high bluff in the northern part of the state. The well-fortified Illinois Indians knew they were unapproachable for

---

[6] The English finally defeated Pontiac and his Indians by knowingly distributing blankets to them which were infected with smallpox.

battle. The Ottawa Indians remained at the bottom of the bluff, and the Illinois Indians starved to death. Not one member of the Illinois tribe remained. The area in the state of Illinois where this took place is now named "Starved Rock State Park."

The Juniata River flows into the Susquehanna River, forming the Wyoming Valley in the state of Pennsylvania. This valley is five miles north of Wilkes-Barre, located in Luzerne County.

Wyoming is an Algonquin name meaning "large prairie or plain." This is the name that was first given to the Pennsylvania Valley, where the Wyoming Valley Massacre took place during the Revolutionary War on July 3-4, 1778. Tory and Indian raiders, fighting under the command of British Maj. John Butler (Butler's Rangers), overwhelmed and massacred 200 inhabitants in these American frontier settlements. This is also the Wyoming Valley mentioned in Longfellow's poem "Hiawatha." When a new territory later became the state of Wyoming in the western United States, it was also called "Wyoming" because it described the area so well.

Shenandoah and Rappahanock are rivers in Virginia.

Potomac is a river in Maryland. The Ohio River forms the southern border of Ohio, Indiana and Illinois; and the northern border of Kentucky and West Virginia.

Gasconade, Meramec, and Chariton are rivers in Missouri. The Neosho River is in Kansas. Lake Itaska forms the headwaters of the Mississippi River, located in Minnesota.[7]

Kansas is a river in the state of Kansas, which was named after an Indian tribe. Utah was named after the Ute Indians.

The Cherokee Indians were in Florida and Georgia. The Winnebago Indians were from Minnesota. The Chippewa Indians were from the Great Lakes area. A Sauk Indian chief named Keokuk was from Wisconsin. Powhatan was chief of the federation of Algonquin tribes in eastern Virginia. He was the father of Pocahontas; his village was called Accomac. Cahokia Indians lived in Illinois. Osage Indians were from Missouri. Sioux Indians use the name Lakota or Dakota; Sioux is what the white man called them. Hiawatha was an Iroquois Indian.

Osceola was a Seminole Indian chief from Florida. He was lured to come to confer under a flag of truce, but was captured and thrown into prison where he died under mysterious circumstances. His head was cut off and put on display in the Fort Moultrie "Medical Mu-

---

[7] Lake Itaska was discovered and named by Henry Schoolcraft. The name comes from the Latin *veritas caput,* or "true head."

seum."[8]

Kansas, a street running east and west, was named for the Kansas Indians. When a subdivision was built near Carondelet Park, the street named Kansas was changed to Holly Hills, the name of the subdivision.

Miami Indians lived in what is now Indiana. Fort Miami was rescued by Gen. "Mad Anthony" Wayne when the fort was surrounded by Indians. The occupants of the fort were so grateful to him that they changed the name to Fort Wayne.

Some of these Indian street names have been changed:

Delaware	to	Geyer and Allen
Pontiac	to	Russell
Susquehanna	to	Arsenal
Hiawatha	to	Pulaski
Powhatan	to	Halliday
Wacousta	to	Crittenden
Rappahanock	to	Magnolia

The street named Ohio, running east and west (indicating it was named after a river), was changed to Lami. We still have an Ohio Street (running north and south) named for the state of Ohio. The Kansas Street that ran north and south was named for the state of Kansas; its name has been changed to Compton Avenue.

Cooper and Pacific were changed to Gratiot Street. Sycamore was changed to Labadie, then to La Salle, because there is a Labadie in North St. Louis. Virginia, running east and west, was changed to La Salle. Crooked and Wood streets were eliminated. Elizabeth became Hickory; Hickory Street in North St. Louis was changed to Wash, then Cole after Richard H. Cole, a school principal. There is a public school named Cole. We have an Elizabeth Street in Clifton Heights, and on The Hill.

Mary Ann became St. Vincent after the cemetery located there. Susan became Eads after James B. Eads, builder of the bridge that carries his name. A public school is also named for Eads.

Henrietta has been retained. It is said that one of the men who built nine of the homes on this street named it after the wife he abandoned in Canada.

Arrow and Kingsbury were changed to Shenandoah. A Kingsbury still is in the Central West End. Martha was changed to Lami for Michael Lami, an early settler. Lami died in St. Louis in 1784.

Russell is for William Russell; Ann is for his daughter; Allen is for

---

[8] At the end of King Philips' War (1675-76), the Indian Chief Metacom (King Philip) was killed and the victorious settlers displayed his severed head on a pike in Plymouth, Massachusetts, for 20 years.

Ann's husband, Robert Allen. These three streets are together in the Soulard area.

Victor, Sidney, Anna (not to be confused with Ann), Louisa, Sarah and Lane streets were all named by William Carr Lane, the first mayor of St. Louis.[9]

Victor was named for Lane's only son; Anna, Louisa and Sarah for his daughters; Lane was for the family name. Anna Street was changed to St. George after the area. The street named Carr Lane still runs north and south. There is also a public school named for Carr Lane. The name of William Carr Lane's favorite daughter was Sarah. He named a street for her, but his nickname for her was Sidney so he also named a street Sidney. Sarah was changed to Rutger, but Sidney Street still exists. Winter was also changed to Rutger for Arend Rutgers, an early land owner.

Lane, running east and west, was changed to Lynch. In the 1830s, B. M. Lynch was a specialist in supplying house servants; quite a pretentious title for a slave trader. During the Civil War, Lynch's slave pens were used as a prison for Confederate soldiers.[10] L'Esperance, Picotte and Trudeau were early settlers. Antoine Soulard married Julia Cerré, Julia Street is for Julia Cerré Soulard. Harper was changed to Dorcas, after the wife of William C. Carr. He built one of the first brick homes in St. Louis in 1813. There is a public school named for him.

Bent was for Judge Silas Bent, whose father participated in the Boston Tea Party. Bent was sent from Ohio to St. Louis in 1806 by Secretary of the Treasury Albert Gallatin to become surveyor general of the Louisiana Territory. The street which was named for him, along with Powhatan, was changed to Pestalozzi.

Bent Street by Tower Grove Park still exists; it was named after Lucy Bent Russell, daughter of Silas Bent. Her sisters married Judge William C. Carr, Joseph McClelland and Lilburn W. Boggs, who became the sixth governor of Missouri.

Johann Heinrich Pestalozzi, a Swiss educational reformer (1746-

---

[9] William Carr Lane and Auguste Chouteau were the candidates in the first election for mayor of St. Louis. Lane received 122 votes, Chouteau 70. It might seem unusual that Chouteau did not win, but it is not surprising that Lane was the victor. Lane, along with most members of the City Council, had all moved to St. Louis from Pennsylvania. This is probably also the reason that the Philadelphia system of naming streets was used when the street names were changed from French to English.

[10] These slave pens were still in existence in the warehouse basement of Meyer Bros. Drug Co. until the building was razed in the early 1960s to make way for Busch Stadium.

1827), was born in Zurich. The training of school teachers is still significantly influenced by standards he recommended during his lifetime. St. Louis has a street and a public school named for him.

Steins was once named Heaven. The area where Jacob Steins, a glazier and innkeeper, lived was called "Steins Town," and the name of the street was changed to Steins. Many of the families settling in the area were from Alsace-Lorraine and were very pro-French, even though they had German-sounding names such as Koeln, Poepping, Primm, Tesson, Courtois, Schirmer, Robert, Lorentz, Espenschied, Marceau, Krauss, Soper and Menard. Each of these names lives on as a street name in this area.

Henri Chattilon married Odile Delor, granddaughter of Clement Delor, the founder of Carondelet. They sold their house to Dr. Nicholas DeMenil and his wife Emile Sophie Chouteau, granddaughter of Pierre Chouteau. It is now known as the DeMenil Mansion on DeMenil Place. Tours are given through the house, and there is a restaurant in what was the carriage house.

Sam Wainwright was a brewmaster with Fritz and Wainwright Brewery. After his death in 1883, his widow Catherine commissioned architect Louis Sullivan to erect a building in downtown St. Louis in his honor. Sullivan completed this assignment in 1891 with the construction of the Wainwright Building, which was considered the first skyscraper.[11] Charlotte Wainright, his sister-in-law, died while the Wainwright Building was being built. Sullivan was asked to design and build a tomb for her in Bellefontaine Cemetery, a request he also fulfilled.

In 1902 Ellis Wainwright, Sam's brother and Charlotte's husband, was indicted for bribing members of the state Legislature; he fled abroad to avoid arrest. After the charges were dropped in 1911, he returned to St. Louis to live as a recluse. He never got over the shame of his downfall. When he died on November 6, 1924, he was buried with Charlotte in the tomb that Sullivan built.

John Street was changed to Lemp for Adam Lemp, who arrived in St. Louis in 1838. In 1840 he started a brewery, which proved to be a profitable business and made him a multi-millionaire. The Lemp Mansion, built in 1860, was a 33-room showplace. Besides the beautiful rooms and appointments, three massive vaults, each 15-feet wide, 25-feet deep and 13-feet high, were built at the rear of the house. The vaults were used to store numerous valuable works of art and other priceless possessions. These treasures and furnishings were changed with the seasons, in the same way that museums rotate their displays. Some servants did nothing

---

[11] The Wainwright Building has been remodeled and houses many state offices.

but polish silver in the "silver polishing" room, located in the basement.

Homes of this era usually had a third floor ballroom; the Lemp mansion didn't. Instead, an auditorium and a swimming pool were created in natural underground caverns. One could only enter these caverns through a tunnel from the basement of the house. Another tunnel led to a cave under the brewery, where barrels of beer were stored.

William Lemp's favorite son, Frederick, died "under mysterious circumstances" in 1901. After grieving for three years, Lemp shot and killed himself in his office in the mansion. His oldest son, William J. Lemp Jr., became president of the brewery. He built a new plant at Cherokee and Carondelet (now South Broadway) and the brewery prospered, rapidly expanding to cover five city blocks. Lemp Brewery was the largest in St. Louis when Prohibition closed the thriving enterprise.

The Lemp family was a symbol of the city's wealth and power. William Lemp Jr.'s wife, Lillian Handlan Lemp, was called the "lavender lady" because she wore a different shade of lavender every day of the week. Her carriages and the trim on her horses matched the color of her clothes for the day. Legend has it that her husband gave her $1,000 a day to spend on herself, and whatever money she didn't spend that day had to be returned to him that night. They ultimately divorced. Before she died, Mrs. Lemp said that "she did not want to be buried near her husband; she couldn't stand him alive, and certainly didn't want to be near him in death." He is supposed to be near the front of the tomb; she occupies the back. The Lemp tomb is across the road from the Wainwright tomb in Bellefontaine Cemetery.

William Lemp Jr.'s sister committed suicide in 1920.

On June 28, 1922, the magnificent group of buildings and machinery, once valued at more than $7 million, was sold to International Shoe Co., for $588,500. Driving south on Highway 55, the name "Lemp" can be seen on one of the buildings. You might also see the shield that was their trademark before Falstaff Brewery purchased it from them.

William shot himself in the later part of 1922 in the same office that his father used. His remaining brother's death was also attributed to a self-inflicted gunshot wound. A street is named after this unfortunate family. The Lemp Mansion Inn is also on DeMenil Place and offers tours, a restaurant and bed-and-breakfast service.

Congress, Senate and President streets are for the titles of the chief executive and the two governing bodies of the United States.

Mott was named for Frederick W. Mott, who organized the Southern Railroad and worked in real estate. He was the first pupil admitted to Blow School. This street was incorrectly spelled "Malt" for a while.

In the Tower Grove area, a few streets named for states ran between Old and New Manchester roads. Missouri became Talmage, Virginia became Boyle and Kentucky is unchanged. Many South St. Louis streets that run north and south are named after states. The streets named Mississippi, Missouri, Illinois and Arkansas are the names of large rivers, but because they run north and south, they are part of the state streets. States not having a street named for them are, for the most part, states that delayed the entry of Missouri into the Union. There are no streets in St. Louis named for the states of Massachusetts, New York, New Jersey, New Hampshire, Rhode Island or Connecticut. We have a street named Connecticut, but it is not named for the state.

The homes in the area south of Tower Grove Park were financed by the Connecticut Mutual Insurance Co. (located in Hartford), whose president was Humphrey Green. There was already a Green Street downtown (remember Prune?), so the street was named for Green's first name, Humphrey. These three streets, Humphrey, Hartford and Connecticut, are located south of Tower Grove Park. Men usually had streets named for them by using their surnames; women usually had streets named after their first names. There are some exceptions.

Gravois is taken from the French and means "gravelly, rubbish, or rubble"; some even say "garbage." Gravois by the "Gravois Coal Diggins" was called "Diggins Road." Gravois was the road to the dump.

West of Jefferson but still in the city, Gravois was muddy and unattractive until paving began in 1915. By 1918, Gravois was paved to the River Des Peres. Busch asked the city to continue paving Gravois to Grant's Farm (his home) and offered to pay half of the cost. When the job was finished, Gravois was the first concrete highway in Missouri, and was six miles long. A public school is named Gravois.

August A. Busch Sr. built Bevo Mill with a 60-foot windmill in 1916 for $250,000. Two short streets near Bevo Mill, Frieda and Gertrude, were named for two of Busch's nursemaids. There is a street and a public school named for Busch.

Records show that the owner of the land at the shallow point or ford on the River Des Peres (on the western boundary of the Carondelet Common Fields), was owned by James Morgan. This became known as "the road to Morgan's Ford." Today we just say Morganford Road. At one time it was also called "The Old Winding Road."

Cologne and Dresden were named after cities in Germany. Bowen was named for Confederate Gen. John Bowen. He had once been a St. Louis neighbor of Ulysses S. Grant. Bowen was one of the Confederate generals who surrendered to Grant at Vicksburg. Grant saw that his friend was very ill and offered the services of his personal physician. Bowen refused. If his men could not have access to these services, neither would he. He died 13 days later. Vicksburg surrendered to Grant on July 4, 1863. Vicksburg did not celebrate Independence Day until years after World War II. Thirty-nine regiments of soldiers from Missouri fought in the battle of Vicksburg; 22 fought for the North, 17 were with the South.

Sigel was named for a Union Civil War general, Franz Sigel.

Henry Blow, who was Ulysses Grant's ambassador to Brazil, married Minerva, the daughter of Thornton Grimsley. Their daughter Susan started the first kindergarten in 1873. Susan approached the school board with her plan; the board agreed that it was a wonderful idea but they had no funds to give her. Susan never received a salary for teaching school for 11 years, and she personally furnished most of the supplies. She did not receive recognition by way of a street name either, as Blow Street is for Henry Blow. There is also a Blow School.

Roswell Field, father of the poet Eugene Field, was one of the attorneys who represented Dred Scott; Mary French was one of his cousins. There are streets named Roswell, Field, Eugene, French Street and French Court. A public school is named for Eugene Field.

Carondelet Park was the estate of Alexander Lacey Lyle, a Confederate sympathizer who left St. Louis during the Civil War. Roswell Field handled his assets while he was gone. Lyle's property, consisting of 180 acres, was purchased for $140,570 by St. Louis in 1875. Since the dedication was held on July 4, 1876, someone suggested they name it "Independence Park."

The Knackstedt Dairy Farm was located south of Carondelet Park; there is still a street by that name. The hill where the cows grazed was called a crude synonym for "Cow Manure Hill." Many people, with a chuckle, will ask me if I know what it was really called. I do — and assume you will, too, from this hint.

One of the developers of Holly Hills was originally from Delaware; he named the streets Dover and Wilmington. William Federer, Don Livingston and Gus Arendes were developers who named streets for themselves. They met at the Coronado Hotel to draft their plans, so they named one of the streets "Coronado." Their wives, MARie Federer, WINifred Livingston and JeanETTE Arendes, also have one street named for the three of them — Marwinette.

The name Tesson came from Michael and Francis Tesson, merchants who also ran a ferry. St. Louis is nearly an island with the Mississippi, Missouri and Meramec rivers surrounding the city; one must cross water to get in or out of the city. That is why we have so many streets with

"Ferry" in their names: New Halls Ferry, Old Halls Ferry, Tesson Ferry, Dougherty Ferry and Lemay Ferry. The Davis Street Ferry was in Carondelet, the Wiggins Ferry was downtown, and North St. Louis had the Captain Lewis Bissell Ferry. Ferry Street led to the Bissell Ferry.

In 1835, the Missouri General Assembly established Manchester Road as the first official state road in St. Louis County because it ran west to Jefferson City, the state capital. Manchester is the only major road leaving St. Louis that does not cross a river. One of the reasons given for choosing Manchester Road on November 11, 1926 to convey U.S. Highways 50 and 66, was the fact that Manchester was the only improved road heading west. These highways were routed on Manchester Road until January 1, 1933, when Watson Road was completed and Highway 66 was relocated there. Highway 50 remained on Manchester Road until 1955, when it was also transferred to Watson Road. Manchester Road is still the route for Missouri Highway 100.

I met the widow of developer August Sturmfels at one of my talks. She asked me if I knew where the name "Marceline Terrace" came from. I told her I knew where it was located and how long it was, but that I didn't know how it was named. She told me that her husband asked her to name it and she gave it the name Marceline Terrace. I asked her if Marceline was her name. "My name is Vera," she replied. "I always liked the name Marceline, so that's what I named it." Sturmfels also named streets for his daughters Lavernell, Ruth and Myrlette.

Frank Trampitsch, a developer, named Salzburger, Austria, Tyrolean, Oldenburg, Heidelburg, Allemania, Hummelsheim, Hamburg, Toenges and Meckelsburg streets, and Martella and Fairfield Place. The last three streets were eliminated when Germania was created. The Trampitsch Insurance Co. and Helena Realty Co. (the latter named for his wife) shared an office on Meramec between Compton and Louisiana.

Hoover Way is a crosswalk, located one block west of Grand at Bellerive. It has a street name, but it is not a street.

Koenig, the German word for king, was the name of the developer who introduced matt brick to the area. The street he lived on was named Kingsland.

Chapter 9

Compton Heights - Shaw - Russell

In 1867 the city purchased 36 acres to use for a water reservoir on the highest point in the city, Compton Hill, which was named for the wife of Mayor James S. Thomas. Compton Avenue took its name from Compton Hill.

The city, which anticipated hosting the Columbian Exposition of 1892, knew a solution must be found to the water problem in St. Louis. It was necessary to draw water the day before it was used and allow it to settle because of the mud in it. They did not even want to consider the effect a brown water cascade would have on visitors to the St. Louis World's Fair. A saying in those days was "St. Louis water was too thick to drink, but too thin to plow." In March 1851, C.G. Rosenberg, Jenny Lind's manager, said this about St. Louis:

"It is muddier in wet, and dirtier in dry weather than any other part of the United States. It is a huge reservoir devoted to the manufacturing of mud on a wholesale scale. ..."

"The air is so rich along the Mississippi River, and the dust from coal smoke falls so thick in the streets, that one is as satisfied by an afternoon walk in St. Louis, as if one had eaten a heavy dinner."

Mark Twain said:

"St. Louis water is good for steamboating, but worthless for all other purposes except baptizing. If you let your glass stand for a half-hour, you separate the land from water as easy as Genesis. Natives do not take them separately; when they find an inch of mud on the bottom of the glass, they stir it up and drink it. Weak as water doesn't apply in St. Louis; you can chew St. Louis water."

Twain also wrote:

"The muddy Mississippi water is more wholesome to drink than the clear water of the Ohio ... there is a nutritiousness in the mud, and a man that drinks Mississippi water could grow corn in his stomach if he wanted to."

By 1860, St. Louis had 40 breweries; whiskey was almost as popular a beverage as water.

Although St. Louis presented the highest bid for the Columbian Exposition, the influence of the New England states won the Exposition of 1892 for Chicago. Undaunted, St. Louis made plans to host the Louisiana Purchase Exposition in 1903. As Chicago was one year late with the Columbian Exposition, St. Louis was also one year late with the Louisiana Purchase Exposition. By March 21, 1904, — two weeks before the fair was to open — every tap in the city was discharging a clear, unfamiliar, pure liquid. Some of the older St. Louisans were suspicious when they first saw the clear water; something *must* be wrong, there was no body to it!

The only building from the 1904 Fair still in use is the former Palace of Fine Arts, now the St. Louis Art Museum. The bird cage in the Zoo is also left from the fair, but it is not considered a building. The so-called "World's Fair Pavilion," was erected in 1910 by the Louisiana Purchase Exposition Company as part of the fair's reconstruction. The Olympic Games were held in St. Louis during the 1904 World's Fair.[12]

Compton Hill is still the site of Reservoir Park with its distinctive water tower. At one time, there were more than 500 water towers like it in the United States; only seven are left. The one in Chicago is one of the few original structures remaining after the Great Fire of 1871. There is one in Milwaukee which is called The North Point Tower; the one in New York is called the High Ridge Tower. I didn't find a name for the one in Louisville. There are three in St. Louis; the tower at 20th and East Grand is the oldest of the three and was used until 1910. Designed by George Barnet and built in 1871, it is the tallest free-standing Corinthian column in the world at 154 feet. The tower was listed in Ripley's "Believe It or Not."

The tallest water tower, designed by William S. Eames, was built at Blair and Bissell streets in North St. Louis. Built in 1885 and used until 1910, the tower stands 190-feet high. The 179-foot Compton Hill Tower, designed by Harvey Ellis and built in 1898, was used until 1929.

These towers regulated the water pressure to neighborhood homes; they also prevented the water pipes in homes from rattling by venting air between the surges caused by the giant one-stroke piston pumps.

---

[12] The Olympics originated in Athens about 490 A.D. The first modern Olympics was held in Athens in 1896, the second in Paris and the third in St. Louis, which was the first Olympics ever held in the United States.

It wasn't until the Grand Boulevard viaduct over the railroad tracks (which took four years to build) was completed in 1889, that any residential building was started. Compton Heights, the Tyler tract, the Shaw area, etc., were all developed after that. Compton Heights subdivision was laid out by Julius Pitzman, the man who designed Vandeventer Place. The residential deed restrictions for Compton Heights were the first used in Missouri. Such zoning restrictions are now widely accepted and have often been copied. Pitzman created two east-west, limited-access streets on his 250 acres. He cut off the six north/south streets of Arkansas, Tennessee, Louisiana, Virginia, Minnesota and Pennsylvania to accomplish this. Pitzman named one of the streets for Henry Wadsworth Longfellow (1807-1882), the first American honored by Westminster Abbey. Longfellow Street and a public school were also named for him. The second street was named for Nathaniel Hawthorne (1804-1864), a New England novelist, classmate and close friend of Longfellow. A street is also named for John Milton.[13]

The development of the Shaw and Tyler areas followed soon after Compton Heights. Most of those homes were built between 1900-1910.

Charles Stockstrom came to the United States when he was 16. He refined the gas stove, and founded Quick Meal Stove Co. (which later became Magic Chef Co.). He needed a lot larger than those available in Compton Heights to build the size house that he wanted. He purchased five lots on Russell facing Reservoir Park, and hired architect Ernst Janssen to design a mansion modeled after French and German castles. His family moved into the house in 1909. Members of his family lived in the house until 1992. The front lawn of this fabulous 30-room house resembles a park, with a long circular drive leading to the front door. There is a 12-room apartment above the carriage house where the servants used to live. After years of neglect, the house was recently refurbished by Shelly and Glynn Donaho, the new owners.

In 1882 the Sisters of the Most Precious Blood, a Catholic religious order, purchased the Schiller home located between Arsenal and Pestalozzi, Louisiana and Tennessee. They used it for a girls' boarding school, calling it St. Elizabeth's Academy. Additional buildings were needed as the school expanded over the years. In 1982, the 2900 and 3000 blocks of Tennessee between Arsenal and Pestalozzi was changed to "St. Elizabeth

---

[13] Longfellow's compositions include the "Song of Hiawatha," "The Courtship of Miles Standish," and "The Midnight Ride of Paul Revere." Hawthorne's works include *The Scarlet Letter* and *The House of the Seven Gables*. John Milton was an English poet who wrote *Paradise Lost*.

Avenue," to honor the centennial of the school in this location.

Kingshighway started as an Indian trail, or trace, to the portage on the Missouri River. Then it became the King's Trace, or the King's Highway, as most roads that ran between the king's land and the common fields were called. At one time, St. Louis was surrounded by streets named Kingshighway — Union Boulevard was called "Second Kingshighway"; what is now Bircher Boulevard was called Kingshighway NE. Christy Boulevard, Holly Hills Boulevard and Bellerive Boulevard were all called Kingshighway SW. South Grand Boulevard, from Carondelet Park to Bellerive, was once called Grand Kingshighway. A church located on the corner of Bellerive and Colorado still uses the name "Kingshighway Methodist Church."

Hiram W. Leffingwell envisioned a broad boulevard extending from the river on the north to the river on the south. He wanted to call it Lindell Boulevard because of its proximity to Peter and Jesse Lindell's property. Leffingwell convinced the Lindells, as well as Henry Shaw and John O'Fallon, how convenient such a broad boulevard would be. The Lindells, however, did not want the boulevard named for them. Leffingwell simply called it a "grand boulevard." It didn't live up to its name at first, mainly because much of it was still a dirt road in 1880.

Benjamin Franklin Howard, a member of Congress from Lexington, Kentucky, was appointed governor of the Upper Louisiana Territory on April 17, 1810, by President James Madison. In 1812, Howard divided the territory into the five counties of St. Charles, St. Louis, Ste. Genevieve, Cape Girardeau and New Madrid. He died on September 18, 1814. A bachelor, Howard left his estate (located southwest of St. Louis) to his favorite nephew, Benjamin Howard Payne. Payne, also a lifelong bachelor, died in 1821. He left this property to his younger brother, Thomas Jefferson Payne, who moved to St. Louis in 1828 after he acquired title to the estate.

Shortly after Henry Shaw arrived in St. Louis, he purchased property in southwest St. Louis. The first time he saw the Prairie des Noyer (the French Common Field southwest of the city), he wanted it. Shaw was probably very happy to loan money to Payne, who used 760 acres of his land as collateral. Payne could not repay the loan, so Shaw foreclosed and acquired the title to land between what is now Grand and Kingshighway, Shaw and Arsenal. This is where Tower Grove Park and Shaw's Garden is located. The "Tyler tract" (belonging to Mary Lawrence Tyler) and a small area of land (at the northwest corner of what is now Tower Grove Park) that Payne retained the title to were not included in the foreclosure. Payne died in 1867 and is buried in Bellefontaine Cemetery.

Shaw gave Tower Grove Park to the city in October 1868. The city agreed to provide funds from a bond issue to develop the park and to make annual appropriations for maintenance. Shaw worked with outstanding botanists to transform an almost treeless prairie into a park considered remarkable for its vast variety of trees and shrubs. Two-hundred feet around the perimeter of Tower Grove Park was reserved to be divided into lots and leased for fine homes to be built on them, as was the custom in England. The rent collected would provide continuing support for the Missouri Botanical Garden, which Shaw gave to the state of Missouri in 1858. He built what could be called a "model home," at Tower Grove and Magnolia avenues; this building is used today as the residence for the park superintendent. Shaw's plan was not successful, however, as no one would build a home on land they could not own.

The pillars at the north entrance to the park on Tower Grove and Magnolia were taken from the Old Courthouse when it was remodeled. The ruins at the reflecting pool were taken from the Lindell Hotel after a fire at the hotel in 1867. There were 12 pavilions and 12 wells in the park; the pavilions are still there but only one capped well remains (located by the administration building at the Arsenal Street entrance). Shaw presented three bronze statues in the park to the city. They recall the English, German, and Italian nationalities of Shakespeare, Humboldt and Columbus. The Steuben Society of America gave a statue of Baron von Steuben (originally a gift from the German government to the 1904 World's Fair) to Tower Grove Park. Tower Grove Park is one of the best-preserved Victorian walking parks in the United States, and one of only four urban parks declared a National Historic Landmark.

According to Shaw's will, the city had a limited amount of time to acquire the Payne tract or they would lose the rest of the park; ownership would revert back to his estate. The Payne tract was acquired by condemnation; the city also took possession of the 200-foot strip of land around the perimeter of the park at the same time. There were four buildings on the Payne tract; three of those buildings were razed, and the remaining one is on Magnolia between Kingshighway and Tower Grove Avenue.

Four Tower Grove Park employees and their families live in the park — in the gate house on Kingshighway, in the Payne house on Magnolia, in a house by the stables and in the superintendent's house.

Shaw owned approximately 1,800 acres in the city. He donated property at Lafayette and Grand to Mount Calvary Episcopal Church; another lot on Grand for the Protestant Episcopal Orphans Home; and land at 20th and Washington for St. Luke's Hospital. He built a four-room, two-story schoolhouse at what is now Vandeventer and South

Kingshighway in 1876 and gave it to the city. It was later moved a few blocks west to Columbia and Macklind. The building is now used as a community school, but it is still called Shaw School.

In the early 1800s, Maj. William Christy purchased a sizable section of land from Charles Gratiot. Christy sold 235 acres to Capt. William Chambers in 1816 for $763.75 (about $3.25 an acre). This land was between what is now Grand Boulevard and Tower Grove, Magnolia and Shaw. Chambers left the land to his daughter, Mary Lawrence Tyler, when he died; the property was called the "Tyler tract." Shaw wanted access from Grand Boulevard to his country home, but needed access through the tract. Shaw discussed the situation with Mary Lawrence Tyler. She agreed to give him a right-of-way if he would buy a strip of land on the north side of the right-of-way and provide funds for its upkeep (this right-of-way was first known as Floral Boulevard). Shaw planned to rent the lots on the property he purchased and use the money to help support the garden. Again, no one wanted to build a house on land they did not own, so no income was collected from that land, either.

As the area developed, Shaw's Garden had to pay $50,000 for the upkeep of Flora Boulevard to provide sewers, landscaping, etc.; the Grand Boulevard entrance alone cost $10,000. The Garden's share of expenses increased until it reached $150,000. Since the Garden did not have the necessary resources to continue this arrangement, the board of directors broke Shaw's will and sold the strip of land.

Mary Lawrence Tyler sounds like a very astute businesswoman. Besides her agreement with Shaw, she sold the land her father purchased for $763 to Richard Klemm, a developer, for $700,000 in 1888. Klemm plotted a subdivision and named two streets, Lawrence and Tyler, for Mary Lawrence Tyler; he also named a street for himself. When the city expanded out to this area, a street in North St. Louis — which had been changed from Webster to Tyler for Mary Lawrence Tyler — already existed; it is located next to Chambers which was named for her father. The street named Tyler in the Tyler tract was appropriately changed to Botanical for the Missouri Botanical Garden. Tyler Place Presbyterian Church at Spring and Russell is the only use of Tyler's name remaining in this area.

Even though St. Louis was 111 years old, Tower Grove Park, Shaw's Garden and the Russell property were the only lands developed west of Grand Boulevard in 1875. Magnolia, between Alfred and Kingshighway, was called Payne until 1881. Pauline, between Oleatha and Tholozan, was changed to Alfred for a relative of Thomas Payne; Maury was named for William L. Maury, a friend of Payne's.

Shaw also owned land north of the Tyler tract, extending as far as property owned by Mary McRee. After her husband, Sam, died in the cholera epidemic of 1849, Mary operated a race track between Old and New Manchester roads. In that area, Old Manchester Road is now called Vandeventer. All that is left of McRee's Racetrack is the street called Race Course Avenue. About 90-feet long, it extends from Vandeventer to Tower Grove. The first street north of Race Course is Hunt, for Charles Hunt, the secretary for McRee's Racetrack. McRee Street also is in the area. Hemp Avenue, the shortest street in the city, is nearby.

Shaw had 10 houses built on Shaw Place that he expected to rent to furnish income for the Garden. In his will, however, Shaw provided that his sister, housekeeper, etc., could live rent-free in some of these houses. When the taxes for Shaw Place rose to $17,000 (and the income only came to $4,000), Shaw's will had to be broken again. In 1915, the trustees of the Garden sold Shaw Place for $55,000. Some of these houses were built with bricked-up windows, which was an English custom to get taxes reduced. The superintendent's house at Tower Grove and Magnolia streets also has bricked-up windows.

Henry Shaw brought James Gurney from England to be chief gardener for the Missouri Botanical Garden and Tower Grove Park in 1866. After Shaw's death, Gurney was appointed the first superintendent of the park, beginning a tradition of three generations of park superintendents in the Gurney family. James Gurney introduced the water lily display in Tower Grove Park and the Garden; his son James Gurney Jr. maintained the park unchanged after his father's death in 1920. James Gurney Jr.'s daughter, Bernice, became superintendent in 1943. She expanded the recreational facilities, and after her retirement in 1976, she became a consultant to the Garden's board of commissioners.

In addition to Shaw Avenue and Shaw Place, Shaw named Flora, Magnolia and De Tonty. Tower Grove was the name of his country home and has a street named after it. He called what is now Spring Avenue "Morisse" for his brother-in-law. It was later changed to "Mercy"; farther north it was called "Cabanne." All these names were changed to Spring when this area was absorbed by the city.

In the early 1920s, the air pollution in the city was so bad that the board of directors of the Garden were afraid the rare flowers, plants and trees would die and become extinct. Part of the Garden, from Kingshighway to Alfred, was sold to facilitate the purchase of land in Gray Summit, Missouri, to move the Garden and save the plants. The pollution in the city was brought under control so the move was not necessary. The property in Gray Summit is now the Arboretum; an adjunct to the Garden and open to visitors.

Gurney and Heger courts were developed by Frederic Heger on Magnolia Street across from Tower Grove Park. Another point of interest in the 4100 block of Magnolia is Hortus Court. Five houses are built on both sides of a sidewalk, which runs at a right angle to the city sidewalk. There is no street, just a sidewalk separating two rows of houses.

In 1888, a single-track extension of the Blue Line Union Depot Horse Car was built as far west as Arsenal and Bent, near what is now the southern entrance to Tower Grove Park. A turntable, used for turning the bobtail car around without unhitching the mules, was located there. This turntable was never removed, it was just paved over. You can't help but notice this large paved area when you enter the park from Arsenal Street.

Politics were definitely involved with the naming of Cleveland Avenue. In 1884, the presidential candidate was Grover Cleveland, and a public school was named for him; A.G. Thurman was the candidate for vice president, and Thurman Street was named for him; Fulsom was named for Cleveland's wife, Frances Fulsom; and Blaine was the name of his opponent in the election, James G. Blaine. What is now 39th Street was once called Tifanny, after Louis Tiffanny, a landowner.

In 1880, the grandson of a prominent neighbor of Henry Shaw attended Oak Hill School at Tholozan and Morganford. He had such a dislike for school that when he was 16 he left home and went west to Montana. His parents hoped that when he experienced the hardships out west, he would be glad to return home and settle down. He came home three years later for a few weeks, but missed the West and was anxious to return. His parents recognized his talent as an artist and persuaded him to at least attend art school. He went for half a day, then quit. As he told his mother, "Heck, they spent the whole morning trying to show me how to hold a pencil. I already know how to draw." The young man returned to his beloved West, and became a friend of Will Rogers. Along with Remington, he is famous for the authenticity of his paintings of Western scenes and Indians. This young man was the artist Charles M. Russell, who died in 1926 at age 62.

James Russell, grandfather of Charles, operated a coal mine at what is now Tholozan and Morganford. He also operated a clay mine at Utah and Morganford, in partnership with his son-in-law, George Ward Parker. What is now Morganford was Russell Lane from Arsenal to Beck; Roger Place was Russell Place. Lucy and Bent streets were named for his wife, Lucy Bent Russell. Their granddaughter married a Portis, Gustine was a relative, Oak Hill was the name of James Russell's country home and streets are named for all of them. A public school is named Oak Hill.

Beck Avenue was named for John Beck, who owned the strip of land between the Russell and Christy estates. He must have been very proud of his block; he called it "Beckville." Fred Beck was postmaster of the post office located there from 1874-1876. Called Beckville Station, it was later merged with Tower Grove Station.

James Russell's tract was started in 1894; the tract named for Lucy Bent Russell was begun in 1912. Russell Boulevard is named for William Russell, brother of James. The Reese family once lived on what is now Humphrey and Morganford; part of Humphrey was once called Reese's Lane. Reese had a butcher shop and grocery store on Morganford, just north of the bridge over the Missouri Pacific railroad tracks.

The Tholozan tract was started in 1871. The development of other residential subdivisions in this area covered a span of 50 years, from 1880 to 1930. The first was Tower Grove Heights, bounded by Arsenal, Louisiana, McDonald and Gustine. Subdividing began in the Christy tract with Beethoven Heights in 1906, Newport Heights in 1908, Ellenwood Park in 1909 and Christy Park in 1910. During this same time, Chester Heights, Humboldt Heights and Rosa Park opened south of Delor. Work started on Grand Boulevard Park and Grand Meramec Park in 1906, and continued into the 1920s. Pomona Court, started in 1942, was one of the last subdivisions developed in the city. Streets are named for all these subdivisions.

Chippewa, west of Grand, was called "Mine Road" because it led to the Russell coal mine, and the Christy and Bingham clay mines. This area was also known as the "Gravois Coal Diggins." Bingham was named after John Bingham, a land and mine owner; Jessica Street is named after his daughter. Along with Osceola, these were the first streets in that subdivision. Christy is named for William T. Christy, who established the clay products plant (which eventually became the Laclede-Christy Clay Products Co.). The plant was located at the intersection of Christy and Delor; it is now the site of a department store.

Laclede-Christy Co. started to use a narrow-gauge railroad in 1889. The tracks ran north on Kingshighway from the plant, and west on an area between Winona and Chippewa to Macklind, where there were five miles of underground mines. When the tracks were removed, this became what is probably the only divided alley in the city of St. Louis. This also was one of the last areas in the city to be developed, due to the settlement of the underground mines. The Christy mansion at Alfred and Taft is now used as the Avalon Nursing Home. Alfred was originally Christy between Beethoven and Eichelberger. Ellenwood was named for Christy's daughter, Ellen. The land east of the Russell and Christy estates was owned by the families of R.F. Phillips, Thomas Grace and John Giles; men who worked in the "Gravois Coal Diggins." Streets in the area are named for them.

A family by the name of Hunt owned property east of what was the site of the House of the Good Shepherd Convent; it is now Gravois Plaza. Hunt Street was named for them. When the city limits extended out that far, the name conflicted with Hunt Street by the McRee Racetrack. Hunt Street by the House of the Good Shepherd was then named for a family who operated a nearby recreation area known as Bamberger's Grove. McDonald, Henry Lierman and James Dunnica also owned property in this area and have streets named for them. A workman who was building houses in this area had a girlfriend named Molly McKean; he named a street for her.

Chapter 10

Southwest St. Louis

Without zoning regulations to control haphazard development during the city's development, many prime locations had been used for commercial purposes, i.e. Mill Creek, Des Peres Valley, Mississippi Bluffs, etc. To protect residential areas from future encroachment of more commercial ventures such as streetcar sheds and switching tracks, property owners started building and maintaining private streets. Deed restrictions and assessments for maintenance, which became the responsibility of the owners, were introduced at this time.

Lucas Place was the first private street to be developed. Benton Place, Vandeventer Place, Shaw Place, Clifton Heights, West Cabanne, Forest Park Terrace, Westmoreland Place, Portland Place, Compton Heights, Lewis Place, Flora Boulevard, Westminster Place, Washington Terrace, Kingsbury Place, Windemere Place, Hortense Place and many others soon followed.

Christopher Schiller purchased land near the western border of the Carondelet common fields (located between what is now Morganford Road and Ulena Street) to develop a private street called "Schiller Place," after he sold his home to the Sisters of the Precious Blood. He had always admired the spacious boulevards on Flora Place, and Shaw Place with its 100-foot median. He definitely wanted the median on Schiller Place to equal or exceed the median on Shaw. When a financial panic occurred, Schiller did not have the money to continue his project and a developer bought the land from him. The developer divided the property into small lots and even sold lots on the land designated for the median. Schiller Place is now the street on the south side of what should be the median; Eichelberger is the street on the north side. Some of the houses built on the median face Schiller, some face Eichelberger, with very little space between the buildings.

Property west of Shaw's Garden and Tower Grove Park was owned by many people: William and Solomon Sublette, James D. Fyler, John Dalton, James F. Cooper, David W. Graham, Wesley Watson, John D. Daggett and Frederick L. Billon. Streets in the area are named for these landowners.

Kemper College, originated in 1837 by the Protestant Episcopal Church on 125 acres at the corner of what is now Kingshighway and Arsenal, was named for Rt. Rev. Jackson Kemper, the first missionary bishop of the Protestant Episcopal Church in America. The college opened in 1840 with Rev. P.R. Minard as its director. The college was closed in 1845 because of financial difficulties, and the property was sold. The college moved to Ninth and Cerre (near the hospital of Dr. Joseph N. McDowell) when it closed on Kingshighway. During the Civil War, the McDowell Hospital was used as a prison for Confederate soldiers and was called the "Gratiot Street Prison."

Peter Lindell and Henry Shaw purchased the college property and held it in reserve for eight years, until they sold land from present-day Kingshighway to 59th Street and Arsenal to Fyler, to St. Louis County for county health institutions. Southwest High School, located on Kingshighway and Arsenal, opened in 1939 and closed in 1990. The building was reopened for Roosevelt High School students to use while their school was being renovated. Roosevelt High School has now been reopened. The Southwest High School building is presently being used by the Mathews-Dickey Boys Club. The first street south of Arsenal at Kingshighway is Kemper; this is all that remains of Kemper College at this site.

An Englishman named Everett Horton sold a large tract of land west of Kingshighway and south of Chippewa, but reserved the right to name the area and streets. Horton called the area Southhampton, and named the streets Nottingham, Devonshire, Lansdowne and Sutherland for places in England. (see Appendix V "K" p. 179) The only frame house built east of Macklind will be found in this Southhampton neighborhood at 5307 Devonshire.[14] Another unusual structure at the time was the concrete block house fabricated to look like stone at 5233 Lansdowne. A public school bears the name Nottingham.

Bancroft was named for George Bancroft, an American historian who was secretary of the navy under President James K. Polk (1844-1848). Winona was named for the daughter of Carl Wimar, the artist who painted the dome of the Old Courthouse.

---

[14] This house was moved from west of Macklind and Bancroft to 5307 Devonshire when it was owned by William Reiter.

Numerous "high-toned" houses of prostitution flourished in St. Louis in the 1860s. William Barrett, the chief health officer declared, "Since prostitution cannot be suppressed, it may be and ought to be regulated. This is an age of progress." Imagine the discussions held over back fences, in homes, churches, taverns, on street corners and in the City Council chambers, concerning this controversial subject in conservative St. Louis! Ten years passed before the City Council enacted the necessary legislation (which passed by a vote of 16-5) requiring prostitutes to have regularly scheduled medical examinations and authorizing a hospital to be built. Since the primary purpose of this hospital was to treat these "social outcasts," the name chosen for it was the "Social Evil Hospital." In 1873, the total amount collected from examination fees for one year amounted to $134,000. The experiment was declared a success.[15]

Opponents to the hospital were concerned that the city was approving immorality so they conducted a campaign against it. A decision was reached by the state Legislature four years later (1874) to nullify the "Social Evil" ordinance. The hospital was renamed the "Female Hospital," because it was used exclusively to treat female patients. It was razed in 1914. The 13.5 acres on which the hospital was located was donated to the city for a park, which was first called Manchester Park because Old Manchester Road was the major border. When the name of that part of Old Manchester Road was changed to Southwest Avenue, the name of the park was changed to "Sublette," after another bordering street. Sublette Park serves a wide cross-section of the population, with a playground for young children, tennis courts, ball fields for team sports and paths for a leisurely stroll.

William Sublette told Frances Hereford before they were married that if he died first, and she remarried and changed her name, she would relinquish all rights to his property. Shortly after their marriage, Sublette asked Thomas Hart Benton to have him appointed superintendent of Indian Affairs in Washington, D.C. He received the appointment and was on his way to Washington in 1845 when he died. Frances did remarry, but she did *not* relinquish any property rights; she married his brother Solomon. Hereford Street is named for her.

(Andrew Sublette, the younger brother of William and Solomon, went to California during the '49 Gold Rush and was attacked by a grizzly bear. The bear's mate joined the fight. Sublette killed both bears but was so badly mauled that he died from the wounds. Some people call that "the good, old days.")

---

[15]At that time, most men earned less than $1 a day.

Some street names in this area were changed: Cooper is now Marconi, most of Billon is now Hampton, Blue Ridge Road is now Sublette, and St. Louis Avenue became Macklind.

Land owners from this area who have streets named after them include Will and James Jamieson, James McCausland, Joseph Weil, Louis Finkman and Lisette, who was a relative of Finkman.

Prather could be named after John Griffith Prather who was born June 16, 1834, in Ohio. His mother died soon after his birth and his father entrusted his care to relatives. At the age of 9 he ran away and floated on a plank down the Ohio River to Cincinnati. He had no formal education (his only learning was from the "school of hard knocks") but he was an industrious boy. He found work in a grocery store, then on riverboats. When notified of his father's death and an inheritance, he refused his share of the estate. He lived in California for a period of time, then came to St. Louis and joined Daniel G. Taylor in the wholesale liquor business. Taylor was elected mayor of St. Louis in 1861 and served until 1863. During the Civil War, Prather was a lieutenant colonel in the Union Army. He retired from business in 1896 and died on December 27, 1903, at the age of 69.

(Or, the street might be named for a landowner, James V. Prather, but John has a better story!)

Hilgard and Kinsey were surveyors who had streets named after them.

Developers who have streets named after them in this area are: Scanlan, Donovan, Moellenhoff, Wenzlick and Cyrus Crane Willmore, who developed Kingshighway Hills and University Hills. While Willmore was supervising the development of St. Louis Hills, he named Crane Circle and Willmore Road for himself. He then allowed two workmen to each name a short street, thinking they would use their names. One man had come from Austria and named a street Vienna; the second man was from Czechoslovakia and named the street Prague.

The road that led to D.W. Graham's Sulphur Springs was called Sulphur; the whole area was called Sulphur Springs. A train station was built when the railroad reached that area. The first train arrived at Cheltenham Station, five miles from St. Louis, on December 9, 1852; the entire area soon accepted that name. At one time, parts of Sublette, Hampton, Sulphur and West Park streets were named Cheltenham. A public school also was called Cheltenham.

Work on the railroad stopped because of a shortage of funds, and trains did not reach Jefferson City until 1855. Most of the Irish laborers built small, long and narrow, one-room-wide houses for themselves to fit the narrow city lots. While they waited for work on the railroad to continue, many found employment in nearby clay mines. St. James the Greater Catholic Church, on Tamm Avenue in Dogtown, was established in 1860 to serve these families. This area was first called Sulphur Springs, then Cheltenham. It is now called Dogtown. The eastern edge is called "The Hill." [16]

Italian men came to America without their families and boarded with German families. Later, the railroad permitted them to sleep in empty, parked boxcars. It is said that the beds never cooled. The men worked in shifts and at least three men probably used every bed, every day and night, while the others worked in the mines and brick works. Shortly before their shift was to end, experienced veterans would remind newer arrivals to "save some energy for the long walk up the hill."

The Italian men missed their family life, so they lived frugally in order to send for their families as soon as possible. The World's Fair provided an unexpected bounty after it closed — the dismantled building materials were offered to anyone who would carry them away. The Italians acquired a substantial amount of this material and built "shotgun" homes, styled like the boxcars they had previously occupied. Some of these buildings are still being used.

I recently read that the Viviano family obtained equipment from the Italian pavilion of the 1904 World's Fair. They acknowledged that the success of their pasta business started after this acquisition.

The Germans built homes on "Blue Ridge," near The Hill area, so they could live near their work when they were building the county institutions. St. Aloysius Catholic Church, established for the Germans in 1892, allowed the Italians to hold services in the basement until their own church, St. Ambrose, was established in 1903.

When the railroad reached Franklin County, work stopped again. The community applied for a post office, to be named the Franklin Post Office. The application was denied because a Franklin Post Office already existed in Howard County, Missouri. They next selected the name of the Pacific Post Office, in honor of the anticipated destination of the Atlantic and Pacific Railroad. The railroad eventually dropped Atlantic from its name, and became known as the Missouri Pacific Railroad.

Pattison Avenue Negro Baptist Church was organized in 1897 at 5232 Pattison in St. Louis. It remained there until 1970 when the site became part of the right-of-way for I-44. Hugh T. Pattison was a clerk of the Criminal Court.

---

[16] The Hill was once called Mount St. Louis. From Kingshighway to St. Louis Avenue (Macklind), Bischoff to Northrup, it was also called "Fairmont Heights."

The Rev. Benjamin St. James Fry of the Methodist Church purchased 35 acres of the D.W. Graham Sulphur Springs tract for a campground retreat. He called it "Clifton Heights," because John Wesley preached at a chapel near Bristol with that name. Clifton Street took its name from the area. Years later, in 1885, Clifton Heights was developed by Julius Pitzman and is well worth seeing today. Large frame Victorian homes sit on the side of the hills that surround a pond, which is snugly nestled in a hollow in the center; it almost has a Currier and Ives appearance. It is located one block west of Hampton Avenue and north of Columbia.

Jamieson Avenue was named for the Jamieson brothers who arrived from Scotland in 1852. James Jamieson operated a clay mine near where Longfellow School was later built. He lived at 6820 Scanlan until 1918, then moved to 51 Westmoreland Place.[17] William Jamieson worked for Christy and discovered clay on the Christy land; Andrew Jamieson worked for Russell and built a home for himself at 3719 Garnier. His daughter lived at 6571 Bradley.

Arthur was named for Vice President Chester A. Arthur, who became president after the assassination of James Garfield in 1881. Arthur died in 1886, two years before Lake Farm was developed into Harlem Place subdivision, which is what this area of the city was first called. Harlem Heights was platted in 1890 in the area south of Fyler and west of Ivanhoe. Lake Street was changed to Ivanhoe.

A street separated the property of two large land owners in the Central West End; each one wanted to name the street after his home state and they finally compromised. Since one was from Delaware and the other from Maryland, the men used the first three letters from the name of each state and formed the name "Delmar." There is a public school named Delmar. The area where a large race track existed in the county on the north side of Delmar is marked by two streets that are still there, Eastgate and Westgate.

Samuel Thomas Rathell, a real estate developer, asked his wife Oleatha Didawich Rathell to name the streets in that area. She named Oleatha for herself, Lindenwood for the college she attended,[18] Marquette for the school her children went to, and Delmar for the street she lived on while growing up. The original Delmar is still used in St. Louis, so she just reversed the spelling and called it Mardel. There are public schools named Lindenwood and Marquette.

---

[17] Mayor Cervantes lived in the house at 51 Westmoreland Place from 1960-1968 while he was mayor of St. Louis.
[18] Some say it was named for the linden trees in the area.

Chapter 11
West End, County and Outstate

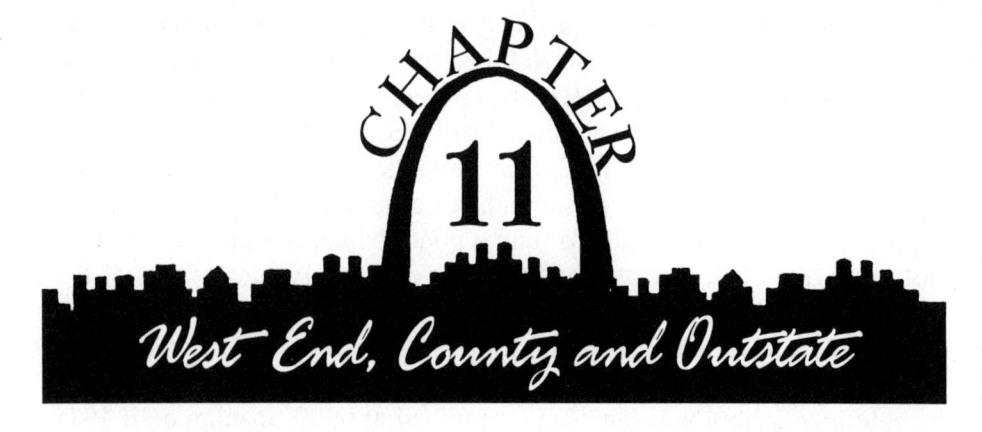

The streets or roads outside the city developed from paths worn by wagons and carriages traveling to various sites, so these routes were usually named for where they led. In St. Louis, the streets extended like spokes from the hub of a wagon wheel. Bellefontaine Road was first called "The Great Trail." There were two trails or roads joined at what is now the Baden wedge; the lower one where Hall Street is now, and the upper one where Broadway is now. Broadway was called "Bellefontaine Road" outside the city limits because it led to the "Big Fountain or Spring" on the Missouri River.

What is now South Broadway was called Carondelet because it led to the village of Carondelet, which was founded in 1767 by Clement Delor. Delor Street is named for him. He first called the village "Prairie a Catalan," after Louis Catalan; then changed it to "Louisburg," after the king of France. In 1794, the name was once again changed to "Carondelet," after Baron de Carondelet, the Spanish governor general of the Louisiana Territory. There is a street named Catalan in that area.

Affton was named for George Aff, a pioneer resident of the area.

The first seat of Missouri territorial government was housed in the Mansion House Hotel at Third and Vine in St. Louis; the second was in the Missouri Hotel at Main and Morgan in St. Louis. When Missouri became a state, the majority of delegates wanted the capital to be located in the center of the state, but there was no city. The delegates agreed to build a city specifically for the capital, and name it the "City of Jefferson."[19] While Jefferson City was being built (1821-1826), St. Charles served as the state capital. The road leading to St. Charles was heavily traveled and

---

[19] Only four presidents have state capitals named for them: Andrew Jackson, Jackson, Mississippi; Thomas Jefferson, Jefferson City, Missouri; James Madison, Madison, Wisconsin; and Abraham Lincoln, Lincoln, Nebraska.

in poor condition; really just a mixture of mud and manure and full of ruts.[20] Oak planks were laid down to try to improve it but this was not successful; when wet the wood was slippery, and it also warped and rotted. The planks were taken up and the road was covered with rocks. It is still called St. Charles Rock Road. The first Capitol in Jefferson City burned in 1837; the second one, completed in 1840, burned on February 5, 1911; the present Capitol was completed in 1917.

Outside the city, Market Street was first called "La Rue Bonhomme" (meaning good man; usually meant farmers) by the French fur traders, then Market Street Road because it was the extension of the city's Market Street. It eventually became Manchester Road because it led to Manchester, the first non-suburban settlement west of St. Louis. Established by James Hoard in 1795, Manchester was first called Hoardstown and used as a tax collection point in 1823. After Hoard died in 1825, the name of the town was changed to Manchester for a city in England. The whole town consisted of only 12 houses, two stores and one tavern.

A road from the Port of St. Louis on the Mississippi River led to Howell's Landing on the Missouri River. This road became a major "farm to market road," and was called the Old Bonhomme Road. It took two days of travel from Port of St. Louis to reach Howell's Landing, so the community at the halfway point became known as Center or Central. The dirt road was first covered with oak planks to improve it, and called the Central Plank Road. Olive Street led to this road from the city. To get to Center (or Central) and Howell's Landing, one took the Olive Street Central Plank Road. Central was first omitted from the name, and it was called Olive Street Plank Road. When the planks were removed, it became Olive Street Road. It is still called Olive Street Road. Center or Central remained a quiet farming community until 1930, when it was incorporated as "Olivette."

The Indian Mound, where Kingshighway and Dr. Martin Luther King Drive now meet, would be called "Bright Hill" in English. The French name is "Cote Brillante," which is what the street is called. There is also a Cote Brillante public school.

Julia Antoinette Cabanne, a granddaughter of Madame Papin, married Capt. James Wilkinson Kingsbury. Her daughter, Sarah Mary Virginia, married Armand Francois Robert Count de Giverville; another daughter, Adele Louise, married Alfred M. Waterman. De Baliviere was the name

---

[20] As late as 1910, 95 percent of Missouri's roads were still dirt roads. As of 1990, although there are 17 states larger in area than Missouri, Missouri ranks sixth in the total amount of road mileage maintained in the United States.

of the Mother Superior at the Convent School her daughters attended. John Sarpy was Julia Kingsbury's brother-in-law, and her mother was Julia Gratiot Cabanne. Cabanne, Papin, Kingsbury, DeGiverville, Waterman, DeBaliviere and Gratiot are all names of St. Louis streets.

In 1796, Madame Marie Louise Chouteau Papin asked the Spanish lieutenant governor of St. Louis to give her a land grant for a small farm on the bank of the River Des Peres. Madame Papin wanted the land so that her servants could have a garden to grow food for her ever-increasing family. If you would stand in front of the Art Museum in Forest Park facing north, most of the land you would see was once part of the grant given to Madame Papin. Her farm extended from what is now Art Hill to Maple Avenue (one block south of Page), and from Union Boulevard to Hanley Road, 2,720 acres. Forest Park, the largest park in the city, is 1,374 acres.

Charles Gratiot was 29 when he married Victoire, daughter of Madame Marie Therese Chouteau, in 1781; they received a Spanish land grant in 1785. The boundaries of this grant would now extend from the middle of Forest Park on the north to Pernod on the south, and from Kingshighway on the east to Big Bend on the west. These 5,712 acres were called the Gratiot League Square. When Gratiot died, it was divided among his sons Henry, Pierre, John, Paul and Charles Jr.

Charles Gratiot's daughters married into the Cabanne, Labadie and DeMun families; his granddaughters married into the Hempstead, Sarpy, Berthold, Kingsbury, De Giverville and Waterman families. Names of streets commemorate all these family names.

John McKnight purchased 629 acres of land from Charles Gratiot in 1816 and sold it to Ralph Clayton in 1821. Clayton married Rosanna McCausland. Some of their neighbors were the Tesson, McCutchen, DeMun, Hanley, Bemis, Skinker, Forsyth, McKnight, Thomas and Gay families. These families are all remembered by street names. The road from St. Louis to Fox Creek ran along Clayton's farm. Once called Fox Creek Road, it is now Clayton Road. When St. Louis seceded from the county, Ralph Clayton gave 100 acres for the County Seat. Wanting to show their appreciation, the county named it after him. The first presiding justice was Henry L. Sutton; his associate was Joseph Conway. Streets in the new Clayton township were named after the existing townships — Central, St. Louis, Meramec, St. Ferdinand, Carondelet and Bonhomme. The first commissioners named streets after themselves — William W. Henderson, Thomas J. Sappington and Robert G. Coleman. Some of these street names have been changed:

St. Ferdinand to Forsyth, after Thomas and William Forsyth.

Henderson to Maryland, after Lindell's Maryland.
St. Louis to Bemiston, after Judson M. Bemis.
Coleman to Brentwood, after J.T. Brent.

Gregorie Sarpy, a fur trader, received a grant for 6,000 acres[21] of land west of the River Des Peres and south of Gratiot League Square from the Spanish government. Kenneth Mackenzie bought some of this land; the Murdoch farm was also located in this area. The road along the west side of the Murdoch farm led to the Laclede train station on the Pacific Railroad. The road took its name from the station, Laclede Station Road. People used to take a "short-cut" through the Murdoch farm; a street called the "Murdoch Cut-Off" is still located there.

Richard J. Lockwood also bought property from Sarpy, and the road running down the middle of his property was named Lockwood. The Frisco Railroad ran its line through Lockwood's "Old Orchard," and appropriately called that stop Old Orchard Station. Old Orchard Street is also in the area. Lockwood's home is now Nerinx Hall, named for Fr. Nerinx of Kentucky, the founder of the Sisters of Loretto.

Hiram Leffingwell, along with Richard S. Elliot, developed a subdivision by the Kirkwood railroad station in 1852. It was named for James Kirkwood. The men named streets after themselves; after presidents — Washington, Adams, Jefferson, Madison, Monroe, Van Buren, Harrison, Taylor, Fillmore and Jackson; and for senators, Clay and Webster. The area took its name from the railroad station. The name of Webster Street was changed to Kirkwood Road, and Jackson was changed to Geyer. Main Street was the name of the east-west street north of the station. It was changed to Argonne Drive for the American battle in France during World War I.

Ballwin was named for John Ball, the first man to settle in that area.

Frederick Niesen, a wealthy St. Louis real estate agent, purchased land from Arman Francois Robert de Giverville and built a large frame house at Dale and Bellevue in 1892. John Rankin Dyer, a developer, bought 120 acres south of Neisen's property; together the men built many homes. Robert E. Lee, a young Army lieutenant who was stationed in St. Louis while working to eliminate Bloody Island from the Mississippi River, often remarked that this part of the country reminded him of his home in Richmond, Virginia. Dyer and Niesen named their development Richmond for the city in Virginia, and added Heights to the name because the land is some of the highest in St. Louis County.

---

[21] It has been written that Auguste Chouteau had Spanish land grants amounting to over 30,000 acres; his brother Pierre had land grants totaling 27,500 acres.

Crestwood was named for a large white oak tree.

The Rev. Artemas Bullard, pastor of the First Presbyterian Church in St. Louis, along with John C. Marshall and Carlos S. Greeley, established a boy's school and called it Webster College after Daniel Webster. Marshall later platted a subdivision nearby which he named Webster Groves, and the train station was called Webster Groves Station. The school was discontinued after Bullard was killed in a train wreck over the Gasconade River in 1855. The building became a soldiers' home; in 1868, it housed the St. Louis Protestant Orphan Home. In 1916, the Sisters of Loretto opened a college in this building and changed the name to Webster College, in honor of Daniel Webster. It is now Webster University. In 1896, five separate communities along the railroad were incorporated to become Webster Groves. The Pacific Railroad made stops at Webster College, Tuxedo Park and Webster Park; the Frisco Railroad stopped at Old Orchard and Selma stations.

The following men also built homes in the area and have streets named for them: Edward M. Avery, L.R. Blackmer, Dr. B.J. Bristol, Matthew Chestnut, William H. Gore, Charles Gray, John P. Helfenstein, James and Edward Lancaster, John C. Swon, George M. Plant, C. Wilshusen, and Edward and Justin E. Joy.

Planning for I-44 began in 1958, resulting in the destruction of 200 homes in Webster Groves for the construction of this interstate highway.

Shrewsbury was named for Shrewsbury, England.

Eureka was a station on the Pacific Railroad line, named for the cry of joy uttered by early travelers when they finally arrived in California.

Pacific is the western boundary that was reached when the Atlantic and Pacific Railroad was being built. The railroad was later known as the Missouri Pacific or MOPAC.

James C. and John L. Sutton originally operated a blacksmith shop on South Church Street in St. Louis; they later moved way out to Manchester and Sutton. James Sutton purchased 334 acres of land for "a dollar and a bit" per acre. Jean Baptiste Bruno, a French farmer, was one of their neighbors; another neighbor was a lawyer, Charles S. Rannells. James Sutton's land was divided among his nine children when he died in 1877. His daughter, Mary Marshall, sold some of her land for a subdivision that was called Sutton City. The name was later changed to Maplewood because of the maple trees planted along the streets. Marshall named streets for these trees and shrubs: maple, elm, myrtle, hazel, vine, cherry, arbor and flora. Sarah and Harrison are named for a Sutton daughter, and Ellendale for a granddaughter. Limit Avenue indicates the boundary between Maplewood and St. Louis.

Rock Hill is located on a rocky hill on the way to Manchester where James C. Marshall and others built a church.

The Lohmeyer family bought land from one of the Sutton sons; Moses Greenwood also acquired some of this land. Greenwood named a street after himself, along with Piccadilly, Cambridge, Oxford, Commonwealth, Manhattan, Canterbury, Linden, Drury and St. James streets.

Sappington Road (63122, 63126, and 63128) was named for Dr. John Sappington, one of the discoverers of quinine. He had four daughters, Gov. Claiborne Fox Jackson married three of them. Meredith Marmaduke, Missouri's eighth governor, married the other one.

William Long, the founder of Fenton, named it for one of his relatives, Rev. Joseph Fenton.

Valley Park was a recreation park in the valley of the Meramec River; it was first called Meramec Valley.

Lemay was first called Luxemburg, then changed to Lemay for Francois LeMais, a ferrymman. Lemay Ferry Road was for the road that led to this ferry. Records indicate that the residents appreciated and wanted to recognize the service provided by the ferryman.

Mehlville was named for Charles Mehl, an early settler.

Edward G. Lewis called his 80 acres "University Heights," because of its proximity to Washington University. He named the streets in this subdivision for the principal eastern universities: Trinity (which he had attended), Cambridge, Cornell, Princeton, Amherst, Dartmouth, Yale, Vassar, Colgate, Tulane, Purdue, Vanderbilt, Harvard, Syracuse and Radcliffe.

University City is located on land once owned by the Kingsbury, Waterman, Ames, de Giverville, Deaver, Sutter, Kingsland, Creveling, Clemens, Cates, von Versen, Hanley, Gannon, Forsyth and Tesson families.

Brentwood was named for its founder, J.T. Brent.

Peter Albert Ladue, a wealthy lawyer, owned several farms in the country; the road that led to his farms was called Ladue Road. Deer Creek was on one of these farms. John and William McKnight, the McCutchan, Woodson and Litzsinger families, Robert A. Barnes, Joseph Conway, John F. Lay, John Warson and Isaac J. Price families were his neighbors. Streets are named for all these landowners.

Benton Missouri was named by Ringrose D. Watson in honor of Thomas Hart Benton. It was first called "The Glades."

Dr. James Jennings arrived in St. Louis in 1839, and considered purchasing land near what is now Grand and Olive. He eventually purchased a larger, less expensive tract of 2,550 acres outside the city. Laura,

Lucille, McLaran, Switzer, Theodore, Ada Wortley Lane, Belle, Florence, Garesche and Jennings Road were named for him and members of his family. His holdings were so large that three railroad stations were located on his property: Heights, Jennings and Woodland. Jennings Station Road led to the central station.

Overland was named for the Overland Trail, a collection of trails that headed westward from the Mississippi River. Originally, it was supposed to be called "Ritenour City," after landowner J.S. Ritenour. He was subsequently honored by having his name given to a school district. The Parkway School District was named for the Daniel Boone Parkway (U.S. 40).

Ferguson was named for William B. Ferguson, a real estate developer. He donated nine acres of land for the construction of the railroad to St. Charles on one condition: that the station be named after him. The city that grew up around the station also took the name.

St. John was named for John L. Ferguson, who owned most of the land in the area. I do not know if he was related to William B. Ferguson.

Black Jack was originally called New Bielefeld, after the German city from which most of the early settlers came. The name "Black Jack" was inspired by three large "blackjack" oak trees growing at the intersection of Old Halls Ferry and Parker roads.

Riverview was named for its geographic location overlooking the Mississippi River.

Charles F. Vatterott, the developer, named St. Ann for the Mother of the Blessed Virgin Mary to honor her. He wanted to provide affordable homes for families having four or more children because he knew they would have a problem finding a home.

One man felt St. Louis was getting too crowded and wanted more open space around his home. He purchased land out in the county, built a fine home and invited all his friends to celebrate with him. One of them mentioned that it looked like he was living on "Easy Street." Everyone enjoyed this remark. As the company left, one of the group put a printed sign proclaiming "easy street" in front of his house. Years later, when street signs were being installed by St. Ann, they saw this homemade sign and replaced it with a regulation street sign. He continues to live on Easy Street.

Hanley Hills was named after Hanley Road, which was named for Martin Hanley, a farmer and Confederate sympathizer.

Bridgeton was originally called "Marais des Lairds," or "Swamp of the Cottonwoods." It was later called "Ville de Robert," and then Owen's Station, after its founder, Robert Owens. It was named Bridgeton in 1843.

Hazelwood was named after the estate of Maj. Richard Graham, son-in-law of John Mullanphy. Rumor has it that when Henry Clay visited Graham's home, he called it "Hazelwood." Graham's home was actually located in what is now Berkeley but it makes a good story. (see Appendix V "L" p. 179)

French Canadian Louis Blanchette built a cabin for his Pawnee wife Angelique and himself in 1769. Before long, other French Canadians came to live in the area and the settlement took the name of "Les Petites Cote," or the "Little Hills." The French settlers did not farm but, like the Indians, hunted for their food. In 1767 Auguste Chouteau surveyed the area and appointed Blanchette commandant of the district.

The Catholic church built on November 7, 1791, was named San Carlos Borromeo. The village also was called San Carlos. (The English translation, St. Charles, has been in use since 1803.) Blanchette died in 1793, and Charles Tayon was appointed commandant. He declared that the land settled by the early French Canadians did not belong to them and granted the property to himself. (How convenient!) St. Charles formally became a village October 13, 1809. It was named as one of the five original Missouri counties in 1811.

During the war of 1812, Maj. Nathan Heald was ordered to evacuate Fort Dearborn, the site of present-day Chicago. The fort was attacked by Indians of several tribes before an orderly evacuation could be held. Major Heald and his wife were each captured by a different band of warriors. After Heald escaped, a friendly Indian offered to rescue and deliver Mrs. Heald in exchange for a mule and a bottle of whiskey. Heald agreed to the terms, and the Indian delivered her as promised. The couple later moved into a cabin in St. Charles County that was built by Jacob Aumwalt. In 1831, the couple was astonished when they were visited by the Indian who had rescued Mrs. Heald in 1812.

In 1786, St. Ferdinand was settled by French fur traders. The name was changed to Florissant in 1939. Flordel Hills used the first four letters from FLORissant for part of its name.

Bellefontaine Neighbors was named for Fort Bellefontaine, an army post established where the Missouri River meets the Mississippi River by a beautiful big spring. The road that led to the spring and fort was named Bellefontaine Road. In 1840 a land owner, Dr. William G. Gibson, extended the name to the surrounding area.

Vinita Park was named by its developer, A.C. Stewart, owner of the Vinita Realty Co.

Bellerive was named for Louis St. Ange de Bellerive, the French commandant who left Illinois and came to St. Louis soon after it was founded. The country club first used his name, and it was later adopted by the surrounding area. Bel-Ridge was originally a subdivision in the BELlerive area; Bel-Nor also takes its name from BELlerive.

Charlack took its name from St. CHARles Rock Road and LACKland Road. Lackland Road was named after Rufus Lakeland, one of the area's first bankers.

Pagedale was named after Page Boulevard.

Breckenridge Hills was named for James Breckenridge from Kentucky, who settled on that land before the Civil War.

Spanish Lake was named for a spring-fed lake which was a favorite recreational spot for the Spanish soldiers quartered in the area.

Kinloch is derived from the Scottish term "kind a' lock," or "at the head of the lake." Some say it was named after a large country club in the area and was given the Scottish-sounding name in keeping with the Scottish origin of golf.

Columbia, Missouri, was founded by Col. Richard Gentry who became the city's first mayor and first postmaster. In 1837, he left to fight the Seminole Indians in Florida and was killed. Sen. Thomas Hart Benton obtained the appointment of postmaster for Gentry's widow. She served in that position for 30 years.

Columbia University was the first university west of the Mississippi; it was established on June 4, 1839. The university was occupied by Union troops during the Civil War. After the war, the Drake Amendment prevented anyone in Missouri accused of being sympathetic to the Confederacy in any way, from voting or holding public office. Out of a population of 2,236 in Columbia, only 238 residents could vote.

Joplin, established after the Civil War in 1873, was named for Rev. Harris G. Joplin, who started the first Methodist Church in Jasper County. Lead deposits were found in the area within two years. This "Klondike" in Missouri had 12 dry goods/clothing stores, 12 blacksmith shops, five hotels, 16 doctors, 16 lawyers, two banks and 75 saloons. The mining company paid their employees with pasteboard checks, which were only redeemable at the company store. A state law, passed in 1891, corrected that injustice.

The site of Hannibal was given to Abraham Bird of New Madrid in exchange for his property that had been destroyed in the earthquake of 1811. When the town was platted, salesmen came to St. Louis to sell lots. The Civil War put an end to most of Hannibal's river commerce.

Louisiana was named after the daughter of John Walter Bayse. He gave her that name because she was born in 1803, the same year as the Louisiana Purchase.

The story most often told about Rolla is that the town was laid out by settlers from North Carolina in 1858. They wanted to name their city after Raleigh, the capital of their home state. They were not great scholars, so they spelled the name the way they pronounced it — Rolla.

Festus, founded in 1886, was named for banker Festus J. Wade.

In 1833, an area in Greene County known as Kikapoo Prairie because the Delaware and Kikapoo Indians lived there, invited all the residents to vote for their choice of a name for the County Seat. A white man married to an Indian woman lived on a creek which took its name from him; his name was James Wilson. He took a jug of white whiskey to the polls on election day. When the people came to vote, he took them aside and said, "I live here. I was born and raised in the beautiful little town of Springfield, Massachusetts. It would please me very much if you would vote to name this town Springfield." He would then produce his jug for voters to sample. When the votes were counted, "Springfield" was the name chosen for the County Seat. Wilson's Creek became the site of the bloodiest battle of the Civil War fought in Missouri.

Washington, established in 1822, was named for President George Washington. Lincoln, established in 1868, was named for President Abraham Lincoln. The 27 presidents of the United States — beginning with Washington in 1789 up to Woodrow Wilson in 1921 — all have either a city, county, place or park named for them throughout Missouri. The exception is Chester A. Arthur, although St. Louis has a street named for him.

Some years ago, the wife of a St. Louis businessman saw a small house for sale in the county west of Florissant and thought it would be nice to use as a summer/weekend home. Her husband bought the house and lot, and ordered a certificate of title. The title examiner found no conveyances, and few mortgages. He thought he might not have been looking for the right property, so he asked the owner to bring the tax receipts to him. When the owner produced a large bundle of paid tax bills, the examiner was astonished. The first paid tax receipt was for "one dollar and two bits," and signed by Alexander McNair, Collector, 1810. The property had been owned by the family of the original purchaser since the title was confirmed by the United States, immediately after the Louisiana Purchase in 1803! (McCune Gill)

Kimmswick was founded in 1859 by Theodore Kimm, a German immigrant who served as the first postmaster.

Farmington, established in 1798, was first known as Murphy Settlement for the Baptist minister, William Murphy. His wife, Sarah Barton Murphy, was the aunt of David Barton, the first senator from Missouri.

Wentzville, established in 1855, was named for the chief engineer of the St. Louis Kansas City and Northern Railroad.

Sikeston was founded in 1860 by John Sikes.

Herculaneum, founded in 1808 by Moses Austin, was named for the ancient Roman town that had been buried under 60 feet of lava by Mount Vesuvius in 79 A.D.

Kirksville was established in 1841 and named for Jesse Kirk, a tavern owner.

Webb City was founded by John Webb in 1873.

Warrenton was named for Gen. Joseph Warren of Massachusetts, who was killed in the Battle of Bunker Hill. In addition to a St. Louis street, there is also a county in Missouri named for him.

Branson, founded in 1881, was named for R.S. Branson, the postmaster.

Gray Summit was founded by Daniel Gray in 1859.

The first white settler in Lebanon in 1820 was Jesse Ballew. The city was first called Wyota after the early Indian inhabitants. Most of the early settlers were hunters and farmers from Tennessee. It was later changed to Lebanon, after a minister's hometown in Lebanon, Tennessee.

Ste. Genevieve is the oldest white settlement in Missouri; it was founded on January 3, 1735, by the French.

Cape Girardeau was established in 1808.

Chapter 12

Duels and Parks

DUELS

In 1810, Dr. Bernard G. Farrar's brother-in-law was caught cheating in a card game with James A. Graham, a lawyer, and was challenged to a duel. Dr. Farrar served as his brother-in-law's second. When his brother-in-law did not appear, Dr. Farrar had to fight in his place, according to the code of honor (even though Farrar and Graham were close friends). Both men were wounded in the fight; Graham more seriously than Farrar. Farrar attended to Graham's wound, but Graham died. Farrar recovered and died in the cholera epidemic of 1849. Dr. Farrar was St. Louis' first American-born physician; Hyde Park was his estate. There is a street named for Farrar.

* * * * *

Henry S. Geyer, a lawyer, and George H. Kennerly, a merchant, fought a duel in 1816; Kennerly was wounded. There are streets named for both men.

* * * * *

Thomas Hart Benton and Charles Lucas, both lawyers, fought a duel in 1817 which resulted in the wounding of Lucas. Benton, however, was not satisfied, and demanded another duel be fought at a distance of 10 feet. When Lucas recovered from his wounds, they fought again on September 27, 1817. This time Lucas was killed and Benton was wounded. Jean Baptiste Lucas, father of Charles, never forgave Benton for killing his son. Lucas Street is named for J.B.C. Lucas, the father of Charles Lucas.

* * * * *

William Smith, born in 1772, arrived in St. Louis in 1810. He became director of a bank, and built one of the early brick houses in the city in 1812. The day after the death of Charles Lucas, Smith was discussing the affair with William Tharp. Suddenly, Tharp drew a pistol and shot and killed Smith, who left a widow and five children. His widow married Lewis Edward Hempstead on December 29, 1827; she lived until October 24, 1832.

* * * * *

Commodore Stephen Decatur fought in the War of 1812 and came home unscathed. He was killed at the age of 41 in a duel with Commodore James Barron in 1815. He is remembered for his statement, "Our Country, may she always be right, but my Country, right or wrong."

* * * * *

In 1818, Capts. Ramsay and Martin, stationed at Fort Bellefontaine, dueled. Martin wounded Ramsay, who consequently died from the wound.

* * * * *

In 1820, the seconds for Alphonse Stewart and William Bennett agreed that guns, without bullets, would be used. However, Bennett secretly loaded his gun and killed Stewart. Bennett was indicted, convicted and hanged; not because he fought in a duel and killed a man, but because he had taken an "ungentlemanly advantage" of his adversary.

* * * * *

There is record of a duel between a man named Waddell and a man named Mitchell in 1823. Both men were killed.

* * * * *

Also in 1823, William Rector, U.S. surveyor general at St. Louis, and Joshua Barton, U.S. district attorney for Missouri (and brother of Sen. David Barton), fought a duel. Barton was killed.

* * * * *

Captain Harrison and Dr. Randolph dueled in 1828; neither man was injured, and both were satisfied.

* * * * *

A man named Tates fought a man named Lelong and wounded him in 1838.

* * * * *

There is record of a duel, with swords as the weapon, between Mr. Heisterhagen and Mr. Kibbe in 1845. Kibbe was wounded.

* * * * *

Thomas C. Reynolds, a lawyer, and Benjamin Gratz Brown, who was later a governor and also a senator from Missouri, fought a duel over the issue of slavery in 1857; they used pistols at 10 paces. Brown was wounded in the knee and limped for the rest of his life.

* * * * *

In 1860, Edward B. Sayers, an engineer, criticized Gen. D.M. Frost; Frost horsewhipped Sayers in his office on Chestnut Street. Frost and

Sayers then fought a duel. When they met on Bloody Island, Sayers fired first and missed; Frost immediately fired into the air. Both men were satisfied.

* * * * *

When John S. Marmaduke was an officer in the Confederate army in 1863, he called Confederate General Walker a coward, and was challenged to a duel. The rules of their duel stated that they were to walk 10 paces, turn, and approach firing their revolvers; Marmaduke's second shot killed Walker. Marmaduke was later governor of Missouri. There is a street named for him.

* * * * *

The Missouri Legislature passed a law forbidding dueling in 1822. In 1835, they passed another law which made dueling a crime even if no one was wounded or killed. Neither of these laws was successful in stopping duels.

The Constitutional Convention of 1865 finally solved the problem. It stated, "Anyone who should hereafter be involved in a duel, act as a second or accept a challenge, could not hold any public office." This ended the practice of dueling in St. Louis. Taking a chance on losing one's life might be considered of little consequence, but losing one's job and/or career was an entirely different matter.

SOME EARLY ST. LOUIS PARKS

Clinton, Jackson and Marion parks in North St. Louis were established by Christy, Wright and Chambers in 1816.

Lafayette Park, in South St. Louis, was part of the common land originally owned by the city. Establishment of the park was initiated by the city in 1836 through the efforts of Thornton Grimsley. Nothing else has ever been on that ground.

Washington Park was purchased by the city in 1840. This is where City Hall was built and now stands.

Carr Park, at 10th and Carr streets in North St. Louis, was donated to the city in 1842.

St. Louis Place, in North St. Louis at 21st Street and St. Louis Avenue, was donated to the city in 1848.

Hyde Park, in North St. Louis at 20th and Farrar streets, was purchased from the Farrar family in 1854.

Missouri Park was purchased from James H. Lucas in 1854. He donated another block called Lucas Garden. They are both in the downtown area adjacent to the Main Library, at 13th and Locust streets.

Benton Park, at Jefferson and Arsenal, was part of the common land owned by the city. It was first used as a cemetery, and converted to a park in 1866.

Tower Grove Park, at Grand and Arsenal, was donated to the city by Henry Shaw in 1868. Because it was located outside the city limits at the time, it was necessary for the state Legislature to pass a bill giving the city permission to accept the park.

Lyon Park, on South Broadway, across from Anheuser-Busch Brewery, consists of one square block. It was donated to the city by the U.S. government in 1869. The statue of General Lyon was moved to this park in the 1960s.

Forest Park was developed primarily through the efforts of Hiram Leffingwell, who wanted the city to purchase 2,754 acres for it, but compromised for the 1,374 acres they finally acquired in 1874 for $800,000. Most of the land was owned by William Forsythe, Thomas Skinker, the Chouteaus and John Cabanne. The formal dedication of Forest Park was held on June 24, 1876. There are streets in St. Louis named for the Chouteau, Forsythe, Skinker and Cabanne families. A public school is also named Chouteau.

The residents of St. Louis did not want Forest Park. "It is too far away," was the reason most mentioned. Not only was it too far "out in the country" for people to use, the park was well beyond the range of affordable transportation. To show their displeasure, *all officials who voted to buy Forest Park were voted out of office at the next election.*

The land remained undeveloped, for the most part, until the World's Fair in 1904. The committee that came to St. Louis to inspect Forest Park for the site of the World's Fair got lost in the woods! A street is named for Leffingwell in St. Louis; it runs north and south and is located two blocks west of Jefferson at Delmar.

The park contains many important statues. One is of a Union general, Franz Sigel, seated on a horse facing north in front of the Municipal Opera. His statue faces a white 30-foot-tall stone monument erected in 1914 in memory of the Confederate soldiers from St. Louis who died in the Civil War. Placing a statue honoring Confederates in Forest Park was quite controversial. The City Council would only accept it if the sponsor, the Confederate Monument Association of St. Louis, would agree to maintain it. No other monument in the park is encumbered in this way. St. Louis has a street and a school named for Sigel.

A statue of Edward Bates, cast in 1871, is also in this park. It was unveiled the day the park was dedicated on June 24, 1876. It had originally been placed near the southeast entrance to Forest Park but was later moved to the present location west of the Art Museum.

Bates served as attorney general in Lincoln's Cabinet. He owned slaves until 1844, and favored the creation of colonies in Africa for the freed slaves. One of his sons served in the Union army, and one son served in the Confederate Army. Bates advised Lincoln that St. Louis had men with skills necessary to produce iron-clad gun boats. The government placed orders for boats, some exceeding 200 feet in length, for use against the Confederates in the Civil War. The boats were given interesting names: *The St. Louis*, *The Mound City*, *The Benton* and *The Carondelet*. A brass relief displaying the likeness of James B. Eads, the builder of these boats, is on one side of the base of this statue.

Lucius Boomer, from Chicago, was given exclusive rights to build a bridge across the Mississippi River at St. Louis with a 25-year charter. Rumors spread that Boomer, the Wiggins Ferry Company[22] and the various steamboat companies, conspired to delay the building of this bridge to further isolate St. Louis. Boomer built the Gasconade River railroad bridge that collapsed on November 1, 1855, killing 44 and injuring 100. This was not an unusual occurrence, as one out of four bridges built in those days collapsed. Numerous accidents also occurred on the railroad bridge over the Missouri River at St. Charles; a total of 129 lives were lost in 1871 on that bridge. In 1879 and again in 1881, freight trains crashed through its spans falling into the river below.

Through the efforts of southern Illinois legislators whose interests were bound to St. Louis, Boomer lost his exclusive rights in 1867. The ferry and steamboat companies still made it difficult for Eads. With the help of engineer Henry Flad, James B. Eads constructed the bridge over the Mississippi River that carries his name. For the dedication ceremony on July 4, 1874, when work on the bridge was finished, Eads parked 14 locomotives (each weighing between 35 and 51 tons for a total weight of 560 tons) to demonstrate the solidity of his bridge. The bridge is still a vital link to Illinois. It is used by automobiles on the top deck, and by the new Metro Link transportation on the original railroad lower deck. Eads Bridge was used as the symbol of St. Louis for many years, until St. Louis acquired the statue of St. Louis after the World's Fair of 1904. (see Appendix V "M" p. 180)

Another brass relief on the Bates statue bears the likeness of Hamilton Rowan Gamble, a lawyer who became provisional governor of Missouri during the Civil War, and who served as secretary of state to Frederick

---

[22]Mary Christy Scanlan, the heir to the Wiggins Ferry fortune, died in 1903. This ferry service was started in 1797 by James S. Pigott, then acquired by Sam Wiggins. He sold it to Andrew and Sam Christy in 1820.

Bates. He wrote the dissenting opinion in the Dred Scott case when he was a judge of the Missouri Supreme Court, prior to being appointed governor.

The third relief commemorates Charles Gibson, a lawyer, and the husband of Archibald Gamble's daughter, Virginia. Gibson used his influence to get Hamilton Rowan Gamble (Archibald's brother) appointed provincial governor of Missouri.

The fourth likeness is of Henry Sheffie Geyer, a lawyer remembered for his participation in the Dred Scott case. He prepared most of the briefs in that famous lawsuit. He became a U.S. senator in 1851, defeating Thomas Hart Benton. (see Appendix V "N" p. 180) There are streets named for Eads, Hamilton Rowan Gamble, Geyer and Gibson.

We have a street named Bates in South St. Louis, but it is named for his brother, Frederick, who served as acting territorial governor of Missouri three times, and was elected the second governor of Missouri. Bates School is named for Edward Bates.

Frank P. Blair, who was largely responsible for keeping Missouri in the Union during the Civil War, served as a U.S. congressman. There is a statue of him in Forest Park at Kingshighway and Lindell Boulevard. Blair Avenue is in 63106 and 63107.

O'Fallon Park, with 159 acres in North St. Louis, and Carondelet Park, with 180 acres in South St. Louis, were purchased by the city in 1876.

Sublette Park, in southwest St. Louis at January and Southwest Avenue, was donated to the city in 1915. It was first called Manchester Park; the name was changed to Sublette Park in 1925.

Francis Park was given to the city in 1916 by former mayor and governor, David Rowland Francis. It covers 60.39 acres at Nottingham and Tamm avenues in southwest St. Louis. Federal Relief Administration funds paid for much of the work done in Francis Park in the 1930s.

Willmore Park in southwest Saint Louis runs along the River Des Peres from Lansdowne to Gravois. Cyrus Crane Willmore, the man who developed St. Louis Hills, donated 70 of the park's 105 acres in 1946. The next year the park was named for him.

Suson Park was acquired from Sidney Solomon Jr. and named for his daughter Susan.

John O'Fallon gave 54 acres to the city in 1854 for Fairgrounds Park. It was dedicated in 1909.

River Des Peres Park covers 145 acres and was acquired by the city in 1934.

Lindenwood Park is 14.08 acres in size and was purchased by the city for $81,000 in 1947.

Rosalie Tilles Memorial Park has 29 acres. St. Louis purchased the park for $380,000 in 1957, using funds received from the sale of Tilles Park in the county.

Aloe Plaza, in downtown St. Louis at 18th and Market streets, was built in 1941 and contains a fountain/sculpture that was originally named "Wedding of the Rivers." It is now known as the "Meeting of the Waters." It was controversial when it was first constructed, as residents were offended by the naked figures and wanted them clothed. To conserve water, the fountain has often been turned off.

Chapter 13

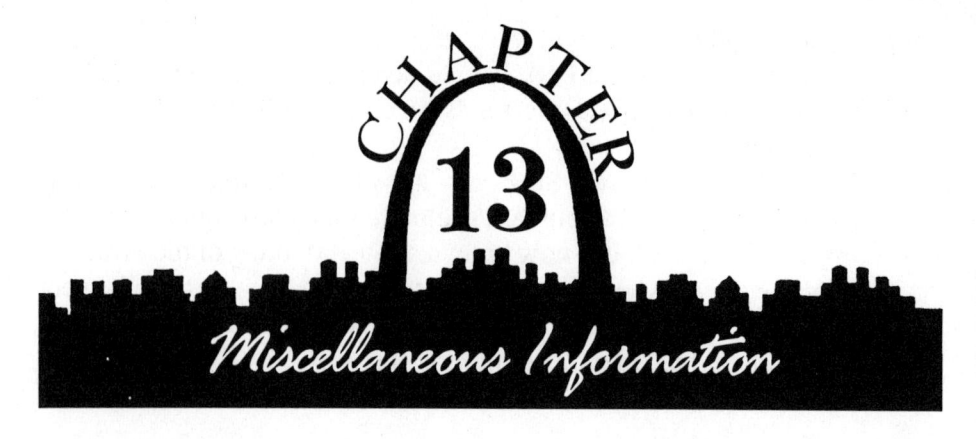

Miscellaneous Information

As St. Louis grew, it expanded upward; forming a series of hills from one level of ground to the next. Third Street was the first terrace, 18th Street the second terrace, Jefferson Avenue the third terrace, and Grand Boulevard the fourth terrace.

St. Louis had 151 streets in 1846. On March 22, 1882, 200 changes were made in street names. An additional 150 names were changed in 1883. In 1898, St. Louis expanded to 962 streets; by 1899, 280 streets had become obsolete. More than 100 streets are named for females; more than 60 have names that I was unable to identity.

We have:
- about 28 streets named after military men.
- more than 100 streets named for a location.
- 10 streets named for birds (the county has 30).
- 15 streets named for Indians (the county has 50).
- 20 streets named for trees (the county has over 100).
- 12 streets named for rivers.
- 20 streets named for other cities.
- 34 streets named for states.
- we had a Government Street and a Capitol Street.
- we still have a Liberty Street.
- we have more than a dozen streets named for U.S. presidents.
- we have one street named President, one street named Senate, and one named Congress.
- we eliminated Pacific but we still have an Atlantic.
- we had a Short Street, but no Long Street.
- we have an End Street, but no Beginning Street.
- we have a Hill Street and a Dale Street; a Mound Street and a High Street; a Plateau Street, a Cave Street, a High Point, a High View, a Valley and a Prairie Street.

- we don't have a Mountain Street; the closest Mountain Street is in Fenton.
- we have a River Street, a Water Street, a Ripple Street, a River Bluff Drive, Wharf, Dock, and Ferry streets.
- we have a Castle Lane, a Kings Drive, a Queens Avenue, a Duke Street, and a Regal Place. The streets named for royalty in the city can't compare with the number of royalty streets in north St. Louis County. One area has Castle, Crown Point, Royal, Empire, Empress, Monarch, Viscount, Lord and Earl streets. It also has King and Queen, Prince and Princess, Baron and Baroness, Count and Countess, and Duke and Duchess streets.
- we no longer have a Wood Street, but we have an Iron Street.
- we no longer have a Soft Street, but we have a Sharp Street.
- we had streets named Summer, Fall, Winter, Spring, and two streets named Autumn. Spring and Fall, located in 63113, are all that are left.
- we have a Park, a Forest, a Gardenville, a Garden and a Fountain streets.
- we have a Northland and a Southland, but no Eastland or Westland streets.
- we have a North Court, East Court, West Court, and a South Court; we also have a Center Court.
- we had a Lucky Street, and a Crooked Street.
- we have a Bent Street, and a Half Street.
- we have a Pleasant and a Mount Pleasant.
- we don't have a Bird Street; we have streets named for birds.
- we have a Magazine Street, but no Paper or Book street.
- we have a Berger and a Hamburg.
- we have a School Street, a College Avenue, and a University Street, but no High School street.
- we have a Grace Avenue, Church Road, and Convent Street but no Rectory street.
- we have a Pope Street, Cardinal Street, and Bishops Place, but no Priest street. The nearest Priest Street is in Ballwin.
- South St. Louis has the highest numbered streets: 37th, 38th, 39th, and 59th Streets.

The tree streets running east and west are called streets. The state streets running north and south are called avenues.

It once was thought that all streets running north and south were avenues, and all streets running east and west were streets. However, in the downtown area, we have Cass, Franklin, Washington, Clark, Chouteau and Park that run east and west and are avenues.

Mullanphy, O'Fallon, and all the tree streets are called streets; they all run east and west. Eighteenth and 20th, which run north and south, are also called streets. In addition to the state streets, Jefferson, Compton, Spring, Macklind, January, Vandeventer and Gravois also run north and south, but they are avenues.

Morganford and Watson are called roads; Nicholson, Waverly, Benton and Roger are called places; Grand and Kingshighway are boulevards; Hortus, Heger and Gurney are courts. They all run north and south.

Many streets in St. Louis are also named for their location. Examples include: Alhambra Court, Arsenal Street, Art Hill, Bamberger, Beacon, Branch, Busch Place, Calvary, Cave Street, Centerre Plaza, Chevrolet, Columbus Square, Convention Plaza, Dock, Eads Bridge, Fairgrounds Place, Fine Arts Drive, Foot of Arsenal, Foot of Haven, Foot of Iron, Kemper, Fountain Avenue, Government Drive, Hampton Village Plaza, Knackstedt, Magazine, Mansion House Center, Mercantile Center, Produce Row, Race Course Avenue, River Bluff Drive, Stadium Plaza, Wharf Street, St. Elizabeth Avenue, St. Mary's Drive and St. Louis Union Station.

Some street names were changed when Carondelet was annexed by the city:

Pennsylvania	became	Bates.
Clark	changed to	Eichelberger.
Hiawatha	changed to	Pulaski.
Termination	changed to	Delor.
Allen	changed to	Fassen.
Berthold	changed to	Bellerive.
Market	changed to	Bowen.
Franklin	changed to	Courtois.
Block	to	Keokuk.
Pritchard	to	Meramec.
Endora	to	Gustine.
Lily	to	Alexander.

Carondelet once had streets running in alphabetical order:
    Adams, now Eiler
    Bates
    Cedar, now Caldwell
    Dover

Elwood
Fillmore
Grundy, eliminated
Illinois, now Iron
Kansas, now Holly Hills
Lafayette, now Soper
Miller, now Mott
Nebraska, now Haven
Olive, now Krauss
Pine, now Loughborough
Quincy
Randolph, now Blow
St. Louis, now Nagel
Taylor, now Robert
Union, now Upton
Vine, now Koeln

Some early landowners who have streets named for them:

Adair, Elizabeth
Adkins, George
Bailey, Elizabeth
Baker, John and Robert
Barnes, Robert A.
Beck, John
Becker, Charles
Berry, Joseph S.
Berthold, Pelagie
Bingham, Caroline and Charles
Bircher, Rudolph
Bittner, Jacob
Block, Phineas
Blow, Henry
Boening, Henrietta
Bompart, Henrietta
Bradley, Mary
Brannon, Louise and Thomas
Bruno, Jean Baptiste
Cabanne, Francis
Carter, Walter R.
Christy, Ellen and Calvin

Clark, Benjamin and Joseph
Clayton, Ralph
Collins, Esther
Davis, J.S.
Davis, J.R.
De Mun, Isabelle
Denny, Andrew J.
Devlin, Charles
Dunnica, James
Eddie, Thomas — Eddie & Park Rd.
Edgar, T.P.
Espenschied, Louis
Field, Roswell M.
Fine, Phillip and David
Finkman, Louis
Forder, Samuel and William
Forsythe, Robert
Gartside, Joseph
Gibson, Charles
Grant, Ulysses S.
Hanley, C.
Harney, William S.

Hawkins, C.M.
Heintz, John
Henry, Fedetio and James
Hoffmeister, William
Hornsby, N.L. and H.
Houck, Philip
Hunt, R.W.
Jennings, William H.
Kennerly, J.S.
Kerth, Peter and Rosina
Koeln, Christian
Lindell, Peter
Litzinger, William and John
Locke, James H.
Luetkemeyer, Bernard
Maffitt, Julia Henry
McCausland, James
McCune, J.S.
McDonald, James
McLaran, Charles
McKnight, John
McRee, Mary and Sam
Mitchell, Stanislaus
Moellenhoff, Rudolph C.
Murdoch, John J.
Musick, Wrenshaw
Oberbeck, Christian
Outley, Elizabeth
Pardee, I.G.
Park, John — Eddie & Park Rd.
Parke, Sam — Green Park Road
   (The "e" has disappeared.)
Parker, George Ward
Pattison, Robert E.

Phillips, Thomas
Prather, J.V.
Reber, Sam
Russell, James
Sappington, John T. & Thomas J.
Schreve, Henry
Shaw, Henry
Sire, Rebecca W.
Skinker, Thomas
Smiley, Mary
Sproule, A.
Steffens, Louise & Fred
Sutton, James C.
Swann, O.C.
Switzer, William N.
Swon, J.C.
Tamm, Jacob
Thatcher, A.B.
Tholozan, John & Adel
Tieman, Catherine
Toll, John
Tyler, Mary Lawrence
Volz, Henrietta
Wallace, John A.
Watson, Wesley
Weber, James F. and Henry J.
Weil, Joseph and Rosa
West, George W.
White, George & Mary Ann
Will, John
Wilshusen, John & Claus
Wilson, S.A.
Yeager, Henry

Chapter 14: Churches

SOME CHURCHES IN EARLY ST. LOUIS

The sights of church spires in towns and the sounds of church bells ringing were probably thrilling and unforgettable experiences in many American cities. It must have been overwhelming in St. Louis. There were 142 churches in St. Louis in 1874:

Catholic:	28
Catholic chapels:	21
Catholic missions:	4
Outlying Catholic	10
Baptist:	9
Christian:	3
Congregational:	4
Episcopal:	10
German Evangelical:	16
Hebrew:	4
Methodist:	18
Presbyterian:	13
Unitarian:	2

The Missouri Conference of the Methodist Episcopal Church was organized in St. Louis in 1848. The Methodists were split during the Civil War, as other churches also were, with most of the churches favoring the South. Ebenezer Chapel on Washington Avenue was closed due to its stand against slavery. In 1862, the Union Methodist Church was started at 11th and Locust. In 1880, it was moved to Garrison and Lucas. On May 11, 1911, the church was destroyed by fire. In 1913, the congregation purchased the First Congregational Church at Grand and Delmar. A branch of the Union Methodist Church was started in Harlem Place in southwest St. Louis on Jamieson Avenue. When Jamieson was widened in 1943, the church was razed. The congregation purchased land at Pernod and Watson to build its church, now calling it Christ Methodist Church. In 1954, they merged with Union Methodist Church and adjusted their name to Union United Methodist Church.

The congregation of a Methodist church, which had been established in Carondelet at Virginia and Haven in 1857, was also split by the Civil War. After the end of the war, Lucy Bent Russell donated land for a mission church. It was established in the "Gravois Coal Diggins" at Tholozan and Russell Lane (Morganford Road) in 1871, and named Holy Innocents Episcopal Church. In 1938, Holy Innocents Church and St. Andrew Mission merged and became St. Mark's Episcopal Church. It is now located at Clifton and Murdoch in St. Louis Hills. Some of the property at Morganford and Tholozan was sold to the Nazareth Evangelical Church.

On July 4, 1865, the Lutheran Young People's Society of St. Louis met at Bambergers Grove to establish St. John's Evangelical Lutheran Church. It met in Holy Innocents Episcopal Church at Morganford and Tholozan until the congregation built a frame church, which was dedicated on September 20, 1868. Dedication of the second building at Morganford and Chippewa took place on November 23, 1884; the present building was dedicated on October 30, 1949.

Holy Trinity German Catholic Church was the first church in Bremen when it was built in 1848 on land donated by Dr. Bernard G. Farrar and Emil Mallinckrodt, before Bremen became part of St. Louis. Farrar also donated land for the Bethlehem German Lutheran Church. Streets are named for Farrar and Mallinckrodt.

In the Census of 1870, St. Louis withheld its count until Chicago's figures were reported. St. Louis then produced figures showing its population was still larger than Chicago. However, 10 years later, the 1880 Census showed that St. Louis had only grown by 40,000 (including Carondelet's annexation) while Chicago had grown by 200,000. It was estimated that St. Louis had inflated the 1870 figures by nearly 100,000 in an effort to beat Chicago.

Daniel Boone (1734-1820) was 65 years old when he came to Missouri in 1799. He had been given 2,000 acres of land by the Spanish government. Boone volunteered his services when the War of 1812 began, but was not accepted because he was 78 years old. He died in 1820 when he was 86. Boone not only had a talent for finding his way through the wilderness, he also had a way with words. When asked if he had ever been lost on any of his many journeys in the wilderness, he replied: "Oh, I was never lost, but I was bewildered once, for three days." A street in

Florissant is named for Boone, and Missouri has a county named for him.

Maj. Isaac von Bibber, the adopted son of Daniel Boone, built a tavern on Boone's Lick Trail. He believed that events recurred every 6,000 years. He sometimes discussed his theory with guests, which once resulted in a group of guests saying they would pay their bill when they returned in 6,000 years. After they all enjoyed a good laugh, von Bibber picked up his rifle and said, "I remember you — you are the same group that left 6,000 years ago without paying your bill, so now you can pay both bills." The story stopped there, so I am unable to share the ending with you.

Chapter 15: Historical Tables

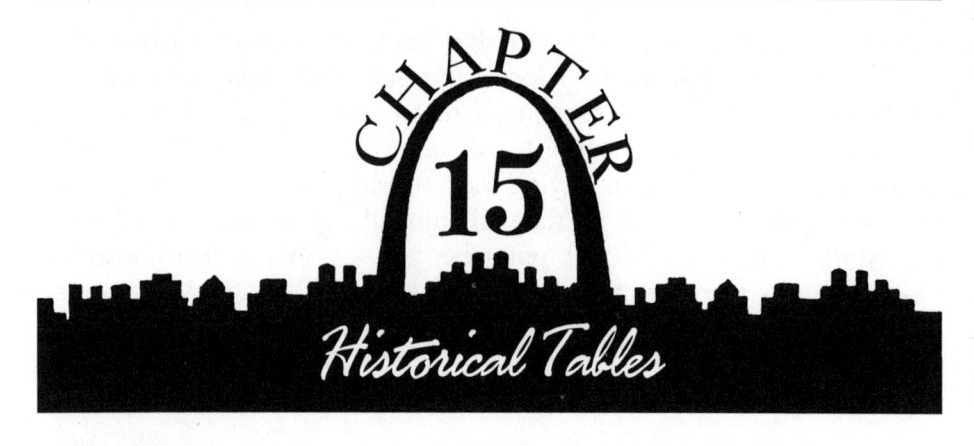

ORDER OF COLONIES AND STATES ENTERING THE UNION.

1. Delaware	Dec. 7, 1787
2. Pennsylvania	Dec. 12, 1787
3. New Jersey	Dec. 18, 1787
4. Georgia	Jan. 2, 1788
5. Connecticut	Jan. 9, 1788
6. Massachusetts	Feb. 6, 1788
7. Maryland	April 28, 1788
8. South Carolina	May 23, 1788
9. New Hampshire	June 21, 1788
10. Virginia	June 25, 1788
11. New York	July 26, 1788

(George Washington was inaugurated as president on April 30, 1789)

12. North Carolina	Nov. 21, 1789
13. Rhode Island	May 29, 1790
14. Vermont	March 4, 1791
15. Kentucky	June 1, 1792
16. Tennessee	June 1, 1796
17. Ohio	Feb. 19, 1803
18. Louisiana	April 30, 1811
19. Indiana	Dec. 11, 1816
20. Mississippi	Dec. 10, 1817
21. Illinois	Dec. 3, 1818
22. Alabama	Dec. 14, 1819
23. Maine	March 15, 1820
24. Missouri	Aug. 10, 1821

25. Arkansas	June 15, 1836
26. Michigan	Jan. 26, 1837
27. Florida	May 3, 1845
28. Texas	Dec. 29, 1845
29. Iowa	Dec. 28, 1846
30. Wisconsin	May 29, 1848
31. California	Sept. 9, 1850
32. Minnesota	May 11, 1858
33. Oregon	Feb. 14, 1859
34. Kansas	Jan. 29, 1861
35. West Virginia	June 20, 1863
36. Nevada	Oct. 31, 1864
37. Nebraska	March 1, 1867
38. Colorado	Aug. 1, 1876
39. North Dakota	Nov. 2, 1889
40. South Dakota	Nov. 2, 1889
41. Montana	Nov. 8, 1889
42. Washington	Nov. 11, 1889
43. Idaho	July 3, 1890
44. Wyoming	July 10, 1890
45. Utah	Jan. 4, 1896
46. Oklahoma	Nov. 16, 1907
47. New Mexico	Jan. 6, 1912
48. Arizona	Feb. 14, 1912
49. Alaska	Jan. 3, 1959
50. Hawaii	Aug. 21, 1959

UNITED STATES AREA IN SQUARE MILES

	YEAR	AREA	COST
Revolutionary War	1783	820,680	
Louisiana Purchase	1803	899,579	$11,250,000
Florida	1819	66,900	$ 5,000,000
Texas	1845	318,000	$ 7,500,000
Oregon Territory	1846	308,052	$ 3,750,000
Mexican War/Purchase[23]	1848	528,955	$11,750,000
Gadsden Purchase	1853	45,535	$10,000,000
Alaska Purchase	1867	586,400	$ 7,200,000

---

[23] The great statesman Daniel Webster said, "I cannot think of anything more ridiculous than acquiring this territory from Mexico. ... I hold it is not worth more than $1."

STATES IN THE ORIGINAL LOUISIANA TERRITORY
AND YEAR OF ENTRY INTO THE UNION

EAST OF THE MISSISSIPPI
(Obtained in 1783 by
Revolutionary War)

Kentucky 1792
Tennessee 1796
Ohio 1803
Indiana 1816
Mississippi 1817
Illinois 1818
Alabama 1819
Michigan 1837
Wisconsin 1848

WEST OF THE MISSISSIPPI
(Obtained in 1803 by
Louisiana Purchase)

Louisiana 1812
Missouri 1821
Arkansas 1836
Texas 1845
Iowa 1846
Minnesota 1858
Kansas 1861
Nebraska 1867
Colorado 1876
Montana 1889
North Dakota 1889
South Dakota 1889
Wyoming 1890
Oklahoma 1907
New Mexico 1912

COMPARISON OF STATES EAST OF THE MISSISSIPPI RIVER
Missouri area in square miles is 68,945:

1. Georgia 58,910
2. Michigan 56,954
3. Illinois 55,645
4. Wisconsin 54,426
5. Florida 54,153
6. North Carolina 48,843
7. Alabama 50,767
8. New York 47,377
9. Mississippi 47,233
10. Pennsylvania 44,888
11. Tennessee 41,155
12. Ohio 41,004
13. Virginia 39,704
14. Kentucky 39,669
15. Indiana 35,932
16. Maine 30,995
17. South Carolina 30,203
18. West Virginia 24,282
19. Maryland 9,837*
20. Vermont 9,273*
21. New Hampshire 8,993*
22. Massachusetts 7,824*
23. New Jersey 7,468*
24. Connecticut 4,872*
25. Delaware 1,932*
26. Rhode Island 1,055*

TOTAL: 51,254*

* These last eight states combined do not equal the area of Missouri.

The Bootheel of Missouri is 1,100 square miles.
Rhode Island is 1,055 sq. mi.

Part II

Appendices

Appendix I

States

States marked with an asterisk (*) have streets named after them. Most of the streets named after states in South St. Louis run north and south and are located in ZIP codes 63104, 63111, 63118.

*Alabama (63111). A French name for the region which was named for a local Indian tribe. The street was named for the state.

*Alaska (63111). It comes from Alakshak, an Eskimo name for the area. The street was named after Alaska when it was still a territory.

*Arkansas (63104, 63118). The name given by the French for a Sioux Indian tribe. The name may mean "down stream people." The street was named for the state.

Arizona. The name taken from an Indian name Arizonac, meaning "little springs," located in southern part of the state.

*California (63104, 63111, 63118). Named by the Spanish. The street was named for the state.

*Colorado (63111). A Spanish name meaning "colored reddish." The name was first given to the river that flows through the state. The street was named for the state.

*Connecticut (63116, 63118, 63139). An Indian name meaning "place of the long river" for the Connecticut River flowing through the state. Connecticut Street runs east and west. The street is not named for the state; it is named for Connecticut Mutual Life Insurance Company.

*Dakota (63111). It was named for the Dakota Territory, which was named for the Dakota Indians that lived in the area; it means "allies." The street is named for the Indian tribe, and it runs east and west.

*Delaware (63104). It was named for Baron De La Warr, the first governor of Virginia (1610-1611) when it was an English colony. The street named Delaware was for the Delaware Indians. It was changed to Geyer and Allen. The first half of Delmar is named for the state of

Delaware. The last half of Mardel is named for Delaware.

*Florida (63102). A Spanish name meaning "having many flowers," it was named by Ponce de Leon. The street named Florida is two blocks long between Broadway and the Mississippi River, one block south of Mullanphy. It does not run north and south, and is not located in South St. Louis with the rest of the state streets.

Georgia. It was named after George II (1683-1760), king of England, when Georgia was founded as a colony.

Hawaii. It was named by the Polynesians.

*Idaho (63111). It was named for tribe of Indians living in the area. The street is named for the state.

*Illinois (63118). A French name for a tribe of Indians in the area. It comes from Indian word "ileniwi" meaning "man." The street is named for the state.

*Indiana (63104, 63118). A made-up word meaning "land of the Indians." The street is named for the state.

*Iowa (63104, 63111, 63118). The name of an Indian tribe in the area. The tribe was called Ayuba meaning "sleepy ones." The street was named for the state.

*Kansas (63111, 63116). A French name for a tribe of Sioux Indians living in the area. It means "people of the south wind." (St. Louis had two streets named Kansas; the one named after the Indians was changed to Holly Hills, the other named after the state was changed to Compton.)

*Kentucky (63110). An Iroquois Indian name 'Kentake," meaning "level land or meadow." The street named Kentucky is not located with the other state streets; it does run north and south. It was named for its location near the McRee Racetrack. The street was named for the state.

*Louisiana (63104, 63111, 63118). The name was given to the area by the French explorer La Salle, who named it for King Louis XIV of France. The street is named for the state.

Maine. It was so named because it was the main part of New England or part of the mainland, apart from offshore islands.

Massachusetts. An Indian name "Massa-adchu-es-et," meaning "big hill."

*Maryland (63108). The state was named after Henrietta Maria, wife of Charles I, king of England. The street named Maryland does not run north and south, and is not located with the rest of the state streets in South St. Louis. The street was named after the state by Peter Lindell. The last half of the street named Delmar is for the state of Maryland; the first half of the street named Mardel is for Maryland.

*Michigan (63104, 63111, 63118). An Indian name "missi-gan," for "big lake." The street was named after the state.

*Minnesota (63104, 63111, 63118). A Sioux Indian name meaning "milky blue water." The street was named after the state.

*Mississippi (63104). The state was named after the river. It is the Indian name for "big river," "missi-sippi." The street was named for the state.

*Missouri (63104, 63118). The state was named after the river, which had been named for a tribe of Indians in the area. It means "people of the large canoes." The street was named for the state.

*Montana (63116, 63118). It was taken from the Latin word "montana," meaning "mountainous region." The street does not run north and south.

*Nebraska (63104, 63111, 63118). It is an Indian name for what is now the Platte River, the name means "flat river." The street was named for the state.

Nevada. It was named after the Sierra Nevada mountains. In Spanish sierra means "mountain," nevada means "snowy."

New Hampshire. It was named after Hampshire County in England.

New Jersey. It was named after the English island of Jersey.

New Mexico. The English translation of Spanish "Nuevo Mejico."

New York. It was named in honor of the Duke of York, brother of King Charles II of England.

*North Dakota (63111). It was given this name because it is north of Dakota Street. It runs north and south and, like Dakota, is named for the Dakota Indians.

North and South Carolina. Named for the English colony of Carolina, which was named in honor of King Charles I of England. Carolina is from the Latin "Carolus" meaning "Charles."

*Ohio (63103, 63104, 63111, 63118). An Iroquois Indian name meaning "large river." The street is named for the state. We had a street, named after the river, that ran east and west; it was changed to Lami.

Oklahoma. It was formed from Indian words, "Okla" meaning "people," and "homma" meaning "red."

*Oregon (63104, 63111, 63118). The name given to what was first called Columbia after the river. The street is named after the state.

*Pennsylvania (63104, 63111, 63118). It was named after William Penn and the Latin word "sylvania," meaning "wooded land." The street is named for the state.

Rhode Island. Originally named "Roodt Eyelandt" by the Dutch, meaning "red island."

*Tennessee (63104, 63111, 63118). The state was named for the

Cherokee Indian village, called Tanasi. The street was named for the state.

***Texas** (63104, 63118). A Spanish name taken from the Indian word "techas" meaning "allies or friends." The street is named for the state.

***Utah** (63116, 63118). It comes from the Spanish "yutta," which came from the Ute Indian tribe who lived in the area. It means "hill dwellers." The street is not named for the state but for the Ute Indians. It runs east and west.

***Vermont** (63111). It is from the French "vert" and "mont," meaning "green mountain." The street is named for the state.

***Virginia** (63103, 63104, 63111, 63118). The state is named for Queen Elizabeth I of England. The street is named for the state.

***Washington** (63101, 63102, 63103, 63108, 63112). The street was named for President George Washington. It is not a state street because it runs east and west.

West Virginia. This was the western part of Virginia that seceded during the Civil War.

***Wisconsin** (63118). It was named for the Indian "wees-kon-san," which means "gathering of waters." The street is named for the state.

***Wyoming** (63116, 63118, 63139). An Indian word meaning "large plain," a name first given to a valley in Pennsylvania. The street was named for this valley, not for the state. The street runs east and west.

APPENDIX II
Governors and Mayors

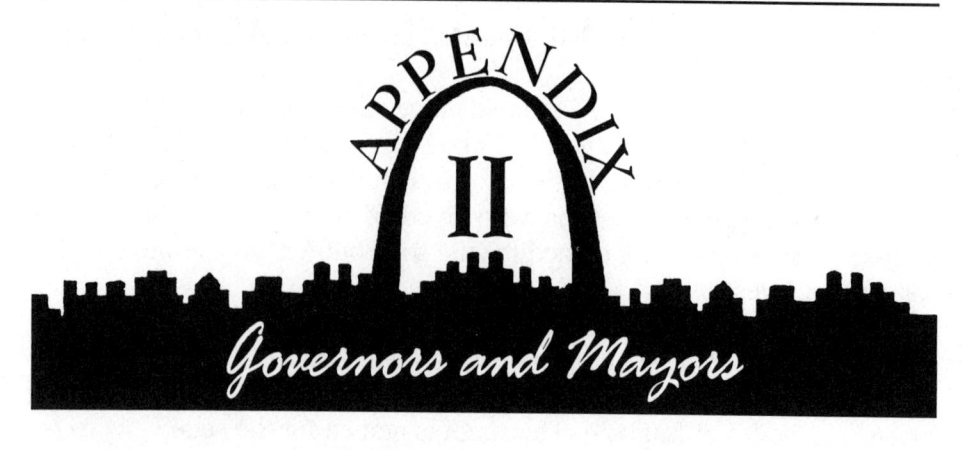

GOVERNORS OF THE MISSOURI TERRITORY

	SERVED
Amos Stoddard	1804
William Henry Harrison	1804-1805
General James Wilkinson	1805-1807
Joseph Browne, Acting	1807
Frederick Bates, Acting	1807
Meriwether Lewis	1807-1809
Frederick Bates, Acting	1809-1810
Benjamin Howard	1810-1812
Frederick Bates, Acting	1812-1813
William Clark	1813-1820

Alexander McNair. Served 1820-1824. Died March 18, 1826

McNair started political life when he was appointed U.S. commissioner of the Indiana Territory in 1804 by President William Henry Harrison. He was appointed sheriff of St. Louis county in 1810, and U.S. marshall in the Missouri Territory in 1811. This led to his election as governor on August 28, 1820. The heavy influx of Pennsylvanians made it possible for him to defeat his opponent William Clark, the territorial governor. McNair received 6,576 votes, Clark received 1,656. McNair died in 1826 at age 51, and is buried in Calvary Cemetery. McNair Street is in zones 63104 and 63118. There is also a McNair School.

Frederick Bates. 1824-1825. Died August 4, 1825

Bates was appointed secretary of the Louisiana Territory in November 1806, and became acting governor of the Territory on April 1, 1807. Before a year ended, Meriwether Lewis was appointed governor. When Lewis died in 1809, Bates was again acting governor. He served until the summer of 1810, when Benjamin Franklin Howard was appointed. Howard left in 1812, and Bates was appointed acting governor a third time, serving from December 1812 until July 1813, when William Clark received the appointment. Bates was secretary until 1820, then became recorder of land titles. He was elected the second governor of the state, defeating William Henry Ashley, but did not live to complete his term of office. He died at the age of 48. Bates Street is in zones 63111 and 63116. Bates School is named for his brother, Edward.

Abraham J. Williams. 1825-1826. Died December 30, 1839

When Lt. Gov. Benjamin H. Reeves resigned to survey a new federal road, Williams, as "pro tempore" of the Senate, became acting governor. He was the only president "pro tempore" to succeed to the office of governor. He served five-and-a half-months, but never lived in the governor's mansion. He died at the age of 58. Williams Avenue is in zone 63143; there is also a Williams School.

John Miller. 1826-1832. Died March 18, 1846

Miller replaced Williams, the acting governor after Reeves resigned, and was re-elected in 1828 without opposition. This is the only time this has happened in the history of Missouri. He was elected to Congress in 1836, 1838 and 1840. He died when he was 65, and was placed in John O'Fallon's private vault on the O'Fallon farm. He was later transferred to Bellefontaine Cemetery. Miller Street is in zone 63104.

Daniel Dunklin. 1832-1836. Died August 25, 1844

Dunklin married Emily Pamelia Willis Haley; they had six children. Dunklin supported providing a state institution for the hearing impaired, abolition of the whipping-post and reform of the penal system. He is best known for his work promoting public schools; he is often called the "father of Missouri's public school system." Three months before the end of his term, he resigned to become surveyor-general of Missouri and Illinois. Dunklin Drive is in zone 63138.

Lilburn W. Boggs. 1836-1840. Died March 14, 1860

Boggs married Julia Ann Bent, daughter of Silas, on July 21, 1817; they had two sons before her untimely death in 1820. He married Panthea Grant Boone, granddaughter of Daniel Boone in 1823; 10 children were born of this marriage. Elected lieutenant governor in 1832, he became acting governor when Dunklin resigned. As acting governor, he delivered a message to the state Legislature on November 22, 1836. The next day, he delivered his inaugural address as elected governor. This is the only time this has happened in Missouri history. Lilburn Avenue is in zone 63115.

Thomas Reynolds. 1840-1844. Died February 9, 1844

Reynolds married Eliza Ann Young in 1823; their son was born in

1824. Governor Thomas Reynolds considered one of the shortest laws ever enacted in Missouri as the greatest act of his gubernatorial career: "Imprisonment for debt is forever abolished." He also issued a proclamation in 1843, setting the fourth Thursday in November as a day of prayer and thanksgiving. This is probably the first Thanksgiving proclamation ever issued by a Missouri governor. He was appointed judge of the 2nd Judicial Circuit when he finished his term as governor. He died of a self-inflicted wound at the age of 48.

Meredith Miles Marmaduke. 1844. Died March 26, 1864

Marmaduke married Lavinia, a daughter of Dr. John Sappington; they had 10 children: three girls and seven boys. He served as lieutenant governor under Reynolds, became governor when Reynolds died, and served until the election of John Cummins Edwards, almost a year later. He was a staunch Union man; two of his sons attained a high rank in the Confederate army. Meredith Marmaduke was the great-great-great-grandfather of actress Ginger Rogers. After leaving office he farmed, became a county judge and a county surveyor, platting the city of Marshall. He died at age 73, and is buried in the Sappington Cemetery, near Arrow Rock, Missouri.

John Cummins Edwards. 1844-1848. Died September 14, 1888

Edwards served one term as congressman, prior to his election as the youngest chief executive ever elected by Missouri until that year. A bachelor, his sister-in-law was his hostess at the mansion. During his administration, new Missouri counties were organized at a greater rate than ever before, or since. A problem concerning the northern boundary line was resolved, the second Constitutional Convention was held, and the new constitution was defeated in 1845. Legislation included memorandums to Congress to improve the Osage River, to build a railroad from Hannibal to St. Joseph, to reclaim the swamplands, and to enact more effective federal laws to recover fugitive slaves. The primary cause of his defeat was a provision putting the judiciary on an elective basis. He married Emma Jeanne Catherine Richard after his term as governor. She was 19 years old and he was 48; they had 11 children. He died in Stockton, California, at the age of 82.

Austin Augustus King. 1848-1853. Died April 22, 1870

King married Nancy Harris Roberts in 1827; they had eight children. His second wife, Martha Anthony Woodson, whom he married in 1858, five years after the end of his term as governor, bore him two daughters. The Legislature passed acts organizing two temperance societies and an act to promote wine production in Gasconade County on the same day! He believed that Congress alone had power to enact fugitive slave laws, and vetoed one bill sent to him for signature. He wrote the Missouri Code of Civil Procedure, which was passed in 1849. The counties of McDonald, Dodge (now part of Putnam), Laclede, Van Buren (later Cass), Dent, Stone, Vernon, Pemiscot and Bollinger were named during his term. He was an opponent of secession, and was elected to Congress after his term as governor. Because of moderate views, he was not re-elected in 1864.

Sterling Price. 1853-1857. Died September 29, 1867

Price married Martha Head; they had five sons and two daughters. He returned a hero after the last battle of the Mexican War. During his four-year term as governor, the public school system was reorganized, new land was opened to settlement and railroad construction grew. Because he considered the aid given to the railroads as "over generous," he vetoed a bill to increase the state debt in order to continue it; the measure passed over his veto. During the Civil War, Price was appointed charge officer of the Missouri militia by Governor Jackson. He died of cholera at the age of 58, and is buried in Bellefontaine Cemetery.

Trusten Polk. 1857. Died April 16, 1876

Polk married Elizabeth Newberry Skinner in 1837; they had one son and four daughters. On January 5, 1857, he was inaugurated as governor. Eight days later he was elected to the Senate, so he resigned on February 27, 1857, to become a U.S. senator. This is the only instance of its kind in the state's history, and the shortest term — only 53 days — served by a governor in the history of Missouri. He was expelled from the Senate on January 10, 1862, because he supported the Confederate cause, and was replaced by Robert Wilson. Polk enlisted in the Confederate army, served as a colonel, was taken prisoner in 1864, and confined on Johnson's Island until the prisoner exchange several months later. Upon returning to St. Louis, he practiced law until his death at the age of 65. He is buried in Bellefontaine Cemetery. Polk Street is in zone 63111.

Hancock Lee Jackson. 1857. Died March 19, 1876

In 1821, Jackson married Ursla Oldham who bore him 11 children. He served four years in the state Senate before he was elected lieutenant governor. A cousin of Missouri Gov. Claiborne Fox Jackson, Jackson served as governor for 237 days, from February 27 until October 22, 1857, when a special election was held. In his message to the legislature, he outlined suggestions for assistance to the credit of the state, development of the railroad system, and information about the effect of the Panic of 1857 on banking. While governor, he contended legislative divorce was invalid.

Robert Marcellus Stewart. 1857-1860. Died September 21, 1871

A bachelor, he won the special election called by Hancock Lee

Jackson. As governor, he stressed the state's material interests, favored a liberal policy toward railroad development, and "became obsessively occupied with the problem of "bleeding Kansas." In his final message to the state Legislature in 1861, he straddled the issue of secession. He is probably best remembered for riding his horse into the executive mansion and having it fed on the mantel. After serving his term as governor, he was considered singular and eccentric; many anecdotes were spread about him. He died in 1871. Stewart Place is in zone 63112.

Claiborne Fox Jackson. 1860-1861. Died December 6, 1862

Jane Sappington was 18 when she married Jackson; she died six months later. He then married her sister, Louisa, who was 23; she bore him two sons, and died six years later. When Jackson went to Dr. Sappington for his third daughter, Mrs. Eliza Sappington Pierson, the oldest of the three sisters, the doctor said, "You can take her, but don't come back again, all that's left is the old woman." Eliza Jackson reared her eight children from her marriages to Pierson and Jackson,, along with her sister's two sons, for a total of 10 children. When the Civil War broke out, Governor Jackson led the effort to guide Missouri into the Confederacy. He was driven from Missouri to the southwestern part of the state by General Lyon and federal troops in 1861. Provisional Gov. Hamilton R. Gamble was appointed the next day. The beating the Confederates took at Pea Ridge upset him so much that he died at the age of 56. He is buried in Sappington Cemetery near Arrow Rock, Missouri. Jackson Street in zone 63111 was changed to Vulcan Street, after the Vulcan Iron Works.

Hamilton Rowan Gamble. 1861-1864. Died January 31, 1864

Gamble married Caroline Lane Coalter in 1827; they had nine children. As the presiding judge in the Dred Scott case, he was overruled when he decided in favor of the slave. Appointed provisional governor of Missouri after Governor Jackson was driven from the state by federal troops, he was the 16th governor of a state almost in civil anarchy. He believed Missouri should remain in the Union, but not become subservient to the federal government. With a firm hand, Gamble guided the state through two-and-a-half years of Civil War. He changed the name of Second Kingshighway Street in St. Louis to Union Boulevard. He died at the age of 66, a year before his term was to end. St. Louis has streets for all three of his names; Hamilton and Rowan are in zone 63112, and Gamble is in zone 63106. There is also a Gamble School.

Willard Preble Hall. 1864-1865. Died. November 3, 1882

Hall married Anne Eliza Richardson in 1847 and they had four children; she died before he was de facto governor. After her death, he married Olivia L. Oliver; they had three children. Serving as the provisional lieutenant governor, he became the 17th governor of Missouri when Gamble died. When the Mexican War began, he enlisted as a private in the 1st Missouri Cavalry. He was ordered to prepare a code of civil law with Colonel Doniphan for governing New Mexico. This code survived for 45 years. He served three terms in Congress. Hall Street was in zone 63107; it has been changed to De Soto.

Thomas Clement Fletcher. 1865-1869. Died March 25, 1899

He married Mary Clarissa Honey, to whom he was betrothed in infancy; they had two children. Missouri's 18th governor was the state's first Republican governor, first native-born governor, and the youngest governor of Missouri at that time. He faced the problem of whether amnesty should be granted to those who joined the Confederacy. He was unable to get a constitutional amendment abolishing test oaths as qualification for voting and engaging in professions passed by the state Legislature. He disposed of the railroads acquired by the state because the railroad companies neglected to pay interest on bonds the state had guaranteed. He reorganized public education. He died at the age of 72, and is buried in Bellefontaine Cemetery. Fletcher Street is in zone 63121.

Joseph Washington McClurg. 1869-1871. Died December 2, 1900

McClurg married Mary C. Johnson and they had eight children; she died several years before he became governor. He started as a teacher, studied law and was admitted to the bar in Texas. He was elected to the U.S. Congress in 1862 as an emancipationist, and voted to abolish slavery (however, he kept his slaves until right before Lincoln's Emancipation Proclamation). He was re-elected as a Radical, and served almost three full terms. While he was governor, the Eads Bridge, and the school of mines and metallurgy at Rolla were built. The college of agriculture at Columbia was established, as were Normal schools (for Teachers) at Kirksville and Warrensburg. He was soundly defeated in his bid for re-election.

Benjamin Gratz Brown. 1871-1873. Died December 13, 1885

Brown married Mary Hansome Gunn in 1858; they had eight children. Following a career in the U.S. Senate, he became the 20th governor of Missouri. He cultivated support from the Germans in St. Louis. In his administration, important changes were made in the taxation and revenue system; income and poll tax laws were repealed, and the assessment and collection of taxes on railroads were made uniform. He started a policy of investing school funds in state bonds, schools for blacks were established and a policy of conciliation followed. He died at age 59; he is buried in Oak Hill Cemetery in Kirkwood. Brown Avenue is in zone 63115; Benjamin Street is in North St. Louis, zone 63107.

Silas Woodson. 1873-1875. Died November 9, 1896

Woodson married Mary Jane McRoberts in 1842; they had one son. Mary died in 1845, and he married Olivia Adams in 1856; Olivia died 10 years later. He married Virginia Juliet Lard in 1866; they had three children. He served as chairman of the Democratic state convention prior to being the first Democratic governor elected after the Civil War. During his term, he reduced the state debt and simultaneously lowered the tax levy. An act was passed to start a state Normal School at Cape Giradeau. His most important legislation was authorizing a popular vote on calling a Constitutional Convention in 1874. The Panic of 1873 occurred during his term. He refused to be a candidate for the U.S. Senate while governor. Upon retirement, he returned to St. Joseph to practice law. He was appointed judge of the Criminal Court and retired in June 1895 because of ill health. He died in 1896 at age 77. Woodson Road is in zones 63114, 63132, and 63134.

Charles Henry Hardin. 1875-1877. Died July 29, 1892

Hardin married Mary Barr Jenkins. At Miami University he and seven fellow students founded Beta Theta Pi, now a national fraternity. He practiced law for five years. He moved to a farm near Mexico, Missouri, during the Civil War, and remained in comparative obscurity until the Liberal Republican movement swept the radicals from power. He re-entered politics as a staunch Democrat, and was serving in the state Senate when he was elected as the last Missouri governor bound to a two-year term by the Drake Amendment. He was called the "driest speaker that ever took the stump in Missouri." During his administration the Constitution of 1875 was adopted, which removed suffrage restrictions and restored the four-year term for governor. He returned to his farm when his term ended, and never again accepted public office.

John Smith Phelps. 1877-1881. Died November 20, 1886

Phelps married Mary Whitney in 1837; they had five children. During the Civil War, Mrs. Phelps turned her home into a hospital; Congress voted to give her $20,000 for this service. She established an orphanage for children of Union and Confederate soldiers with the proceeds. Phelps served 18 years in Congress before being elected governor. During his administration, the practice of making biennial appropriations in one bill was started. Funds for a building to house the Supreme Court, the state library, and the attorney general's office were appropriated. There was concern about strikes by railroad employees, but he suppressed the strikes vigorously. He favored more liberal support of the public schools. He sent biennial appropriations to the state university for the first time. Phelps Drive is in zone 63043. (see Appendix V "O" Page 180)

Thomas Theodore Crittenden. 1881-1885. Died May 29, 1909

He married Caroline Wheeler Jackson in 1856; they had four children. He was appointed attorney general of Missouri in 1865 before being honorably discharged from the army. He served in Congress from 1873 to 1879, and was elected the 24th governor the following year. He helped found the Missouri Bar Association, and remained a member until his death. During his term the state sued for and collected with interest $3 million which had been loaned to the Hannibal & St. Joseph Railroad in 1851 and 1855. He broke up the James gang while governor; Jesse was killed on April 3, 1882, by Bob Ford, "the dirty little coward who shot Mr. Howard." [See Appendix V, "V," Page 183.] Crittenden went to Kansas City to practice law, served as U.S. consul general in Mexico from 1893 to 1897, and returned to Kansas City to serve as a referee in bankruptcy cases from 1898 until his death on May 29, 1909, at the age of 77. Crittenden Street is in zone 63118.

John Sappington Marmaduke. (His father served as the eighth governor of Missouri). 1885-1887. Died December 28, 1887

John S. Marmaduke, a West Point graduate, resigned his commission when the Civil War broke out and joined the Confederacy against his father's wishes; he was wounded at Shiloh. He was a bachelor when he served as Missouri's 25th governor. Two nieces served as hostesses at the mansion. During his administration, the question of local option first became a bitter battle. Railroad regulation was also an urgent matter because the first railway strike occurred during his term. He handled the problem so well that there were no lives lost and little loss of property. He sponsored a bill to regulate the railroads, but it was defeated. He called a special session and threatened to have continuous special sessions until a regulatory measure was passed. He died in office at the age of 54, a year before the expiration of his term. Marmaduke Avenue is in zone 63139.

Albert Pickett Morehouse. 1887-1889. Died September 30, 1891

He married Martha E. McFadden; they had three children. He qualified as a teacher, studied law, won admission to the bar and practiced law, and then founded a newspaper. He supported changing the constitution to permit disfranchised Missourians to vote. When the constitutional amendment was passed, it enhanced his prestige and popularity. He worked to establish Northwest Missouri State Teachers College, which became a reality after his death. Lieutenant governor at the time of John Marmaduke's death, he served the rest of Marmaduke's term, then retired and became a farmer. While driving cattle in 1891, he suffered from heat prostration and ruptured a blood vessel in his brain. Fearing insanity, he committed suicide at the age of 56.

David Rowland Francis. 1889-1893. Died January 15, 1927

Francis married Jane Perry in 1876; they had six sons. A successful grain merchant, he was prominent in both national and state circles. After completing a term as mayor of St. Louis, he was elected the 27th governor of Missouri. Called the "second father" of the University of Missouri, Francis believed the greatest achievements of his administration were getting a Civil War direct tax of $600,000 added to the University's endowment, and establishing a nine-man, bipartisan board of curators.

After serving as governor, he was appointed secretary of the interior by President Cleveland in 1896. He then became the catalyst for, and director of, the Louisiana Purchase Exposition (St. Louis World's Fair) in 1904. He was also president of the Olympics that year, and the stadium at Washington University was named for him. He became ambassador to Russia in 1916, and was living in Russia during its revolution. In 1916, he donated land to St. Louis for Francis Park. He died at the age of 77, and is buried in Bellefontaine Cemetery. Francis Street is in zone 63106.

William Joel Stone. 1893-1897. Died April 14, 1918

Stone married Sarah Louise Winston in 1874; they had three children. Few equaled, and probably no one excelled, Stone as a practical politician. During his administration, the state's bonded debt was materially reduced, the main building at the University of Missouri was built, and his opposition to an organized railroad lobby led to the Railroad Fellow Servants Law. After completing his term as governor, he practiced law in St. Louis. He succeeded George G. Vest[24] in the U.S. Senate in 1903. He was re-elected twice, and served until his death.

Lawrence "Lon" Vest Stephens. 1897-1901. Died January 10, 1923

Stephens married Margaret Nelson in 1880. During his term, the state fair at Sedalia started on its road to permanency, and the Federal Soldiers' Home at St. James and a Confederate Soldiers' Home at Higginsville, were established. Stephens Place is in 63074, and Stephens Road is in 63017.

Alexander Monroe Dockery. 1901-1905. Died December 26, 1926

He married Mary E. Bird in 1869; six of their children died as infants, and two others at a very young age. Mary died while her husband was in office; her death marked the first time this had happened during a governor's term. Dockery worked as a physician, banker and congressman for many years before he was nominated by acclamation and elected governor. Several important laws were passed during his administration.

---

[24]George Graham Vest served in the Confederate Congress as well as in the United States Congress. St. Louis has a Vest Avenue in zone 63107.

A beer inspection law was revised; preference was given to using Missouri stone in public buildings; franchises of public utilities were taxed; the first law for the consolidation of school districts was passed; new election laws, both general and primary, were enacted; and the state Legislature appropriated $1 million for the Louisiana Purchase Exposition. This was the largest sum ever voted by any state. He returned to his home in Gallatin after serving his term, was twice elected treasurer of the Democratic State Committee of Missouri, and appointed third assistant postmaster general from 1913 to 1921. He died in 1926.

Joseph Wingate Folk. 1905-1909. Died May 28, 1923

Folk married Gertrude Glass in 1896. In 1900, he was elected circuit attorney of St. Louis. Between 1901 and 1902, he exposed an alliance of corrupt business and politics in St. Louis government, and also assisted in investigations of alleged bribery and graft in the Missouri Legislature and among certain state administrative officials. Since he exemplified honesty in public affairs, he was swept into office on a tidal wave of reform. His personal popularity brought support from rural counties, even though it was the first time since the Reconstruction period that the Republican Party was victorious in the state election. He felt that the executive was the steward of public welfare. He wrote direct primary, and direct legislation, devices into the constitution and the laws of the state. He was defeated when he ran for the Senate after he finished his term as governor. To eliminate him from Missouri politics, he was endorsed for U.S. president in 1910 and was abandoned two years later. Political analyses showed that he faced strong urban opposition in every campaign for elective office. St. Louis never forgave him for prosecuting some of its influential citizens; a large majority always voted against him. He never won another election. He suffered a nervous breakdown in 1922, and died the next year. Folk Street is in zone 63143.

Herbert Spencer Hadley. 1909-1913. Died December 1, 1927

He married Agnes Lee, a newspaperwoman, in 1901; they had three children. He was elected attorney general of Missouri in 1904 and became a national figure, prosecuting with success cases against a major oil company, the railroads, and the Harvester Insurance and Lumber trusts. He was in 1908 the first Republican-elected governor since the Civil War, but he rose to fame under a Democratic administration. He recommended a public service commission, a corporate franchise tax, general inheritance tax, income tax, petroleum products tax, wholesale liquor tax, Workmen's Compensation Act, and the simplification of criminal procedure during his administration; none were approved. (The Workmen's Compensation Act that he recommended in 1911 was finally approved in

1925.) He moved to Colorado for his health, and served as a professor of law at the University of Colorado for six years. Returning to Missouri in 1923, he became chancellor of Washington University. As a member of the National Crime Commission in 1926, he helped start a reform movement in American criminal justice, and prepared a model code of criminal procedure that was adopted in May 1930. Hadley was made a trustee of the Rockefeller Foundation before his death in 1927 at the age of 55. Hadley Technical School is named for him. Hadley Street is in zones 63101, 63106, and 63107.

Elliot Woolfolk Major. 1913-1917. Died July 9, 1949

He married Elizabeth Myers in 1887; they had three children. He was elected to the state Senate in 1896. He was nominated without opposition for the office of attorney general of Missouri in 1908. He served four years and was able to conclude many corporation prosecutions instigated by Governor Hadley, resulting in the state collecting more than $500,000 in fines. He was praised for having "secured the passage of more progressive legislation than was enacted in any previous period of 25 years." Construction of the present state Capitol was begun. During his term, the Public Service Commission, a state Highway Department, a grain inspection department, an insurance department and a Board of Pardons and Parole, were created. Some cities were authorized to develop a commission form of government, and the amendment for direct election of U.S. senators was ratified. Absentee voting laws were adopted, and an official state flag of original design combining the national red, white and blue with the state coat-of-arms was adopted. A system of dragged roads to connect county seats in one general system in the state was established, and a county Highway Board was appointed.

Frederick Dozier Gardner. 1917-1921. Died December 18, 1933

He married Jeanette Vosburgh in 1896; they had three children. In 1913, as a private citizen, he studied old-world land credit systems and evolved a Missouri Land Bank plan for making long term loans to farmers at low rates of interest. He presented this plan to the Missouri Legislature. The first land bank plan by either the federal government or any state legislature was started. The Federal Land Bank System was modeled after the Gardner plan. He recommended establishing a bipartisan state highway commission, and a $60 million bond issue for roads paid from automobile license fees. He won passage of a state tax commission law, and a corporation franchise tax, inheritance tax and income tax. The penitentiary became self-supporting, and penal institutions were consolidated under one management. A 1917 law established the state park system, and set aside 5 percent of hunting and fishing license receipts for the purchase of land. Land for Sequiota Park, the first state park, was bought and a state Highway Department was created. After the United States entered World War I, he issued a state war proclamation to carry out the wishes of the President, organized the Missouri Council of Defense, and administered the Missouri Selective Service Law. He signed the Missouri suffrage bill granting women the right to vote for presidential electors; it was ratified on July 3, 1919.

After his term as governor, he served as chairman of the finance committee of the Democratic State Committee in the 1932 campaign. In 1933, he became a member of the executive committee of President Franklin D. Roosevelt's Business Planning and Advisory Council. Gardner Drive is in 63136, and Gardner Lane in 63134. At one time, there was also a post office named for him; it was consolidated with another.

Arthur Mastick Hyde. 1921-1925. Died October 17, 1947

Hyde married Hortense Cullers in 1904. The second Republican-elected governor since Reconstruction, Hyde was fortunate to have a Republican majority in both houses of the state Legislature. He removed every Democrat from office and replaced them with Republicans; even guards at the penitentiary were replaced. The general property tax rate for state revenues was reduced from seven to five cents; the hawthorn was adopted as the state flower; a state highway system, on a non-political basis, was developed. He unsuccessfully sought the Republican vice-presidential nomination before his term as governor ended. He became secretary of agriculture from 1929 to 1933 under President Herbert Hoover.

Sam Aaron Baker. 1925-1929. Died September 16, 1933

Baker married Nellie Tuckley, who was a stenographer for the clerk of the Supreme Court; they had one daughter. He was the second Jefferson City resident elected governor. He was particularly interested in the state's educational program. The Workmen's Compensation Law was passed, more adequate banking laws were adopted, and he supported the $75 million road improvement bonds in the 1928 election. Sam A. Baker State Park in Southeast Missouri is named for him.

Henry Stewart Caulfield. 1929-1933. Died May 11, 1966

He married Frances Alice Delano; they had four children. He was carried into office in the landslide that sent Herbert Hoover to the White House. He was the first St. Louisan in 56 years elected governor. When the Great Depression started, he cut state expenses and reduced salaries. He named a fact-finding commission on state administration and institutions. This led to a legislative program that triggered one of the most bitter controversies in Missouri's history. It centered around an increase in the state income tax recommended by the commission. As a result of the survey, a $15 million bond issue to build a new penal and charitable institution was approved, Algoa Reformatory was completed, a state budgetary system established, the state Highway Patrol instituted, and a small loans law was passed.

In 1941, he was named director of Public Welfare of St. Louis and served eight years. He shared an office with the law firm of Bartlett, Muldoon, Stix and Bartlett until his death in 1966.

Guy Brasfield Park. 1933-1937. Died October 1, 1946

Park married Eleanora A. Gabbert in 1909; they had one daughter. He was absolutely unknown nationally, and practically unknown to the majority of Missourians at the time of his election. He was chosen to replace the nominee from the August primary who died a few weeks before the election. He conducted an active and effective campaign and defeated his opponent by some 339,000 votes, the then-greatest plurality ever given a candidate for governor of Missouri. He presented the state Legislature with 35 economy bills affecting every department and public institution, with the exception of the judges of the Supreme Court. His accomplishments include: consolidating separate agricultural and horticultural units into the Department of Agriculture; transferring duties of the Bureau of Geology and Mines to state geologists; consolidating the Blind Commission and Board of Charities duties into a Charity Board; establishing a state budget department; and starting a centralized purchasing system for all state institutions and county budget and audit systems.

Lloyd Crow Stark. 1937-1941. Died September 17, 1972

Stark married Margaret Pearson Stickney in 1908; they had two sons. She died in 1930. In November 1931, he married Katherine Lemoine Perkins; they had two daughters. Missouri's 39th governor had been a businessman, horticulturist, farmer, naval officer and soldier. A political battle for the Democratic nomination for a Supreme Court judge — an open fight between Stark and the Kansas City Democratic organization which tried to punish him for "his lack of compliance with its wishes on various occasions" — was the highlight of his administration; the organization lost. His pleadings for farm-to-market roads gave him the title "father of the Farmers Highway system." A comprehensive Social Security law was passed, the state's first unemployment insurance bill came into being, and state hospitals for the treatment of cancer and trachoma were established.

Forrest C. Donnell. 1941-1945. Died March 3, 1980

Donnell married Hilda Hays in 1913; they had two children. Because the election results were so close, a committee was appointed to investigate the election and recount the ballots. Governor Stark vetoed the resolution, and the Supreme Court ordered the state Speaker of the House to declare Donnell's election. He became Missouri's 40th governor by 3,613 votes. During his administration, the biggest problems stemmed from World War II: operation of the draft, establishment of the Missouri Guard, and organization of a civil defense and administration of war regulations. During his term, a new code of civil procedure was adopted, a new corporation code was written, a judicial conference of trial judges and appellate judges was established, and a legislative council with a research director and staff was created. He was elected to the U.S. Senate after completing his term as governor. Donnell Avenue is in zone 63137.

Phil M. Donnelly. 1945-1949/1953-1957. Died Sept. 12, 1961

He married Juanita McFadden; they had one son. Donnelly served as Missouri's 41st and 43rd governor. He had the distinction of being the first Missouri governor ever elected to two separate four-year terms. He faced a Republican-controlled general assembly in 1945 and 1947, and successfully opposed the federal Social Security Administration, insisting that Missouri be allowed to operate its own state employment service. Their threat to withhold certification of federal unemployment tax credits collapsed. He instituted, and the voters approved, a $75 million bond issue to modernize state institutions. He filled judicial appointments on the basis of legal qualifications rather than party affiliation. He clashed with labor organizers in St. Louis when they attempted to unionize the Police Department. He directed the quelling of prison riots, which attracted national attention in 1953, and moved against crime and gambling. He probably set an all-time record when he vetoed 26 major measures in 1955. The dogwood was named the official tree of Missouri while he was governor. He joined his son to practice law when he left office, and died after suffering a paralytic stroke.

Forrest Smith. 1949-1953. Died March 8, 1962

Smith married Mildred Williams in 1915; they had two children. He was the first person ever elected to a fourth term for a major state office in Missouri. Known as the "father of the Sales Tax Act," he brought the retail sales tax to Missouri in the 1930s. When he was elected governor in 1948, he received the largest majority then-accorded a gubernatorial candidate in Missouri, carrying 102 of 114 counties. He advocated a use tax on products purchased in other states for use in Missouri. His efforts to inaugurate a multi-million dollar highway improvement program were considered outstanding. During his term a new driver's license law was passed, and the Jefferson Building and a building for the Missouri Division of Employment Security were erected. He recommended establishing a four-year medical school at the University of Missouri; installing voting machines in metropolitan areas, and investing surplus state funds in interest-bearing bonds rather than scattering the funds in banks which paid no interest. He was named Federal Civil Defense coordinator for Missouri in 1957. He planned to participate in a television company in Jefferson City, but died of a heart attack in 1962.

Phil M. Donnelly. 1953-1957. Second term.

James T. Blair Jr. 1957-1961. Died July 12, 1962

Blair married Emilie Garnett Chorn in 1926; they had two children. He was elected president of the Missouri Bar Association in 1930, and elected mayor of Jefferson City in 1947. He resigned in 1948 after being elected lieutenant governor, and was re-elected in 1952 to another term in that office. Then he was inaugurated governor in 1957 for a four-year term.

He set up the state's first effective Budget Review and Control office. Idle funds of the state were invested to produce added income; a pay-as-you-go system for financing capital improvements was introduced; the Division of Procurement was brought within the Division of Budget and Comptroller; a planning and construction unit was added. A motor vehicle speed limit was set; the size of the state Highway Patrol was increased from 355 to 455 men; he won extension of the Patrol's search and seizure powers; effected the reorganization of the division of mental diseases; and created a five-member state mental health commission with a professional director. Also during his tenure, a licensing and inspection law for nursing homes was created; a governor's council on higher education was established; the Missouri Squires, a state atomic energy commission; and a commission on human rights, were created. He recommended the establishment of state-supported junior colleges and scholarships; a 10-year state mental health program, a point system for drivers licenses; and establishment of a fire marshal's office. He also recommended that part of the secrecy provision of the state juvenile code be lifted.

When their son was married in the great hall of the governor's mansion in February 1959, it was the first such wedding for a governor's son. Toward the end of his term he called a special session to increase legislative salaries. He and his wife were found dead in their home in 1962, victims of carbon monoxide fumes. Blair Street is in zones 63106, 63107. There also is a Blair public school, but both the street and the school are named for Frank Blair.

John M. Dalton. 1961-1964. Died July 7, 1972

He was married to Geraldine Hall; they had two children. He was senior member of a law firm and an active cotton farmer in southeast

Missouri when elected attorney general in 1952. He served two terms and then was elected governor by one of the greatest margins ever given a Missouri gubernatorial candidate — a majority of 303,069. In his administration, he emphasized industrial development. He achieved reorganization of the Division of Resources and Development into the Division of Commerce and Industrial Development. He started tours to the East and West coasts and to Europe to attract industry; he had a geological survey building constructed at Rolla; and he established a water resources board. A bill requiring seat belts in all new cars beginning with 1965 models won approval, and a bill to provide state parking facilities in Jefferson City was approved. Branches of the University of Missouri were established at St. Louis and Kansas City, the School Foundation Program was fully financed for the first time, a state commission on higher education was established, and a junior college system was begun with state support. His administration also supported development of Ozark Rivers National Park. He signed a bill creating a national monument at Wilson's Creek battlefield. Bills were passed establishing the first Missouri State Capitol Restoration Commission to aid in rebuilding the Old Capitol in St. Charles, and to help plan for Missouri's 150th anniversary celebration in 1971. Three intensive mental health treatment centers at St. Louis, Columbia and Kansas City were the outcome of his term, a uniform commercial code was adopted, and legislation ensuring equal pay for women was introduced.

Warren E. Hearnes. 1964-1972

Hearnes married Betty Sue Cooper; they had three daughters. This was the first family with young children to live in the mansion since Lloyd Stark's family in the 1930s. He was elected to the state Legislature after retirement from the Army. He practiced law from 1952 to 1961, when he was elected to the House of Representatives. He was the youngest person ever elected at that time. He won re-election to the House four times; in 1957 and 1959 he was the majority floor leader. He was the 30th secretary of state in 1961. A constitutional amendment enabled him to become the first governor in Missouri history to be re-elected to a second consecutive four-year term (when he was re-elected in 1968 by more than 60 percent of the popular vote).

His wife renovated the exterior of the mansion while he was governor. Hearnes was on the executive board of the National Governors Conference and served as vice-chairman of the Midwestern Governors Conference. They are now living in Charleston.

Christopher S. Bond. 1972-1976

Bond married Carolyn Reid; they had one son and adopted another.

He ran for governor in 1972 while he was serving as state auditor. He was only the ninth Republican elected to the post, and the youngest governor in Missouri and the nation at age 33. He served during a difficult financial time in the state and the nation. He worked to attract jobs to the state, and led a drive to acquire public approval for the boldest public works program in the history of the state. When it was approved in June 1982, it created thousands of jobs. He established a merit system of hiring, led a petition drive for a strict campaign contribution law, and reorganized the state government. Under his guidance, the state became a leader in alternative care for senior citizens in their own homes. He is currently representing Missouri as one of our U.S. senators in Washington, DC.

Joseph P. Teasdale. 1976-1980

He married Theresa Ferkenhoff. He earned a law degree and served as a law clerk for a judge, became assistant U.S. attorney in Kansas City, and was the youngest prosecuting attorney in Jackson County. He was elected governor for a four-year term after he walked across the state to personally visit with Missouri residents. He was fondly called "Walkin' Joe." As governor, he was proficient at professionalizing the office in two years. He and his family now reside in Kansas City.

Christopher S. Bond. 1980-1984 Second Term

John Ashcroft. 1984-1992

He met his wife Janet at law school where she was completing her legal education in 1967; they have three children. He served eight years as attorney general and Missouri state auditor before running for governor. He won the election for governor by more than 280,800 votes, receiving 57 percent of the vote. He carried 107 of Missouri's 114 counties in one of the largest Republican gubernatorial victories in the history of the state. He was the first Republican governor to succeed another Republican governor since 1928.

While living on a farm near Springfield, the Ashcrofts practiced law together and both taught at SMSU. They also co-authored two textbooks. The central focus of Ashcroft's administration was to provide citizens of Missouri with an environment of growth, opportunity and development. He was successful in getting assistance for economic development when the Excellence in Education Act passed in 1985, creating a favorable business climate in the state. He served as national chairman of the Education Committee of States in 1987 and 1988, and chairman of the National Governors Association Task Force on Adult Literacy. When elected for a second term, he received 64 percent of the vote, the largest winning percentage since the Civil War. He is now a U.S. senator from Missouri.

Mel Carnahan. 1992-

He and his wife Jean have four children. After graduation from George Washington University, he served as a special agent for the Office of Special Investigators in the Air Force. He was appointed a municipal judge in Rolla at age 26. Elected to serve in the House of Representatives at age 28, he served as majority floor leader during his second term. Elected state treasurer in 1980, he saved taxpayers millions of dollars by using modern money management. Many parts of Missouri were devastated by floods twice in this term of office. He is the present governor.

ST. LOUIS MAYORS

Dr. William Carr Lane. Served 1823-1829

Lane originally came from Pennsylvania, as did many other settlers. He received 122 votes in the election; Auguste Chouteau received only 70. The population of the city reached 4,000 during his term of office and was divided into three wards. He was appointed governor of the New Mexico Territory in 1852 by President Millard Fillmore. He died on January 6, 1863, and is buried in Bellefontaine Cemetery. Carr Lane Avenue is in zone 63104; a public school is also named for him.

Daniel D. Page. 1829-1833

The city limits were extended to Seventh Street during his term, and the population increased to 4,977. He was involved in the incorporation of the Missouri Pacific Railroad and Boatmen's Bank. He died on April 25, 1869, and is buried in Bellefontaine Cemetery. Page Boulevard is in zones 63106, 63112, and 63113.

John W. Johnston. 1833-1835

He represented the government in trading with the Sauk and Fox Indians. He married the daughter of Chief Keokuk; they had three daughters. After the death of his wife, he moved to St. Louis with his children and married Mrs. Lucy Honeywell Gooding, who raised the three girls. The population of the city reached 8,000 and grew to four wards while he was mayor. He died on June 1, 1854, at age 80, and is buried in Calvary Cemetery. We have a street named Keokuk in zones 63116 and 63118.

John F. Darby. 1835-1837

He married Mary, the daughter of Captain Wilkerson and granddaughter of Francis Valle of Ste. Genevieve. Lafayette Park was begun during his term. Taxpayers considered it a waste of money because it was too far out in the "country." He was elected to Congress in 1850. He died on May 11, 1882, and is buried in Calvary Cemetery. Darby Avenue is in zone 63120.

William Carr Lane. 1837-1840 Second Term

John F. Darby. 1840-1841 Second Term
John D. Daggett. 1841-1842

He married Sarah Sparks in 1821; they had 12 children. The population of the city reached 16,469 during this time. He was one of the founders of the Gas Light Co. The ground for Soulard Market was given to the city by Julia Soulard during his term. He died May on 10, 1874, and is buried in Bellefontaine Cemetery. Daggett Avenue is in zone 63110.

George Maguire. 1842-1843

He was born in Ireland, so he was the first foreign-born mayor. He married Mary Amelia Provenchere. The city grew large enough to be divided into six wards during his term of office. He died on October 11, 1882, and is buried in Bellefontaine Cemetery. Provenchere Street, 63118, was named for Mary Amelia's father.

John M. Wimer. 1843-1844

He served as Mayor 1843-1844, Postmaster from 1844-1857, then was re-elected mayor and served from 1857-1858. He also served as president of the Missouri Pacific Railroad. The first paid Fire Department in St. Louis was started in 1857 during his tenure as mayor. He was arrested and confined in the Gratiot Street prison in 1862 for being a Southern sympathizer. He was transferred to the Alton prison in August, escaped in December and rejoined Confederate Gen. Emmet McDonald. He was killed on January 11, 1863, and is buried in Bellefontaine Cemetery.

Bernard Pratte. 1844-1846

He has the distinction of being the first St. Louis-born mayor. He married Louise Chenie in 1824; they had seven children. Carr Square was given to the city by William C. Carr in 1844; the levee was paved with cobblestones; gas street lights were installed; and City Hospital was opened in 1846 during his term of office. He also served as president of the Bank of the State of Missouri. He died on August 10, 1866, and is buried in Calvary Cemetery. The street, once named Pratte, in zone 63104, was changed to Jefferson.

Peter G. Camden. 1846-1847

He married his cousin Anna in 1830. He was mayor when the St. Louis Police Department was established, and appointed James McDonough chief of the Department in 1846. He died on July 23, 1873, and is buried in Bellefontaine Cemetery. Camden Court is in zone 63130.

Bryan Mullanphy. 1847-1848

He was the city's first bachelor mayor. Telegraph service was started in St. Louis while he was in office. He died on June 15, 1851, and is buried in Calvary Cemetery. There is a Mullanphy Street in zones 63102 and 63106 named for his father, John. There is a public school named for Bryan.

John M. Krum. 1848-1849

He was first elected mayor of Alton, Illinois, in 1837. Elizah P. Lovejoy was killed during his term. He married Ophelia Harding in 1839; they had five children. He served as a Union colonel in the Civil War. Two of their sons attained the rank of general in the war; one in the Union forces, the other in the Confederate army. The sewer system was started and the School Board was authorized to levy a tax during his term. He also served as director of Washington University. He died on September 13, 1883, and is buried in Bellefontaine Cemetery. Krum Avenue is in zone 63113.

James G. Barry. 1849-1850

Born in Ireland, he served as mayor of St. Louis during the flood, the cholera epidemic and the great fire of 1849. In the 1850 Census, the population reached 77,860. He was a member of the Missouri Historical Society. He died on May 9, 1880, and is buried in Calvary Cemetery. Barry Court is in zone 63122.

Luther M. Kennett. 1850-1853

He married Martha Ann Boyce, daughter of Colonel Boyce; she died after their daughter was born. In 1842, he married his cousin Agnes A. Kennett; they had seven sons. A quarantine station was established on Arsenal Island in 1850 due to the 1849 cholera epidemic, the worst epidemic the city had ever experienced, and the influx of immigrants. He served as president of the Iron Mountain Railroad and was elected to Congress, defeating Thomas Hart Benton. He died on April 12, 1873, and is buried in Bellefontaine Cemetery. Kennett Place is in zone 63104.

John How. 1853-1855

He ran against Charles R. Chouteau and won. One of his sons married the daughter of James Eads. During his administration, $36,250 was paid for 14.5 acres for Hyde Park. The block where the Main Public Library now stands was purchased from James H. Lucas for $95,500, and the Workhouse was moved to Broadway and Meramec. He later served as an Indian agent in Elco, Nevada. He died on January 3, 1885, and is buried in Bellefontaine Cemetery. How Avenue is in zone 63130.

Washington King. 1855-1856

He married Cynthia M. Kelsey in 1836; they had two children, and lost everything when the city burned in 1849. The city limits were extended to Grand while he was in office. Mayor King and former Mayors How and Wimer were on the train to Jefferson City on November 1, 1855, when the Gasconade Bridge collapsed. Thirty-one people were killed;

How and Wimer were injured along with many others. He died August 27, 1861, and is buried in Calvary Cemetery.

John How. 1856-1857 Second Term

John Wimer. 1857-1858 Second Term

Oliver D. Filley. 1858-1861

He married Chloe Velina Brown in 1835; they had three sons and four daughters. He served as the first mayor during the Civil War, and was the first mayor to serve two years in office. The population of St. Louis more than doubled to 160,773 by 1860; in the 1850 Census, it had only been 77,860.

He worked for a stove manufacturer, and also served as director of the Bank of the State of Missouri. The Police Department was put under state control during his term. He introduced fire prevention measures, indicating chimney and stove pipe specifications in detail. Inspectors checked every building once a month to be sure they were safe. He died on August 21, 1881, and is buried in Bellefontaine Cemetery.

Daniel G. Taylor. 1861-1863

He married Angelique Henri, they had two children before she died in 1858. He married Emilie Lebeau, and she bore him three children. A captain of a river boat, he lost his business in the great fire of 1849. He died on October 8, 1878, and is buried in Calvary Cemetery. Taylor Street is in zones 63108, 63110, 63113, 63115.

Chauncy I. Filley. 1863-1864

He married Anne Dams in 1855. He didn't complete his full term as mayor because of poor health. He resigned from office in April 1864, and lived until he was 93. He died on September 24, 1923. He is buried in Bellefontaine Cemetery.

James S. Thomas. 1864-1869

He was a banking partner of L. A. Benoist. He married Curtis Skinner; after her death, he married Susan H. Hackney. New water works were developed, and Tower Grove Park was accepted by the city during his term of office. He served as a member of the Board of Education. He died on September 26, 1874, and is buried in Bellefontaine Cemetery. Thomas Street is in zone 63106.

Nathan Cole. 1869-1871

He married Rebecca Fagin in 1851. The new City Charter was accepted in 1870 and Carondelet was annexed during his term. He established the St. Louis Grain Elevator and was a director of the Bank of Commerce. He was elected to the U.S. Congress in 1876. He died on March 4, 1904, and is buried in Bellefontaine Cemetery. Cole Street is in zone 63101 and 63106.

Joseph Brown. 1871-1875

He married Virginia Keach in 1854; they had two daughters. While he was mayor of Alton, Illinois, he owned and operated river boats until the Civil War; then he went into the real estate business. He also served as president of the Missouri Pacific Railroad. The city purchased land for Forest Park, O'Fallon Park and Carondelet Park; the Eads Bridge was also completed during his term. He died on December 3, 1889, and is buried in Alton.

Arthur B. Barrett. 1875

He was married to Anna Farrar Sweringen in 1869; they had three children. He died on April 24, 1875, one week after inauguration at age 39. He is buried in Calvary Cemetery.

James H. Britton. 1875-1876

He was a banker and postmaster of Troy, Missouri. He was declared the winner of a special election held on May 15, 1875, to replace Mayor Barrett. He served as mayor until February 9, 1876, when he was unseated by Henry Overstolz, after a recount of the votes. He died on January 27, 1900, and is buried in Calvary Cemetery.

Henry Overstolz. 1876-1881

The first German-born mayor of St. Louis was married to Philippine Espenschied. He was the first mayor to serve under the Charter of 1876, which provided for separation from the county and a four-year term for the mayor. The new city limits were set at Skinker Boulevard, and the city was divided into 28 wards at this time. According to the Census of 1880, the population of St. Louis was 350,518. He died on November 29, 1887, and is buried in Bellefontaine Cemetery. The street named Espenschied, in 63111, was for Philippine's father, Louis.

William. L. Ewing. 1881-1885

A great-grandson of Pierre Chouteau, he worked as a banker. He was married to Mary Fleming; they had one son. While he was mayor, 12 miles of business streets were paved with granite blocks and cable cars were introduced to St. Louis. He died on June 4, 1905, and is buried at Vincennes, Indiana. Ewing Street, in zones 63103 and 63104, is named for his father.

David R. Francis. 1885-1889

He married Jane Perry, daughter of John D. Perry in 1876; they had six sons. He helped arrange for the building of Merchants Bridge while he was mayor. He died on January 15, 1927, and is buried in Bellefontaine Cemetery. Francis Street is in zone 63106.

Edward A. Noonan. 1889-1893

He married Margaret Brennan in 1876; they had one son and two daughters. Union Station construction was started, and City Hall was erected on Washington Square while he was in office. By 1890, electric street lights were in place and the first smoke ordinance had been passed. The population of St. Louis reached 451,770 in 1890; in the Census of 1880 it had been 350,518. He died on September 23, 1927, and is buried in Calvary Cemetery. Noonan Avenue is in zone 63143.

Cyrus P. Walbridge. 1893-1897

He married Lizzie Merrell in 1879; they had one son. He was the first mayor to appoint women to serve in city government. During his term, the public school library became the free public library; the collection and disposal of garbage was started; all telephone wires were put underground in the downtown area; and the Chain of Rocks Water Works was completed. He served as president of Bell Telephone Co. of Missouri. On May 26, 1896, a tornado struck St. Louis. City Hospital was damaged, and the House of Good Shepherd convent was used as a temporary city hospital. He died on May 1, 1921, and is buried in Bellefontaine Cemetery. Walbridge Place is in zone 63115.

Henry Ziegenheim. 1897-1901

He married Catherine Henkle in 1869; they had nine children. The population was 575,238 by 1900, and St. Louis was the fourth largest city in the United States. The citizens approved a bond issue for $5,000,000 that year to finance the World's Fair. He died on March 17, 1910, and is buried in St. Marcus Cemetery.

Rolla Wells. 1901-1909

He married Jennie Howard Parker in 1878; they had five children. After her death, Carlot C. Wells became his second wife. Wells worked with his father, Erastus, in the street car business. During his term, Fairgrounds Park was purchased for $700,000. He died on November 30, 1944, and is buried in Bellefontaine Cemetery. Wells Avenue in zones 63112 and 63113 was named for his father.

Frederick Kreismann. 1909-1913

He married Pauline Whiteman in 1902; they had two children. He was an insurance man. The population in 1910 was 687,029, and St. Louis was still the fourth largest city in the United States. Significant construction during his term included the Municipal Courts Building and the Main Public Library. He died on November 1, 1944, and is buried in Bellefontaine Cemetery.

Henry W. Kiel. 1913-1925

He married Irene H. Moonan in 1892; they had two sons and two daughters. He was a builder by trade. The election results were so close that he thought he lost the election. He took a train bound for Texas, and was notified he was the victor while en route. He has the distinction of being the first mayor elected to three, four-year terms. Governor Caulfield appointed him president of the St. Louis Police Board. He died on November 26, 1942, and is buried in Oak Grove Cemetery.

In addition to Kiel Auditorium, Henry Kiel's contracting firm was involved in the construction of other buildings that include: Soldan, Central and McKinley high schools; the Missouri, Delmont, Loew's State and Ambassador theaters; the Post-Dispatch Building at 12th and Olive; the Coronado Hotel; the 18th Street Garage, and the Hamilton-Brown Building.

Victor J. Miller. 1925-1933

He married Mabel Katherine Cooney in 1918. He was president of the St. Louis Police Board and elected mayor when he was only 36. During his term of office, the Delmar Wabash Railroad Station was built and the Civil Courts Building was completed. Also, the Fire Department became fully motorized while he was mayor; they did not use horses after 1927. He died on January 6, 1955, and is buried in Mount Hope Cemetery in Joplin, Missouri. Miller Street in zone 63111 was named for him; it has been changed to Haven.

Bernard F. Dickmann. 1933-1941

The Republicans lost the mayor's office for the first time in 24 years in 1933 when Dickmann, a staunch Democrat, was elected. The first bachelor to serve as mayor in 50 years, he worked in real estate with his father. Forty city blocks along the river in downtown St. Louis were cleared for the Jefferson National Expansion Memorial. An anti-smoke ordinance was passed forbidding the use of soft coal in the city; Raymond Tucker was appointed smoke commissioner to enforce this ordinance.

After Dickmann served two terms as mayor, a Republican was again elected. Dickman was appointed postmaster of St. Louis in 1943. He married Beula Pat Herrington, postmistress from Mount Olive, Missouri, in February of 1949. He died on December 9, 1971.

William. D. Becker. 1941-1943

He was admitted to the bar in 1901 and married Margaret Louise McIntosh in 1902; they had two children. He practiced law for 15 years before he was elected to the Court of Appeals for a 12-year term and re-elected in 1928 for another 12 years. The Republican candidate defeated Dickmann in 1941. He supported the merit system for city workers which was the start of the Civil Service system. Mayor Becker and five other city and county leaders were killed on August 1, 1943, in a glider crash at Lambert Field. He is buried in Bellefontaine Cemetery. Becker Road is in zone 63129.

Aloys P. Kaufmann. 1943-1949

He practiced law, served as president of the Republican Central Committee, president of the Board of Aldermen, and became mayor upon the death of Mayor Becker. He married Margaret Uding in 1943; they had one son. During his term of office, Lambert Field increased in size from 350 to 1,400 acres; the city refuse collection started in 1947; the first earnings tax was passed but declared unconstitutional; the rat control section of the Health Department was started; a new city building code was passed; the River Des Peres drainage project was completed; general street improvements were made; water service repairs were made; new athletic fields, and three new public swimming pools were built; a Central police station was built; a new elephant house was built at the Zoo; a new Grand Boulevard viaduct was built; and repairs were made to the Art Museum. He later served as president of the Chamber of Commerce. He died on February 12, 1984.

Joseph M. Darst. 1949-1953

He was married to Lucille Rose in 1930, and worked in real estate. Public housing was started during his term with the building of the John Cochran apartments and the Land Clearance Authority was established. He died on June 8, 1953 and is buried in Calvary Cemetery.

Raymond R. Tucker. 1953-1965

He married Mary Edythe Leiber in 1928; they had a son and daughter. He taught mechanical engineering at Washington University, and served as secretary to Mayor Dickmann from 1934-1937 and as secretary to the Survey and Audit Committee from 1939-1941. He was also director of Public Safety. He received the St. Louis Award for rallying citizens to work for civic improvement. He was a proponent of planning on a regular basis, and a strong supporter of the Metropolitan Sewer District in 1954. A Plaza bond issue passed while he was mayor. After many heated discussions, city water was fluoridated to help children's teeth. After he served three terms as mayor, he returned to work at Washington University. He died on November 23, 1970. Tucker Boulevard is in zones 63104 and 63102.

Alfonso J. Cervantes. 1965-1973.

He married Carmen Davis; they had six children. He had many business interests, among them an insurance agency and the Laclede Cab Co. He served as an alderman and president of the Board of Aldermen before he was elected mayor; he was called the "salesman mayor." He was successful in fighting crime, managing the city finances and in avoiding race relation problems. He brought African-Americans into city government with 95 city commissions appointments. He brought the revival of the Mounted Police, started the St. Louis Ambassadors, and the Area Office of Aging and Beautification Committee. The Citizens Service Bureau was added to the mayor's office, and the Land Reutilization Authority was created to take over vacant properties and group them for re-use. He was successful in bringing the Spanish pavilion from the 1964 New York World's Fair to St. Louis, and later the replica of the *Santa Maria*; neither one was successful. He presided at ceremonies to celebrate the completion of the Arch. He tried to establish a new airport south of East St. Louis; this controversy helped defeat his try for a third term. He wrote a book, *Mr. Mayor,* taught at St. Louis University, and was active in business. The St. Louis Convention Center was named for him. He died on June 23, 1983, and is buried in Calvary Cemetery.

John Poelker. 1973-1977

He married Ruth Combron in 1940; they had one son and two daughters. In 1942, he worked for the FBI as a special agent on financial frauds. In 1953 he served as city assessor; in 1957 he served as comptroller when Milton Carpenter became Missouri Director of Revenue. He was one of the best comptrollers to serve St. Louis; he left the city with a $6.5 million surplus for the pending budget. He died on February 9, 1990, and left his personal papers to the Washington University library.

James Conway. 1977-1981

He married Joan C. Newman; they had five children. He was serving as state senator when elected mayor. He put a sign in the mayor's office "UNDER NEW MANAGEMENT," removed all the former mayor's assistants (except for Roger Duffe), and brought in a whole new staff. Many differences of opinion with Comptroller Percich on interpretations of the city charter, resulted in lawsuits and threats of lawsuits. Consolidating the services of City Hospital and Homer G. Phillips Hospital brought him into conflict with African-Americans on the North Side. He was unsuccessful in his attempt to take control of the police department from the state. After serving his term as mayor, he was appointed president of the Board of Police Commissioners.

Vincent Schoemehl. 1981-1992

After serving as alderman in the 28th Ward from 1975-1981, he defeated Conway to become mayor. "He performed a difficult job well for eight years, brought energy, vision, and even daring to the job," is a quote from an evaluation of his first two terms in office. He made use of Urban Development Action grant programs to stimulate city projects, and arranged financial inducements for redevelopers. Some of the highlights of his term include the creation of the Regional Medical Center to handle both city and county patients, a network of shelters for the homeless,

Operation Brightside, Operation Safestreet and Operation Conservation. They all reflect his innovative approach to urban problems.

The renovation of the riverboat, The Admiral, was not as successful as he had hoped it would be. Constant battles occurred between this mayor and the comptroller also. He was called a "dictator" while serving a third term, because of his impulsive statements and actions when he was working intensely for a project. He was involved in planning the new football stadium/enlarged Convention Center, and began generating interest to bring a football team back to St. Louis. The Kiel Center sports arena, built at the former site of Kiel Auditorium, was also planned during his term.

He reversed his position on abortion when he ran for governor, and alienated many St. Louis voters and the Democratic party. He was defeated by Mel Carnahan and returned to the business world.

Freeman Bosley Jr. 1992-

After graduation from law school, he served as staff attorney for Legal Services of Eastern Missouri. He was the first African-American circuit clerk of the 22nd Judicial Circuit, a job he held for 10 years, and was 3rd Ward Democratic committeeman since 1984. He is also the first African-American elected mayor of St. Louis. He married Darlynn Cunningham Bosley; they have a daughter.

He comes from a civic-minded family. His father has been a member of the Board of Aldermen for some time. The mayor does not believe having material posessions is as important as what he can do for humanity. He compared the situation of the races in St. Louis to a piano keyboard, asking for harmony between blacks and whites because both colors need to be used if one wants to play the piano. He hopes his constituents will feel the need to cooperate in like manner.

Appendix III
St. Louis Public Schools

The first school in Missouri was started in St. Louis in 1774 by J.B. Tribeau; it lasted 40 years. In 1812, the Missouri Territory provided land for public schools. The first public school in St. Louis was established in 1817; each student attending school was charged $10 per year. The first public schools in Missouri were supported not by taxes but by tuition, or fees, which ranged from 50 cents to $2.50 per student per quarter. Poor children were excused from this obligation. People thought free schooling was "charity" at that time rather than a basic right.

The first School Board was established in 1817. Members included William C. Carr, Alexander McNair, Thomas Hart Benton, William Clark, H. L. Hoffman, and Auguste Chouteau. The first free public school in St. Louis opened in 1850, and the first tax was levied to support the schools the same year. Most of the public schools in Missouri were closed during the Civil War by Governor Jackson. The money usually spent on the schools was used to buy arms for the state militia.

The first Negro public school opened in 1866; the first kindergarten in the nation was established in St. Louis by Susan Blow in 1873. A compulsory school attendance law was passed in 1905. A state law required that all teachers must have a high school education to qualify for a teachers certificate in 1927. By 1961, a bachelor's degree became the minimum requirement.

By 1987, there were 129 schools in St. Louis which dated from 1910 to 1930. A capital improvement program was begun in 1988, with the projected completion date of 1996. A complex of three new schools, the first in the city since 1970, was completed in time for the 1995-96 school year. Located on 18 acres of the former Pruitt-Igoe site, this includes a one-story special education school, the Michael School for orthopedically-challenged students, a two-story elementary school, and a three-story middle school.

Other new schools scheduled for completion in 1996 are: the Investigative Learning Center Middle School adjacent to the St. Louis Science Center; The Lexington Elementary School; The Metro-Area High School; and the Stix Early Childhood Center. When all this building is finished, the St. Louis Public School System will have remodeled 98 schools, built six new ones, closed 23 schools, and left 106 open. Vashon High School is stil open but was not scheduled for renovation.

Secondary (9-12): Regular 4, Magnet 5, Alternative 3
Middle (6-8): Regular 15, Magnet 6
Elementary: Regular 53, Magnet 14
Special Schools: 6
Total 106
Total Enrollment 9/30/94 — 42,622

Chester Edmonds, the spokesman for the St. Louis Public Schools in 1995, stated that while more than 80 schools were closed in the last 30 years, 20 have been reopened for magnet or alternative school programs, school offices or warehouses. At least 10 have been razed. Dozens have been sold, 11 are for sale, and 18 schools are in mothballs for possible future use.

ST. LOUIS CITY PUBLIC SCHOOLS
* Indicates Street With Same Name

(In the following information, where it is known, the dates of a school's opening and/or closing is mentioned. If a telephone number is listed, it is assumed the school is still active.)

CENTRAL ADMINISTRATION - 911 Locust St., 63101 (231-3720).

PUBLIC AFFAIRS - 911 Locust St., 63101 (231-3720, ext 222).

BOARD OF EDUCATION-TRANSPORTATION - 1520 S. Grand Blvd., 63104 (533-6725).

AAA-BUSCH MIDDLE SCHOOL - 5910 Clifton, 63109 (352-1043). *See Busch School.*

ACADEMIC and ATHLETIC ACADEMY - Curriculum Services - Student Leadership - 5910 Clifton Avenue, 63109 (352-1043). *See Busch School.*

ACADEMIC BASIC INSTITUTION - 25 S. Compton, 63103 (533-1944). *See Waring School.*

ACADEMY OF BASIC INSTRUCTION - 7417 Vermont, 63111 (353-1353). *See Lyon School.*

ACADEMY OF BASIC INSTRUCTION - 6020 Pernod, 63139 (352-9212). *See Mallinckrodt School.*

*ADAMS ELEMENTARY SCHOOL - 1311 Tower Grove, 63110. It was opened in 1878, and named for the second and sixth presidents of the United States (John Adams1797-1801, John Quincy Adams 1825-1829). This school is closed.

ADULT EDUCATION - 3815 McCausland, 63109 (781-6615). *See Lindenwood School.*

ADULT BASIC EDUCATION-GED - 5078 Kensington, 63108 (367-5000). *See Clark School.*

ADULT VOCATIONAL EDUCATION - 3405 Bell Ave., 63106 (534-6401). *See Vashon School.*

ALDRIDGE SCHOOL - Originally called Colored School #11, at Switzer and Christian, 63147. It was later called Baden Colored School. It opened in 1870; the name was changed to Aldridge in 1890 for Ira Aldridge, a black actor. It was closed in 1908.

AMES SCHOOL - 2900 Hadley, 63107. It was opened in 1955, and now is the Visual and Performing Arts School (241-7165). The original Ames School at 1313 Hebert St. was opened in 1873 and named for Henry Ames, a meat packer and hotel owner.

ANNIE MALONE SPECIAL SCHOOL, CHILDREN AND FAMILY SERVICE CENTER - 2612 Annie Malone Dr., 63113 (531-0120). Founded by Sarah Newton in 1888 as the St. Louis Colored Orphan's Home, it was originally located at 1427 North 12th St. In 1905 it was moved to 4316 Natural Bridge, and in 1922 to Goode Ave., (now Annie Malone Drive) and Kennerly Ave. In 1946, the home was named for Annie Turnbo Pope Malone (1869-1957), one of the world's wealthiest black women in the 1930s. In 1918 she established Poro College, and was involved in a variety of philanthropic projects.

*ARLINGTON ELEMENTARY SCHOOL - 1617 Burd Ave., 63112. It was opened in 1899. It originally opened in 1881 on St. Charles Rock Road near Rinkleville. It was named for the district in which it was located, which was named for Arlington, Virginia. There was also a branch at 5420 Cote Brilliante Avenue, 63112. Arlington School was closed in 1968.

*ASHLAND ELEMENTARY SCHOOL - 3921 N. Newstead, 63115 (385-4767). It opened in 1909; it is now a pre-school (382-9440). The original school opened in 1874 on Bridgeton Road, one mile west of Fair Ground. There is a branch at 4415 Margaretta, 63115 (261-9957). It was named for Ashland County in Kentucky, the home of Henry Clay. Clay once owned the land on which this school stands.

ATTUCKS ELEMENTARY SCHOOL - It originally opened as Colored School #12 at Columbus (now Eighth) and Barry; it was also called

Arsenal Colored School when it opened in 1880. A branch was at 1897 Arsenal, 63118, near the Marine Hospital. In 1885 it was moved to Seventh and Hickory. In 1890, it was renamed for Crispus Attucks who was born a slave in Farmington, Massachusetts. He became the leader of a band of American patriots, and was the first man to fall in the Boston Massacre when five men were killed by British soldiers. It was closed in 1910. A school, established in the former L'Ouverture School at 2612 Papin in 1950, was also named Attucks; it closed in 1971. A branch was established at 2022 Papin Street, 63103, in 1949; it closed in 1970. A branch at 2135 Chouteau, 63103, was established in 1945, and closed in 1970.

AUDIOVISUAL SERVICE - 1517 Theresa, 63104 (865-4550).

*BADEN ELEMENTARY SCHOOL - 8724 Halls Ferry Road, 63147. It was opened in 1907; it is now used for a pre-school (388-2477). The original building was at Church Road and Bittner Street, 63147. It was named for Baden, Germany, the city from which many of the early inhabitants of this area had come.

BANNEKER ELEMENTARY SCHOOL - It was opened as Colored School # 5 in 1873 at 18th and Conde (Montgomery Sts.), 63106. In 1890, it was moved to Montgomery and Leffingwell. The name was changed to Banneker, after Benjamin Banneker, a black astronomer, mathematician, and one of the architects who laid out the city of Washington, D. C. In 1932, it was moved to the Stoddard School Building, which had been built in 1873 at Lucas and Ewing, and Stoddard School took the name Banneker. The building was razed in 1959, and a new school was built at 2840 Sam Shepard Dr. (was Lucas). In 1992 it was changed to accommodate grades pre-school through fifth. (533-1872).

*BATES ELEMENTARY SCHOOL - 1912 N. Prairie, 63113. It was opened in 1916 and named for Edward Bates, an early St. Louis school director, lawyer and member of President Lincoln's Cabinet. The original school opened in 1872 at Collins and Bates (Dickson), 63102. Bates School closed in 1980, and was sold in 1983 (Bates Street in 63111 and 63116 is named for Frederick Bates, second governor of Missouri and brother of Edward).

*BEAUMONT HIGH SCHOOL - 3836 Natural Bridge, 63107 (533-2410). It was opened in 1926. It was named for William Beaumont, a surgeon, scientist, and the author of a book on digestion. He was assigned to the St. Louis Arsenal as surgeon and medical officer. There was also a Beaumont School at 3000 Prairie, 63107. Parents as Teachers is now also at 3836 Natural Bridge, 63107 (534-8720).

*BELL AVENUE SCHOOL - on Bell Avenue, one-half mile west of

Grand Boulevard, 63108. (The street named Bell was named for Daniel M. Bell, a merchant.)

*BENTON ELEMENTARY SCHOOL - 2847 N. Kingshighway Blvd., 63115. It was opened in 1894. It was named for Thomas Hart Benton, a member of the first St. Louis School Board, a Missouri lawyer and statesman, who served for 30 years in the U.S. Senate. The original school opened in 1841 at Sixth and St. Charles, 63101. Benton School was also called Central School, when it was opened as the first public high school west of the Mississippi in February, 1853. It was staffed by a principal and four teachers; 70 pupils attended. Until 1904, there were only two public high schools in St. Louis, one for the white population and one for black population. Benton School closed in 1980.

BENTON STATION SCHOOL - 1870-1888 - Near Benton Station on Manchester Road.

BEVO-LONG COMMUNITY SCHOOL - 5028 Morganford, 63116 (353-1034). *See Long School.*

BILINGUAL EDUCATION - 450 Des Peres, 63112 (863-7266).

*BLAIR ELEMENTARY SCHOOL - 2708 N. 22nd St., 63106. It was opened in 1882. It was named for Frank P. Blair, a lawyer, soldier, Republican newspaperman and politician. A school was also located at 2707 Rauschenbach Avenue, 63106. This school was closed in 1980, and the building was converted to apartments.

BLEWETT ELEMENTARY SCHOOL - 1927 Cass Ave., 63106. It was opened in 1956. The first building opened in 1905 at 5351 Enright, 63112. It was named for Dr. Ben Blewett, who served as superintendent of schools from 1908-1917. He established the Jessie Parsons Blewett Fund to be used for relief of teachers and for professional training. It is now used as a middle school. (231-7738)

*BLOW ELEMENTARY SCHOOL - 516 Loughborough Ave., 63111. It was opened in 1903; it is now used as a middle school (353-1349). The original Blow School opened in 1866. The original building opened in 1858 at Fifth (Compton) and Pine (Loughborough) in the Carondelet area. At one time, Catholic schools which had been established in 1836 were the only schools in Carondelet. The Sisters of St. Joseph were paid $87.50 every quarter by the city to teach the children. Henry T. Blow, a wealthy businessman, congressman ,and commissioner to South America, was a Presbyterian and the father of Susan Blow. He introduced the concept of public schools to Carondelet.

CARONDELET BLOW COMMUNITY SCHOOL is also located at 516 Loughborough, 63111.

BOARD OF EDUCATION-TRANSPORTATION CHARTERED -

1520 S. Grand, (533-6725).

*BOOKER T. WASHINGTON VOCATIONAL SCHOOL - 1909 - 814 N. Ninth, 63101. *See Franklin School.* It was named for Booker T. Washington, the famous black educator and founder of Tuskegee Institute. (Washington Street is named for President George Washington.)

BRANCH HIGH SCHOOL NO. 1 - Seventh and Chouteau, 63104.

BRANCH HIGH SCHOOL NO. 2 - 18th and Christy (Lucas), 63103.

BRANCH HIGH SCHOOL NO. 3 - Carroll and Second Carondelet (18th Street), 63104.

*BRYAN HILL ELEMENTARY SCHOOL - 2128 Gano Ave., 63107. It was opened in 1912; it is now a pre-school (534-0370). The original building was at 2041 John, 63107. It was named for the area owned by Dr. John Gano Bryan. (Bryan Street was changed to Prairie.)

BUDER ELEMENTARY SCHOOL - 5319 Lansdowne Ave., 63109 (352-4343). It was opened in 1920. It is named for Mrs. Susan R. Buder, a St. Louis jewelry store owner and philanthropist.

BUILDINGS GROUNDS AND PROPERTY MANAGEMENT - 3431 School, 63106 (535-2500).

*BUSCH ELEMENTARY SCHOOL - 5910 Clifton, 63109. It was opened in 1953. It was named for Adolphus Busch, a St. Louis brewery owner and philanthropist. Busch School was closed in 1980, and the building is now used for THE ACADEMIC & ATHLETIC ACADEMY located at 5910 Clifton, 63109 (352-1043).

CARING COMMUNITIES OFFICE - 5019 Alcott, 63113, (261-8282). *See Walbridge School.*

CARONDELET ELEMENTARY SCHOOL - 8221 Minnesota Ave., 63111. It was opened in 1871. It was named for the city of Carondelet which received its name from Don Francisco Hector el Baron de Carondelet, a former Spanish governor of Louisiana at New Orleans. The first location was Third and Hurck, 63111. The school was closed in 1975.

CARONDELET-BLOW COMMUNITY SCHOOL - 516 Loughborough, 63111 (353-1599). *See Blow School.*

*CARR ELEMENTARY SCHOOL - 1421 Carr St., 63106. It was opened in 1908. It was named for William C. Carr, a lawyer and judge who was born in 1783 in Virginia. He arrived in St. Louis in 1804, married Anna Marie Elliot in 1808, and was elected to the board of trustees of St. Louis with Auguste Chouteau, Edward Hempstead, Jean Cabanne and William Christy. He was appointed a circuit court judge in 1826, his wife died the same year. In 1829, he married Dorcas Bent, a daughter of Silas Bent. He was also a friend of Henry Shaw. He served as a member of the first School Board with Alex McNair, Thomas Hart

Benton, William Clark and Auguste Chouteau. The original school was opened in 1855 at 15th and Carr, 63106. Carr School was closed in 1977 (Dorcas Street is named for William Carr's second wife).

*CARR LANE ELEMENTARY SCHOOL - 1004 N. Jefferson, 63106. It was opened in 1959. It was named for the first mayor of St. Louis, William Carr Lane. It is now the VISUAL AND PERFORMING ARTS MIDDLE SCHOOL (231-0413). The original school building opened in 1870 at 2308 Carr, 63106. There was also a branch at 24th and Carr streets in 1875. In 1949, there was a branch at 1422 N. 22nd St., 63106. Carr Lane Branch closed in 1976.

*CARROLL SCHOOL - at Buell (10th) and Carroll, in the Soulard area, 63104. It was opened in 1858 and closed in 1971 (Carroll Street in 63104 was named for C.C. Carroll, an early landowner).

CARVER ELEMENTARY SCHOOL - 3325 Bell Ave., 63106. (It was formerly Wayman School, named for Wayman Crow which had opened in 1882.) Carver school opened in 1943. It was named for Dr. George Washington Carver, the scientist who was born into slavery and became a college professor. He developed many new uses for the peanut. It is now a pre-school (533-7020).

CARVER COMMUNITY SCHOOL is also located there (535-5618).

CENTRAL HIGH SCHOOL is now a Secondary Magnet School.

CENTRAL VISUAL AND PERFORMING ARTS HIGH SCHOOL - HONORS ARTS - HONORS MUSIC and MASS MEDIA STUDIES. The original school opened February 11, 1853, in the Old Benton Building, on Sixth Street between Locust and St. Charles, 63101. It was named after James Yeatman, who was president of the Western Sanitary Commission. A Central High School, established in 1856 at 15th and Olive, 63103, is now in the building formerly known as Yeatman High School, 3616 N. Garrison, 63107 (371-1045) which was erected in 1904.

CHAPTER 1 - 5183 Raymond, 63113 (361-5500). *See Clark School.*

*CHARLESS ELEMENTARY SCHOOL - 2226 Shenandoah Ave., 63104. It was opened in 1895. It was named for Joseph Charless Jr., a promoter of welfare in St. Louis. The original school, called Devolsey, opened in 1859 at Kingsbury (now Shenandoah) near Gravois in South St. Louis, 63104. The school was closed in 1980.

*CHELTENHAM - It was opened in 1868 near Clayton Road, five miles from the St. Louis courthouse. (Cheltenham Street's name was changed to Hampton in 63110 and 63139. Part of West Park in 63110 and 63139 was named Cheltenham; some of Sublette in 63110 and 63139 was also named Cheltenham. The Cheltenham area is now referred to as "Dogtown" and the Clayton-Tamm area).

CHILDREN'S STUDY SCHOOL - CLASSICAL JUNIOR ACADEMY - 3827 Enright, 63108. *See Enright School.*

*CHOUTEAU ELEMENTARY SCHOOL - 1306 S. Ewing, 63104. It was opened in 1894. It was named for Auguste Chouteau, the cofounder of St. Louis, a leading citizen and a member of the first St. Louis School Board. The original building was opened in 1859 on Chouteau Avenue, west of Jefferson Avenue, 63103. The school was closed in 1980.

*CLARK ELEMENTARY SCHOOL - 1020 N. Union Blvd., 63113. It was opened in 1907. It was named for William Clark, one of the leaders of the Lewis and Clark expedition, who was appointed Indian agent in St. Louis by President Thomas Jefferson. He later was the governor of the Missouri Territory. Clark also was a member of the first St. Louis School Board. The original building opened in 1845 at Seventh and Hickory (now Labadie), 63115. It was was once called First Ward School. Branch # 1 was located at 5078 Kensington Ave., 63108; and Branch # 2 was located at 5183 Raymond, 63113. Branches 1 and 2 were closed in 1984. Branch #2 is now used as LAW AND EDUCATION, (361-5500).

PRE-SCHOOL ACADEMY is now located at Clark School (367-1505).

CLASSICAL JUNIOR ACADEMY - 5351 Enright, 63108 (367-0555). *See Enright School.*

CLASSICAL JUNIOR ACADEMY - 5031 Potomac, 63139 (353-8875). *See Kennard School.*

CLASSICAL JUNIOR ACADEMY MIDDLE SCHOOL - 2156 Russell Blvd., 63104 (773-0027). *See McKinley School.*

*CLAY ELEMENTARY SCHOOL - 3820 N. 14th St., 63107 (231-9608). When it was opened in 1905, it was the first public school in St. Louis with a gymnasium. It was named for Henry Clay, American statesman, Kentucky senator, and orator. The original building opened in 1856 at Bellefontaine Road (now North Broadway) and Mallinckrodt in Bremen, 63147.

*CLEMENS AVENUE PRIMARY - 5858 Clemens Ave., 63112. Clemens Avenue was named for James Clemens, who married Elizabeth Mullanphy.

*CLEVELAND HIGH SCHOOL - 4352 Louisiana Ave., 63111. It was opened in 1915; it is now known as the NAVAL Jr. ROTC ACADEMY (832-0933). It was named for Grover Cleveland, the 22nd and 24th president of the U.S. (1885-1889, 1893-1897)

*CLINTON ELEMENTARY SCHOOL - 1224 Grattan St., 63104. It was opened in 1940; closed in 1977. The original school opened in 1868 at 1109 Grattan, 63104. It is now used for the ELEMENTARY STUDY - LEARNING RESOURCE CENTER (231-9277). It was named for George Clinton, the vice-president under presidents Thomas Jefferson and James Madison, 1804-1812.

*COLE ELEMENTARY SCHOOL - 3935 Enright, 63108. It was opened in 1931. The school was named for Richard H. Cole, a public school teacher who served as principal at the Simmons School for fifty years. Cole School was closed in 1974, and reopened for pre-school to fifth grade in 1992 (533-0894). Cole branch # 1 opened in 1950 at 3963 West Belle Place, 63108. A branch also opened in 1967 at 5890 Etzel, 63112. Cole branch closed in 1974. Cole Street (63101, 63106) was named for Nathan Cole, a St. Louis mayor.

COLORED SCHOOL # 3 opened in 1866 at 24th and Morgan (Delmar), 63106. It was moved to 14th and Christy in 1868; the next move was to 11th between Carr and Biddle, 63106, in 1880 (11th St. School).

*COLUMBIA ELEMENTARY SCHOOL - 3120 St. Louis Ave., 63106. It was opened in 1929 and named for Christopher Columbus. It is now a pre-school (533-2750). A COMMUNITY SCHOOL is also at this address (533-2750).

COMMUNITY EDUCATION SCHOOLS - 1517 Theresa, 63104 (773-7926).

*COMPTON SCHOOL - The original building opened in 1858 at Compton Hill in 63104 on Henrietta Street near Arkansas/Theresa Avenue. Compton Hill was named for the wife of St. Louis Mayor James S. Thomas. Compton Avenue (63103, 63104, 63106, 63111, and 63118) took its name from Compton Hill. Under construction at 5130 Oakland Ave., 63110, is the Dr. Arthur H. Compton/Dr. Charles R. Drew Investigative Learning Center Middle School. The school is named in honor of Dr. Compton, an atomic science pioneer and former Washington University Chancellor, and Dr. Drew, the first director of the American Red Cross Blood Bank.

CONTINUED EDUCATION PROJECT - 814 N. Ninth, 63101 (231-7316). *See Franklin School.*

CONTINUED EDUCATION - 2030 S. Vandeventer, 63110 (771-4041). *See Wade School.*

CONTINUED EDUCATION - 814 N. 19th, 63106 (231-7316). *See Franklin School.*

*COOK ELEMENTARY SCHOOL - 5935 Horton Place, 63112 (725-2346). It was opened in 1964. The school was named for the Rev. James Cook, pastor of Antioch Baptist Church. He was executive secretary of the Pine Street YMCA, and known for his work with black youths. Cook branch was located at 5890 Etzel, 63112. Cook Avenue in 63106 and 63113 was named for John E. Cook, an early landowner.

*COTE BRILLIANTE ELEMENTARY SCHOOL - 2616 Cora Ave., 63113 (531-8680). It was opened in 1904. It was named for the district or subdivision which was called "Cote Brilliante," after an Indian mound which was once in the neighborhood. Cote Brilliante means "shining hill." The original school was located at Kennerly Street west of Taylor Avenue, 63113.

*COTTAGE AVENUE SCHOOL was established in 1922 at 4248 W. Cottage, 63113. Cottage Avenue was named after the subdivision.

CROW SCHOOL was established in 1882 at Bell and Channing avenues, 63106. It was named for Wayman Crow, a merchant and state senator. *See Carver School.*

*CUPPLES ELEMENTARY SCHOOL - 4908 Cote Brilliante, 63113. It was opened in 1917. Cupples School was named for Samuel Cupples, a St. Louis wooden ware merchant and philanthropist. He was a civic leader and donated large sums of money to Washington University. It is now a pre-school (367-2414). Cupples branch at 1617 N. Euclid, 63113, closed in 1967.

CURRICULUM SERVICE BLDG. - 450 Des Peres Ave., 63112 (863-7266).

CURTIS ELEMENTARY SCHOOL - 2824 Madison St., 63106, originally opened as Penrose in 1894; it was renamed Curtis in 1943 for bothers Thomas A. and William P. Curtis; both men were early black pioneers in St. Louis, one a dentist and the other a physician. A branch opened in 1949 at 2825 Howard, 63106. Curtis School and branch closed in 1973.

DELANEY SCHOOL was first called Colored School # 6. It was established in 1873 at 6138 Virginia, 63111, in the Carondelet area. It was named for Maj. Martin R. Delaney, a black Union soldier and physician. *See Maddox School.*

*DELMAR SCHOOL - 5883 Delmar, 63112. Delmar School closed in 1980 but was re-opened as a SPECIAL HIGH SCHOOL (367-1025). The school was named for the street. The street in ZIP codes 63103, 63108, and 63112 was named for the first three letters of the states Delaware and Maryland.

*DES PERES SCHOOL - 6307 Michigan, 63111, was where Susan Blow started the first kindergarten in 1873. The superintendent of schools at that time was William T. Harris. It was first opened at Fourth and Illinois (Iron) in Carondelet, 63111. This school is now owned and maintained by the Carondelet Historical Society. The school took its name from the street. Des Peres Avenue, 63112, was named after the River Des Peres; it means "river of the fathers."

DESSALINES ELEMENTARY SCHOOL - It was opened as Colored School # 2 in 1866 at 10th and Chambers, 63106. It was named Dessalines, for Jean Jacques Dessalines (1758-1806), who served as lieutenant general under the Haitian liberator, Toussaint L'Ouverture. In 1803 he was appointed governor general, and proclaimed himself Emperor Jean Jacques I in 1804. He was assassinated by his own followers near Port au Prince in 1806. In 1871 the school was moved to 12th and Webster (Brooklyn), 1725 N. 12th St. (Hadley), 63106. It was reconstructed in 1904 and closed in 1973.

DEVELOPMENT SCREENING - 4130 Lexington, 63115 (652-6909). *See Farragut School Branch #1.*

DROP OUT PREVENTION - 4130 Lexington, 63115 (531-1455). *See Farrgut School Branch #1.*

*DEWEY ELEMENTARY SCHOOL - 6746 Clayton Ave., 63139, was opened in 1917. It was named for George Dewey, admiral of the American Far Eastern Fleet and a hero of the Spanish American War. Dewey School is now used as a MIDDLE SCHOOL, SCHOOL FOR INTERNATIONAL STUDIES (645-4845).

DISTRICT RECORDS CENTER/ARCHIVES - 1615 Hampton Ave., 63139 (645-2648). *See Gratiot School.*

DIVOLL ELEMENTARY SCHOOL - 2918 Dayton St., 63106. It was opened in 1872. It was named for Ira Divoll, the founder of the Public School Library System, who served as superintendent of schools from 1859-1867. A branch was opened at 2908 Dayton, 63106, in 1950. Divoll School was closed in 1974; the branch closed in 1975.

*DODIER SCHOOL - Dodier and St. Louis Place, 63107. The street was named for Gabriel Dodier, one of the earliest St. Louis residents.

*DOUGLAS SCHOOL - BRANCH HIGH SCHOOL NO 4 - 11th and Howard, 63106.

The street in ZIP code 63147, could be named for Maj. Thompson Douglas who married Cornelia, daughter of Daniel Bissell.

DOZIER ELEMENTARY SCHOOL - 5749 Maple, 63112. It had originally been opened in 1887. It was opened in 1964. It was named for James Dozier, a St. Louis steamboat owner who also owned a bakery. It was closed in 1977.

DUMAS ELEMENTARY SCHOOL - Opened as Colored School # 1 in 1866 at Fifth and Gratiot, 63104. It was moved to 1409 North 15th St., 63106, in 1870. It was moved to Lucas and 14th in 1880, and renamed

Dumas in 1895 for Alexander Dumas, a French romantic novelist who wrote *The Count of Monte Cristo"* and *The Three Musketeers.* There was also a Dumas School at 1241 S. Third, 63104. Dumas School was closed in 1969.

DUNBAR ELEMENTARY SCHOOL - 1415 Garrison Ave., 63106. It was opened in 1912 as Glasgow School at Sheridan and Garrison, 63106. It is now a pre-school (533-2526). It was renamed in 1937 for Paul Laurence Dunbar, a black poet and writer who was distinguished for his collection of prose and poetry.

*DUNNICA SCHOOL - 3824 Dunnica Ave., 63116. It was opened in 1937 and named for James Dunnica, a steamboat captain.

*EADS SCHOOL was opened in 1859 at 15th and Pine streets, 63103. It was named for James B. Eads, who built the bridge that bears his name.

EARLY CHILDHOOD CENTER #3 - 1530 S. Grand Blvd., 63104 (865-2600). Has been renamed Dr. William Kottmeyer Early Childhood Center. Kottmeyer was a St. Louis public school teacher, administrator and superintendent. He died in 1989.

EARLY CHILDHOOD EDUCATION UNIT - 5183 Raymond, 63113 (361-5500). *See Clark School.*

ELEMENTARY STUDY-LEARNING RESOURCE CENTER - 1224 Grattan, 63104 (231-9277). *See Clinton School.*

*ELIAS MICHAEL - 4568 Forest Park Blvd., 63108. *See Michael School.*

*ELIOT ELEMENTARY SCHOOL - 4242 Grove St., 63107. It was opened in 1898. It was named for William Greenleaf Eliot, who was secretary, and president of the School Board. He also founded Washington University, and was the first Unitarian minister west of the Mississippi. It is now a pre-school (535-0096). The original school was established in 1868 at 15th and Walnut streets, 63102. It was moved to 15th and Pine, 63103, and then in 1867 to a rented building at 12th and Pine, 63103. There is a street named Elliot (spelled with two l's) in ZIP code areas 63106 and 63107, named for Richard Elliot, a real estate developer.

*EMERSON ELEMENTARY SCHOOL - 5415 Page Blvd., 63112. It was opened in 1901. It was named for Ralph Waldo Emerson, American essayist, lecturer and poet. It is now a pre-school (367-9030). A branch was opened in 1928 at 5234 Wells Ave, 63113, and closed in 1980.

*ENRIGHT MIDDLE SCHOOL - CLASSICAL JUNIOR ACADEMY now located at 5351 Enright, 63112 (367-0555). It was erected in 1905 and named for Thomas Enright, one of the first soldiers from St.

Louis to die in World War I. The street Enright in 63108 and 63112 was originally named Von Versen after the granddaughter of John Mullanphy.

*EUCLID ELEMENTARY SCHOOL - 1131 N. Euclid, 63113. It was opened in 1893; a Montessori school now occupies the building (367-4385). A Euclid school branch opened in 1965 at 1341 N. Kingshighway, 63113, and closed in 1973. A branch opened in 1967 at 5057 Ridge Ave., 63113, and closed in 1977; it has been reopened as a pre-school (367-8816). The street Euclid (63108, 63113, and 63115) was named for a street in Cleveland, Ohio. Euclid was a Greek mathematician, considered the father of geometry.

EUGENE FIELD HOUSE - 634 S. Broadway, 63102 (421-4689).

EVERETT SCHOOL - Eighth Street south of Cass Avenue, 63106. It was opened in 1859, and was named for statesman Edward Everett, the main speaker at Gettysburg when Lincoln gave his famous address.

*FAIRMONT GRAMMAR AND PRIMARY SCHOOL at the intersection of Bellefontaine Road (Calvary) and North Broadway, 63147. It was opened in 1859. Fairmont Avenue in 63139 is located in South St. Louis; it is named for the subdivision.

FANNING ELEMENTARY SCHOOL - 3417 Grace Ave., 63116. It was opened in 1907; it is now a middle school (772-1038). Fanning Community School is located at 3510 Giles, 63116 (865-4894). It was named for Rose Wright Fanning, who was a teacher for 47 years and the principal of Pestalozzi School.

*FARRAGUT ELEMENTARY SCHOOL - 4025 Sullivan Avenue, 63107. It was opened in 1905; it is now a pre-school (531-1198). It was named for David G. Farragut, the Union naval commander in the Civil War who captured Mobile Bay ("Damn the torpedoes! Full speed ahead!"). FARRAGUT BRANCH #1, DEVELOPMENT SCREENING, DROP-OUT PREVENTION, ROLE MODEL is located at 4130 Lexington, 63115 (531-4228).

FARRAGUT BRANCH #2 - 3000 N. Prairie, 63107.

*FIELD ELEMENTARY SCHOOL - 4466 Olive St., 63108. It was opened in 1900. Field Elementary School was named for Eugene Field, a St. Louis-born poet who wrote the poems "Little Boy Blue," and "The Gingham Dog and The Calico Cat." It is now a pre-school (533-4935). A branch was opened in 1958 at 721 Pendleton Ave, 63108, and closed in 1977. It was closed in 1995 and it is now known as GATEWAY ELEMENTARY (534-1795).

FORD ELEMENTARY SCHOOL -1383 Clara, 63112. It was opened in 1964 and is now a community school (383-0836). It was named for Henry and Edsel Ford, automobile manufacturers who established the

Ford Foundation. A branch at 5599 Ridge Ave., 63112, is now a preschool (361-4855).

*FRANKLIN SCHOOL - 814 N. 19th St., 63106. It was opened in 1909. It was named for Benjamin Franklin, printer, publisher and a member of the committee which drafted the Declaration of Independence. He was also one of the signers and a member of the Constitutional Convention of 1787. The original school was located at Seventh and Chestnut, 63101, in 1860. It was moved to 17th and Christy (Lucas), 63103, in 1874. A vocational school for blacks was opened in 1931 at Franklin School. It was renamed Washington, for Booker T. Washington, in 1934. In 1985 it was changed to a magnet school, "The Center for Management, Law and Public Policy." It is now known as the SCHOOL OF CONTINUING EDUCATION & MANAGEMENT (Expectant Mothers) (231-7316).

*FREMONT ELEMENTARY SCHOOL - 2840 Wisconsin Ave., 63118. It was opened in 1897. It was named for Gen. John C. Fremont, an explorer and soldier in the Mexican-American War who also commanded the St. Louis headquarters of military government during the Civil War. Fremont School was closed in 1980, and the building was reconstructed as apartments for the elderly.

FROEBEL ELEMENTARY SCHOOL - 3709 Nebraska, 63118, (776-3580). It was opened in 1895. It was named for Frederich Wilhelm August Froebel, the originator of the kindergarten.

GALLAUDET SCHOOL - 1616 S. Grand, 63104 (771-2894). This is a school for the hearing-impaired; it was opened in 1926. It was named for Thomas Hopkins Gallaudet, the founder of instruction for the deaf.

*GAMBLE SCHOOL - Fifth and Poplar streets, 63102. It was opened in 1860. It was named for Missouri provisional Civil War Gov. Hamilton Rowan Gamble. It was also located at Gamble (Scott) and Mercer (22nd), 63103, and in a rented building at Fourth and Cedar, 63102.

*GARDENVILLE ELEMENTARY SCHOOL - 6651 Gravois Ave., 63116. It was opened in 1907. It was named for the neighborhood location which was once occupied by market gardeners. The original school was located at 6212 Gravois, 63116. Gardenville School closed in 1980; it is now used as a community center (352-1350).

*GARFIELD ELEMENTARY SCHOOL - 2612 Wyoming, 63118 (776-3713). It was opened in 1937. It was named for James A. Garfield, the 20th president of the United States, 1880-1881. The original school opened at the same location in 1882.

GARNET SCHOOL - opened as Colored School #9 at Bellefontaine and O'Fallon in 1877. It was named for Rev. Henry Highland Garnet, an orator, statesman and United States minister to Liberia in 1881. It was moved to Bulwer and Adelaide, 63147, in 1885. The name was changed to Garnet in 1890. The school was closed in 1980; the building is now used for a community center (352-1350).

GATEWAY INSTITUTE OF TECHNOLOGY - 5101 McRee, 63101 (776-3300). *See O'Fallon School.*

GATEWAY ELEMENTARY SCHOOL - It is located on the Pruitt-Igoe site. It was opened in 1995.

GATEWAY MIDDLE SCHOOL - It is located on the Pruitt-Igoe site. It was opened in 1995.

*GLASGOW SCHOOL- Sheridan and Garrison, 63106 (Glasgow Avenue), 63107. It was named for William Glasgow, a wine merchant. *See Dunbar School.*

*GOODFELLOW SCHOOL - 4257 Goodfellow Ave., 63120. Goodfellow Boulevard (63112, 63120, and 63147) was named for David W. Goodfellow, a landowner.

GOVERNMENT AFFAIRS - 5183 Raymond, 63113 (361-5500). *See Clark School.*

*GRANT ELEMENTARY SCHOOL - 3009 Pennsylvania, 63118. It was opened in 1893; it was named for Ulysses S. Grant, general of the Union army during the Civil War, and the 18th president of the United States (1869-1877). It was closed in 1993.

*GRATIOT ELEMENTARY SCHOOL - 1615 Hampton Ave., 63139. It was opened in 1882. It was named for Charles Gratiot, the first presiding judge (1804) of the Court of Quarter Sessions, Louisiana Territory, District of St. Louis. It was used for CONTINUED EDUCATION of expectant mothers, but this program has been moved to Franklin School. Gratiot School is now used as District Records Center/Archives (781-3378).

*GRAVOIS School opened in 1867 at Gravois Road and Wyoming, 63116.

GREENHOUSE - 3808 Blow, 63116 (353-3961).

GRISCOM SCHOOL opened in 1965 at 3847 Enright, 63108 (531-3600). It was named for John W. Griscom, who established the school. It is for juvenile offenders.

GUIDED EDUCATION AND LEARNING CENTER - 6031 Southwest, 63139 (645-1201). See Mason School.

GUIDED EDUCATION AND INVESTIGATIVE LEARNING CENTER - MISSOURI BOTANICAL GARDEN - 4221 Shaw, 63110 (772-0994). *See Mullanphy School.*

GUIDED EDUCATION AND INVESTMENT LEARNING CEN-

TER - 6131 Leona, 63116 (481-8585). *See Woerner School.*

GUNDLACH ELEMENTARY SCHOOL - 2931 Arlington, 63120, opened in 1931. It was named for John H. Gundlach, a real estate agent and supporter for public improvements. It is now a pre-school (383-0913).

*HADLEY TECHNICAL SCHOOL opened for whites in 1931. It was named for Missouri Governor Herbert Spencer Hadley. In 1963 the name was changed to Vashon. *See Vashon School.*

*HAMILTON ELEMENTARY SCHOOL & Community School - 5819 Westminster Place, 63112. It was opened in 1917. It was named for Alexander Hamiliton, the first secretary of the treasury. It is now a pre-school and community school (367-0552). It was at 23rd and Dickson, 63106, in 1859. It originally was at 24th and Biddle, 63106, in 1856. The street named Hamilton in 63112 and 63120 is named for Hamilton Rowan Gamble.

*HARRIS TEACHERS COLLEGE - 1517 Theresa Ave., 63104. It was established in 1857 and opened in 1905 at 1517 Theresa, 63104. It was named for William Torrey Harris who was superintendent of schools from 1867 to 1880. Mr. Harris arrived in St. Louis in 1857 and left in 1889. Harris Teachers College merged with Stowe to become Harris-Stowe State College in 1954. In 1963 it moved to 3026 Laclede Ave., 63104 (340-3366). The street named Harris (63107, 63115, 63147) was named for the daughter of John O'Fallon.

*HARRISON ELEMENTARY SCHOOL opened in 1896 at 4163 Green Lea Place, 63115. It was named for Benjamin Harrison, the 23rd president of the United States (1889-1893). It was closed in 1995.

HEALTH CAREERS HIGH SCHOOL is located at 1530 S. Grand, 63104 (664-1111).

*HEMPSTEAD ELEMENTARY SCHOOL - 5872 Minerva, 63112, was opened in 1907 (385-2011). It was named for Edward Hempstead, a member of the first St. Louis School Board, a U.S. congressman who advocated federal land grants for schools, and the speaker of the Missouri house of representatives. Branch #1 was established in 1967 at 1437 Laurel, 63112; Branch #2 was at 1260 Hamilton Ave., 63112. Branch #2 was closed in 1972.

*HENRY ELEMENTARY SCHOOL - 1220 N. 10th St., 63106, was opened in 1906. It was named for Patrick Henry, an American orator and patriot. It is now a pre-school (231-7284).

HERZOG ELEMENTARY SCHOOL - 5831 Pamplin, 63147 (385-2212). It was opened in 1936. It was named for Peter Herzog who was a teacher and principal at Blair School for 50 years. The original school was located at 5830 Mimika, 63147.

HICKEY SCHOOL - 3111 Cora Ave., 63115 (383-2550). It was established in 1965 and named for Philip J. Hickey, the superintendent of schools from 1942-1963.

HIGH SCHOOL was established in 1853 in the Old Benton School on Sixth Street, between Locust and St. Charles, 63101. *See Central School.*

HIGH SCHOOL - in 1856 at 15th and Olive, 63103. *See Central School.*

HIGH SCHOOL OFFICE - 721 Pendleton, 63108 (535-3726).

HODGEN ELEMENTARY SCHOOL - 2748 Henrietta Street, 63104. It was opened in 1884. It was named for Dr. J.T. Hodgen, M.D., who was nationally known as surgeon general of the Western Sanitary Commission. It is now a pre-school (771-2539). A branch school was established in 1891 at 2627 Eads, 63104; it was closed in 1975.

*HOWARD ELEMENTARY SCHOOL - 2333 Benton St., 63106. It was opened in 1902 and named for Professor Charles L. Howard, a former principal of Columbia School. It was closed in 1980. Howard Street in 63102 and 63106 was named for Benjamin Franklin Howard, a Missouri territorial governor, .

*HUMBOLDT ELEMENTARY SCHOOL - VISUAL AND PERFORMING ARTS - 2516 S. Ninth St., 63104. It was named for Alexander Humboldt, a German scientist, naturalist and explorer. This school is closed. The original school opened in 1908 on Third Street near Russell, 63104.

INTERNATIONAL STUDIES MIDDLE SCHOOL, ACADEMY OF MATHEMATICS & SCIENCE/DeANDRIES - 4275 Clarence Ave., 63115 (382-7186, 389-0033).

INTERNATIONAL STUDIES - 918 Union Blvd., 63108 (367-9222). *See Soldan School.*

INVESTIGATIVE LEARNING CENTER MIDDLE SCHOOL - located adjacent to the St. Louis Science Center. To be opened in 1996.

*IRVING ELEMENTARY SCHOOL - 3829 N. 25th St., 63107. It was opened in 1871 and named for Washington Irving, a historian, novelist and essayist. He was the author of "Rip Van Winkle." The school was closed in 1993.

*JACKSON ELEMENTARY SCHOOL - 1632 Hogan St., 63106. It was opened in 1898. It was named for Andrew Jackson, the seventh president of the United States (1829-1837). It is now a pre-school (231-8464). The original school was in a rented building at Broadway and Howard, 63102, in 1859.

*JEFFERSON ELEMENTARY SCHOOL - 1301 Hogan St., 63106.

It was opened in 1959. It was named for Thomas Jefferson, the third president of the United States (1801-1809). It is now a pre-school (231-2459). It originally opened in 1848 at Ninth and Wash (Cole), 63101. A branch school was at 10th and Carr, 63101.

JOHNSON SCHOOL - 2841 Laclede, 63103. It was established in 1945. It was named for James Weldon Johnson, a poet, author and diplomat. It was closed in 1959.

KENNARD ELEMENTARY SCHOOL - 5031 Potomac St., 63139. It was opened in 1930. It was named for Samuel M. Kennard, a St. Louis businessman. It was closed in 1984. It has since reopened as the CLASSICAL Jr. ACADEMY (353-8875).

KENT SCHOOL was located on Grand Boulevard opposite Fairgrounds Park, in a rented building, 63107.

KINDERGARTEN SCREENING OFFICE - 905 Locust, 63101 (231-1634).

*KING SCHOOL - 1909 S. Kingshighway, 63110. St. Louis purchased the William Cullen McBride School from the archdiocese of St. Louis in 1971. It was opened as KING MIDDLE SCHOOL in 1972, after the death of Dr. Martin Luther King Jr. Now it is named the TRI-A OUTREACH CENTER (361-0423). There is a street named Martin Luther King.

*LACLEDE ELEMENTARY SCHOOL - 5821 Kennerly, 63112. It was opened in 1914. It was named for Pierre Laclede, a co-founder of St. Louis. It is now a pre-school (385-0546). It was originally opened in 1838 at Fourth and Spruce, 63102. It was located at Sixth and Poplar, 63102 in 1850, and on Fifth near Gratiot, 63102, in 1868.

*LAFAYETTE ELEMENTARY SCHOOL - 815 Ann Ave., 63104. It was opened in 1907. It was named for Marie Joseph Paul Yves Roch Gilbert du Motier, the Marquis de Lafayette (1757-1834). He was a French general and statesman during the Revolutionary War; he was wounded at the battle of Brandywine. It is now a pre-school (771-8666). The original school was at Ann Ave. and Decatur Street (Ninth), 63104.

LANGSTON ELEMENTARY SCHOOL - 5511 Wabada Avenue, 63112. It was opened in 1964. It was named for John Mercer Langston of Virginia and his son, Arthur. John Langston received a bachelor's and law degree from Oberlin College before the Civil War. He was the only black congressman from Virginia in the 53rd Congress. He organized the law school, and was acting president of Howard University. He also served as U.S. minister to Haiti, and as president of the Virginia Normal School. His son, Arthur, was a teacher in the St. Louis Public Schools from 1877 until his retirement as principal of Dessalines School. It is now a middle school, (383-2908). A branch at 5579 Labadie, 63120, closed in 1973.

LAW AND EDUCATION - 5183 Raymond 63113 (361-5500). *See Clark School.*

*LEXINGTON - 5030 Lexington Ave., 63115 (385-2522). It was opened in 1961. The street was named by Henry Clay, after the city in Kentucky. A new Lexington School is under construction and due to open in 1996.

LIBRARY SERVICE - 1100 Farrar, 63107 (436-4664).

*LINCOLN SCHOOL - 2236 Walnut St., 63103. The original school was at 2221 Eugenia St., 63103, in 1867. It was named for Abraham Lincoln (1861-1865), the 16th president of the United States.

LINCOLN HIGH - METRO - WORK STUDY - 5017 Washington Ave., 63108. It was closed in 1980.

*LINDENWOOD ELEMENTARY SCHOOL - 3815 McCausland Ave., 63109. It was opened in 1929. It was named for the area, which at one time was covered with linden trees. The street was also named for Lindenwood College. The elementary school closed in 1982. The building is now used for VOCATIONAL-TECHNOLOGY DEVELOPMENT - OFF CAMPUS WORK/STUDY PROGRAM - ADULT EDUCATION (645-0357) (781-6615).

LONG ELEMENTARY SCHOOL - 5028 Morganford Rd., 63116. It was opened in 1922. It was named for Edward Long, a superintendent of schools from 1880-1895. It is now used for a middle school (481-3440). BEVO LONG COMMUNITY SCHOOL is also located at 5028 Morganford Rd., 63116 (353-1034).

*LONGFELLOW ELEMENTARY SCHOOL - 6593 Smiley Ave., 63139. It was opened in 1891. It was named for Henry Wadsworth Longfellow, a famous American poet. (The building was recently sold and razed.) It was originally located at 3134 Ivanhoe, 63139.

L'OUVERTURE ELEMENTARY SCHOOL - It was originally opened as Colored School # 4 in 1866 at Cozens St. (Papin) east of Jefferson (Pratte), 63106. It was moved to 2612 Papin, 63103, in 1885, and given the name L'Ouverture in 1890 for Haitian general, Pierre Dominic Toussaint L'Ouverture (1743-1803). He led the fight to eliminate the slave trade. Branch #1 was opened in 1945 at 2135 Chouteau using portable buildings; Branch #2 was opened at Lasalle and Caroline. All were closed in 1950. A new school was opened at 3021 Hickory, 63104 in 1950, and is now a middle school (664-3579).

*LOWELL ELEMENTARY SCHOOL - 1409 E. Linton Ave., 63107 (534-5050). It was opened in 1926. It was named for James Russell Lowell, an American poet. It was originally at Adelaide and Belleview

(Von Phul) 63107. It is now a pre-school.

LYON ELEMENTARY SCHOOL - 7417 Vermont, 63111. It was opened in 1909. It was named for Nathaniel Lyon, the Union general who captured the Missouri state troops at Camp Jackson, in Lindell's Grove, during the Civil War. The original building at Eighth and Pestalozzi is now owned by Anheuser Busch. It is now the ACADEMY OF BASIC INSTRUCTION, (353-1353).

MADDOX ELEMENTARY SCHOOL - opened as Colored School #6 in 1873 in South St. Louis at Fifth and Market (now Virginia and Bowen). In 1890, it was named Delaney for Martin R. Delaney, a black phsician. A new school was built at 6138 Virginia in 1911, and renamed Virginia Avenue School in 1935. It was renamed Maddox in 1953 for John J. Maddox, superintendent of instruction from 1921-1929. The school was closed in 1980. There was a branch at Minnesota and Bowen.

*MADISON ELEMENTARY SCHOOL - 1118 S. Seventh, 63104. It was opened in 1910. It was named for James Madison, the fourth president of the United States (1809-1817). The original South Freeman School was established at Seventh and Hickory, 63104, in 1855; also at Seventh and Labadie (La Salle), 63104, in 1870. TRI-A OUTREACH CENTER is also located here (231-1778).

*MALLINCKRODT ELEMENTARY SCHOOL - 6020 Pernod, 63139. It was opened in 1940. It was named for Edward Mallinckrodt, a native St. Louis chemist and philanthropist. It was originally built at 6012 Pernod, 63139, in 1928. It is now the ACADEMY OF BASIC INSTRUCTION and a pre-school (352-9212).

MANN ELEMENTARY SCHOOL - 4047 Juniata, 63116 (772-4545). It was formerly known as Oak Hill branch, which started in 1890 in one room of the old Russell homestead. When they needed four rooms, a small school building was opened at 4047 Juniata, in 1900. In February 1902, the name was changed to Horace Mann, a Pennsylvanian known as the "father of the American public school system." The school was built and opened as a result of the efforts of Nephi Moyle, who lived at 4048 Hartford.

MARK TWAIN ELEMENTARY SCHOOL - 5316 Ruskin Ave., 63115. It was opened 1911. It was named for Mark Twain (Samuel Clemens), the American writer, humorist and steamboat pilot. It is now a pre-school (381-1616). A branch was opened at 5036 Thekla, 63115.

*MARQUETTE ELEMENTARY SCHOOL - 4015 McPherson, 63108. It was opened in 1894 and named for Jacques Marquette, a Jesuit priest and missionary who explored the Mississippi River with Louis Joliet. It was razed in 1995.

*MARSHALL ELEMENTARY SCHOOL - 4342 Lucky (Aldine) Ave., 63113. It was opened in 1900. It was named for John Marshall, who was chief justice of the Supreme Court for 34 years. It is now a pre-school (371-1642). A branch was opened at 4322 Aldine, 63113 (652-4951) in 1952. Branch #2 was opened at 4213 W. North Market, 63113, and closed in 1970. (Marshall Avenue in 63119 and 63143 was named for the daughter of James Sutton.)

MASON ELEMENTARY-MIDDLE SCHOOL - 6031 Southwest, 63139. It was opened in 1919. It was named for businessman Isaac Mason, who also served as the sheriff and auditor of the city of St. Louis. It is now used as the GUIDED EDUCATION AND LEARNING CENTER, (645-1201).

MATH & SCIENCE HIGH SCHOOL - 4275 Clarence, 63115 (389-0033).

*McDONALD - Gravois Road near Grand, 63118. It was opened in a rented building. The street in ZIP code 63116 was named for an early landowner in that area.

*McKINLEY HIGH SCHOOL - 2156 Russell Blvd., 63104. It was opened in 1903. It was named for William McKinley, the 25th president of the United States (1897-1901). It is now used as a magnet middle school and called the CLASSICAL Jr. ACADEMY (773-0027).

*MERAMEC ELEMENTARY SCHOOL - 2745 Meramec St., 63118 (353-7145). It was opened in 1910, and named for the street on which it is located. It was originally at Meramec and Iowa. The street was named after the Meramec River; Meramec is an Indian word meaning "catfish."

METRO HIGH SCHOOL - MAGNET - 5017 Washington, 63108 (367-5201). A new Metro Area High School is due to open in 1996.

MICHAEL SCHOOL - 4568 Forest Park, 63108 (361-1511). This school for orthopedically-handicapped children opened in 1924. It was named for Elias Michael, a member of the Board of Education. The street named Elias in Baden was named by a group of Orthodox Jews who lived in that neighborhood. In 1995, MICHAEL SCHOOL opened on the Pruitt-Igoe site, (241-0993). The building at 4568 Forest Park is now vacant.

MIDDLE SCHOOL OFFICE - 721 Pendleton, 63108 (535-3725).

MISSOURI HILLS - 13300 Bellefontaine Rd., 63138.

*MITCHELL ELEMENTARY SCHOOL - 955 Arcade Ave., 63112. It was opened in 1964. It was named for Joseph and William Mitchell, founders and publishers of the *St. Louis Argus*. They were crusaders for better education for blacks, and were very active in the Pine Street YMCA/YWCA, the NAACP and the Urban League. It is now used as a pre-school (367-0930). Branch #1 was established at 5436 Bartmer Ave., 63112, in 1956. Branch #2 was at 1141 Belt Ave., 63112; Branch #2 was closed in 1968. Mitchell Avenue, Mitchell Place and Mitchell Terrace, 63139, were named for John F. and Robert S. Mitchell, who were architects.

*MONROE ELEMENTARY SCHOOL - 3641 Missouri Ave., 63118. It was opened in 1899 at 3701 S. Broadway, 63118. It was named for James Monroe, the fifth president of the United States (1817-1825). It was closed in 1980.

*MOUND SCHOOL - Eighth and Howard, 63102. It was opened in 1846, and named for the large Indian mound in the area.

MOUND - Labeaume Street at Broadway, 63102. It was opened in a rented building in 1868.

*MOUNT PLEASANT ELEMENTARY SCHOOL - 4528 Nebraska, 63111. It was opened in 1900. The name was for the district and subdivision in South St. Louis where the school is located. It was closed in 1980.

*MULLANPHY ELEMENTARY SCHOOL - 4221 Shaw Blvd., 63110. It was opened in 1914, and is now used for the GUIDED EDUCATION AND INVESTIGATIVE LEARNING CENTERS PROGRAM IN CO-OPERATION WITH THE MISSOURI BOTANICAL GARDEN (772-0994).

MULLANPHY COMMUNITY SCHOOL - 1633 Tower Grove, 63110 (771-4640). It was named for Bryan Mullanphy, a federal judge, mayor of St. Louis and founder of the Travelers Aid Society. Mullanphy Street in 63102 and 63106 was named for John Mullanphy, the father of Bryan.

*NATURAL BRIDGE SCHOOL - was first located at Natural Bridge and Plank Road, 63121, in a rented building. The street was named for a natural limestone bridge that was once in the area.

NEW BENTON BUILDING - opened in 1870 at Ninth and Locust, 63101.

NEW BERLIN SCHOOL - was at Chippewa and California, 63118.

NJROTC Academy/Cleveland - 4352 Louisiana Ave., 63111 (832-0933). *See Cleveland High School.*

NORTHWEST HIGH SCHOOL - Middle School - 5140 Riverview Blvd., 63120 (385-4774). It was opened in 1962, and named for the location.

*NOTTINGHAM ELEMENTARY SCHOOL - 4915 Donovan, 63109. It was opened in 1953. It was named for a street in the subdivision that used English names. The street named Nottingham, 63109, was named for Nottingham, England. It is now used for a middle school (352-6085), and a community school (352-1163).

*O'FALLON TECHNICAL HIGH SCHOOL - 5101 Northrup, 63110. It was opened in 1956. O'FALLON was named for Col. John O'Fallon, a promoter of early railroad companies. He was a financier who made large gifts to local universities. In 1867, a technical school was established at 16th and Cass, 63106; in 1870, it was moved to 1409 N. 15th St., 63106. A branch was opened at 5101 McRee Ave., 63110. It is now known as the GATEWAY INSTITUTE OF TECHNOLOGY (776-3300).

*OAK HILL ELEMENTARY SCHOOL - 4300 Morganford Rd., 63116 (481-0420). The first Oak Hill School was located just north of the bridge, over the railroad tracks on Morganford Road. Oak Hill was the name of the country home of the Russell family who had extensive land holdings in the neighborhood. The second school, located on Tholozan and Morganford, was built in 1870. The third and present school opened in 1907 at 4300 Morganford at Bingham. A branch was established at 4047 Juniata, which later became Horace Mann School. *See Mann School.*

OLDEST # 3 (Originally called Colored School # 3) - Broadway & Sixth, 63102.

PAIRING AND SHARING - 4130 Lexington, 63115 (652-1505). *See Farragut School.*

PARENTS AS PARTNERS - 4130 Lexington, 63115 (652-6909). *See Farragut School.*

PARENTS AS TEACHERS - 4300 Gravois, 63116 (671-1535).

PARENTS AS TEACHERS - 5183 Raymond, 63113 (361-5500). *See Clark School.*

PARENTS AS TEACHERS - 3836 Natural Bridge, 63107 (534-8720). *See Beaumont School.*

PARENT INFANT INTERACTION PROGRAM - 3405 Bell, 63106 (531-9028). *See Vashon School.*

*PEABODY ELEMENTARY SCHOOL - 1224 S. 14th St., 63104 (241-1533). It was opened in 1957. It was named for George Peabody, a St. Louis philanthropist and educator. The original school was opened in 1872 at 1606 S. 18th St., 63104. It is now used as a pre-school.

*PENROSE SCHOOL - 2824 Madison, 63106. It was opened in 1894 and named for Clement Biddle Penrose, an adjuster of land claims. *See Curtis School.*

*PESTALOZZI ELEMENTARY SCHOOL - 1428 S. 7th St., 63118, also 721 Pestalozzi, 63118. It was opened in 1870, and named for the street. The street was named for Johann Heinrich Pestalozzi, a Swiss educational reformer. When this school was closed, the building was used as an office building for a long time by Busch Brewery.

*POPE ELEMENTARY SCHOOL - 3108 Laclede, 63103. It originally opened in 1872 at 2841 Laclede, 63103. It was named for Charles Pope. In 1920 it was re-named for Oscar Minor Waring, the first black principal at Sumner High School. A new school building was built in 1940; it was used as a magnet school in the 1970s. In 1992, it became The WARING ACADEMY OF BASIC INSTRUCTION. The street Pope, in ZIP codes 63115 and 63147, was named for a son-in-law of John O'Fallon.

PRUITT ELEMENTARY SCHOOL - 1212 N. 22nd St., 63106 (231-1443). It was opened in 1955. It was named for Wendell O. Pruitt, a graduate of Sumner High School who became an Air Force captain. He was decorated for distinguished service while serving as a member of the 332nd Fighter Group and the 99th Squadron. It was used as Pruitt Tutorial School before it was closed in the early 1980s. It was reopened as PRUITT MILITARY ACADEMY in 1984.

PUBLIC SCHOOL RETIREMENT SYSTEM - 501 N. Seventh St. (241-7763).

RHODA SCHOOL - 5599 Ridge, 63112 (361-4855).

READING TO ACHIEVE MOTIVATIONAL PROGRAM - 4130 Lexington, 63115 (652-6818). *See Farragut School.*

RIDDICK ELEMENTARY SCHOOL - 4136 Evans, 63113. It was opened in 1870 and named for Thomas Fiveash Riddick, who made a dramatic ride to Washington D.C. to obtain land grants for free schools in St. Louis. It was closed in 1980. There was also a branch at 4146 Garfield St., 63113.

ROCK SPRINGS ELEMENTARY SCHOOL - 3974 Sarpy Ave., 63110. It originally opened in 1873, and in the Rock Springs area in 1899. It was named for the area which is now known as Tower Grove.

ROE ELEMENTARY SCHOOL - 1921 Prather, 63139 (645-1207). It was opened in 1922. It was named for John J. Roe, a steamboat captain, meat packer and contributor to the construction of the Eads Bridge. It is used as a pre-school. The original school was built in 1888.

ROLE MODEL EXPERIENCE PROGRAM - 4130 Lexington, 63115 (652-6818). *See Farragut Branch #1.*

*ROOSEVELT HIGH SCHOOL - 3230 Hartford St., 63118. It opened in 1925. It was named for Theodore Roosevelt, the 26th president of the United States (1901-1909). When it was relocated to SOUTHWEST HIGH SCHOOL, it was called ROOSEVELT AT SOUTHWEST (776-6040) while extensive renovation work was done on Roosevelt School. It reopened at 3230 Hartford for the 1995-96 school year (773-1795).

ST. LOUIS BOARD OF EDUCATION-TRANSPORTATION - 1520 S. Grand Blvd., 63104 (533-6725).

ST. LOUIS PUBLIC SCHOOLS BOARD OF EDUCATION - GED -

5078 Kensington, 63108 (367-5000). *See Clark School.*

SCHOOL #1 SOUTH - Spruce and Fourth, 63102. It was opened in 1838. *See Laclede School.*

SCHOOL # 2 NORTH - Federal (North Broadway) and Hickory (Martin Luther King), 63102. It was opened in 1837.

SCHOOLHOUSE #3 opened December 8, 1841.

*SCHROEDER - 7306 Gravois, 63116. It was opened in 1930. It was named for John H. Schroeder, a merchant.

SCRUGGS ELEMENTARY SCHOOL - 4611 S. Grand Blvd., 63111. It was opened in 1917. It was named for Richard M. Scruggs, a St. Louis dry goods merchant and one of the founders of Scruggs-Vandervoort-Barney department store. He also served as a director of the Mercantile Library Association. It is now a pre-school (752-0604).

SCULLIN ELEMENTARY SCHOOL - 4160 N. Kingshighway, 63115 (383-4200). It was opened in 1928 and named for John Scullin, a bank director and the founder of Scullin Steel Co.

SEVENTH STREET SCHOOL - Seventh between Franklin and Wash (Cole), 63101. It opened in 1858.

*SHAW ELEMENTARY SCHOOL - 5329 Columbia, 63139. It was opened in 1907. In 1876, Henry Shaw built a school at Old Manchester Road (Vandeventer) and Kingshighway, 63110, and gave it to the city. He named it for himself. Shaw was a hardware merchant, the founder of the Missouri Botanical Garden (Shaw's Garden) and developer of Tower Grove Park. He gave the park to the city, and the garden to the state. It is now the VISUAL AND PERFORMING ARTS CENTER (776-5091) and SHAW COMMUNITY SCHOOL (776-4327).

*SHENANDOAH ELEMENTARY SCHOOL - 3412 Shenandoah Ave., 63104. It was opened in 1926. It was named for the street, which had been named for the Shenandoah River in Virginia. Many streets running east-west in South St. Louis are named for rivers. It is now a pre-school (772-7544).

*SHEPARD ELEMENTARY SCHOOL - 3450 Wisconsin Ave., 63118. It was opened in 1905. It was named for Elihu H. Shepard, who formed the first public school committee to organize the public school system. He was also a founder of the Missouri Historical Society. It was orginally located on Carondelet (South Broadway) and Marine; in 1859, it was relocated to Marine near Miami, 63118. It is now a pre-school (776-3664). Shepard Street, 63103, is named for Samuel Shepard Jr., a black teacher. Sam Shepard Street was part of Lucas.

*SHERMAN ELEMENTARY SCHOOL - 3942 Flad Ave., 63110 (776-2626). It was opened in 1898. The school was named for William

Tecumseh Sherman, a Union general who captured the city of Atlanta. He lived in St. Louis before and after the Civil War. It is now a pre-school. It also serves as a community center (772-9550). A branch established at 2206 S. Spring Ave., 63110, was closed in 1980.

SHIELDS SCHOOL - 1119 N. Seventh St., 63101.

*SIGEL ELEMENTARY SCHOOL - 2050 Allen, 63104 (771-0010). It was opened in 1906. It also is a PRE-SCHOOL ACADEMY (772-0682).

SIGEL COMMUNITY SCHOOL - 2039 Russell, 63104 (865-5050). It was named for Franz Sigel, a German-American Union general who helped capture the state troops at Camp Jackson in Lindell's Grove during the Civil War.

SIMMONS ELEMENTARY SCHOOL - It was opened as Colored School #8 in Elleardsville (Prairie Place) in 1873. It is now used as a MIDDLE SCHOOL (535-5844). It was also known as Elleardsville Colored School #8 when it was located on Belle Glade near North Market, 63113; the name was changed to Simmons in 1891. It was named for William J. Simmons, a St. Louis Baptist clergyman and educator. In 1898, it was moved to 4318 St. Louis Ave., 63115. There was a branch at 4430 Labadie, 63115, until it was closed in 1973. Elleardsville, which was named for Charles M. Elleard, a landowner, extended from what is now Annie Malone Drive to Newstead; Martin Luther King to Cote Brilliante. This area was annexed by the city in 1876. The Ville, as it is now called, extends from Martin Luther King to Taylor; St. Louis Avenue to Sarah.

SMITH, HAROLD C. ELEMENTARY SCHOOL - 1110 Victor, 63104. It was closed in 1984.

SMITH ACADEMY - 17th and Washington, 63103.

SOLDAN HIGH SCHOOL - 918 N. Union, 63108. It opened in 1956. It was named for F. Louis Soldan, the superintendent of schools from 1895-1908. A school using this name originally opened in 1909. It is now called SOLDAN INTERNATIONAL STUDIES (367-9222).

SOUTH FREEMEN SCHOOL - Seventh and Hickory, 63104. *See Madison School.*

*SOUTHWEST HIGH SCHOOL - 3125 S. Kingshighway Blvd., 63139. It was opened in 1937. The school was named for the area of the city in which it was built. The school was closed in 1992, but the building was used temporarily while Roosevelt High School was being renovated (776-6040). The Roosevelt students returned to 3220 Hartford in the fall of 1995. Mathews-Dickey Boys Club moved some of its operations to Southwest High School for at least a year, due to the use of its facilities by the St. Louis Rams football team in 1995. Shaw Elementary School is using space for part of its Community Education Center, and the St. Louis Public Schools High School League is also using some of the office space and the outdoor field space. The street named Southwest Avenue in 63110 and 63139, was once named Old Manchester Road.

SPECIAL EDUCATION - 2135 Chouteau Ave., 63103 (621-1462).

SPECIAL SERVICES-SECURITY 1517 S. Theresa, 63104 (865-4550).

SPECIAL STUDENT CONCERNS - 1517 Theresa, 63104 (865-4550).

*ST. GEORGE MARKET SCHOOL - Spring Avenue and North Market Street, 63113. The street named St. George, 63104, in South St. Louis, was named for the area. It previously had been known as Anna Street.

STATE AND FEDERAL PROGRAMS - 5183 Raymond, 63113 (361-5500). *See Clark School.*

STEVENS ELEMENTARY SCHOOL - 1033 Whittier, 63113. It was opened in 1964. It was named for the Rev. George E. Stevens, the pastor of Central Baptist Church. He was a crusader for integrated schools and worked for good government. He was an able leader in community activities and known as the "teacher's pastor." It became a MIDDLE SCHOOL in 1981 (533-8550).

STIX ELEMENTARY SCHOOL - 226 S. Euclid, 63110. It was opened in 1922 and named for William Stix, a dry goods merchant and founder of the Rice-Stix Dry Goods Co. of St. Louis (a new Stix Early Childhood Center is due to open in 1996).

*STODDARD - 26th and Morgan (Delmar), 63103. It was opened in 1859. The street named Stoddard, 63106, was for Capt. Amos Stoddard, an army officer and the first governor of the Missouri Territory. The school was moved to 2840 Lucas, 63103, in 1873. In 1932 the name was changed to Banneker. *See Banneker School.*

STOWE SCHOOL - Originally opened in 1890 and merged with Harris Teachers College in 1954 at 1517 Theresa, 63104. In 1963, Harris-Stowe moved to 3026 Laclede, 63103. In 1967, Stowe School re-opened as a middle school at 5759 Lotus, 63112. (382-7310)

SUMNER HIGH SCHOOL - 4248 W. Cottage Ave., 63113 (371-1048). The first all-black high school west of the Mississippi opened in 1875 at 11th and Spruce in the formerly all-white Washington School. It was named for Charles Sumner, a United States senator and noted abolitionist who fought for black rights. It was moved to 15th and Walnut in 1895. In 1910, it was moved to the Ville. Sumner High School was renovated in 1991. There was a branch at 1912 N. Prairie, 63113, in 1917.

TECHNOLOGY DEVELOPMENT - 5101 McRee, 63110 (776-1644). *See O'Fallon High School.*

TRANSPORTATION - GARAGE - 3418 Cook, 63106 (533-1722).

TRANSPORTATION DIVISION - 1520 S. Grand Blvd., 63104 (771-9200).

TRI-A OUTREACH CENTER - 1909 N Kingshighway Blvd., 63113 (361-0423). *See King School.*

TRI-A OUTREACH CENTER - 1118 S. 7th St., 63104 (231-1778). *See Madison School.*

*TURNER ELEMENTARY SCHOOL - 2615 Pendleton (now Billups), 63113. It was opened in 1925. It was named for Dr. Charles Henry Turner, an early black faculty member of Sumner High School who is famous for his research on behavior using ants and bees. It is now a MIDDLE SCHOOL (535-7767). A branch opened in 1938 at 4235 W. Kennerly, 63113 (535-8482). Turner School was originally the home of Stowe Teachers College, the St. Louis training school for black teachers. Stowe was combined with Harris Teachers College in 1954. Billups Street was named for Kenneth Brown Billups, an African-American school teacher and musician. The street Turner, in 63115, was named for Maj. Henry S. Turner, the husband of Julia M. Hunt, daughter of Theodore and Ann Lucas Hunt.

TURNER OPEN AIR SCHOOL FOR CRIPPLED CHILDREN was founded in 1925 and phased out by 1961.

VASHON HIGH SCHOOL - O'Fallon at Vashon. This was the original Colored School #10, also called the Cheltenham Colored School. It was opened in 1877 on Davis near Manchester. Vashon was named for George Boyer Vashon and John Vashon, who were outstanding black educators. They provided 75 years of consecutive leadership in education, both locally and nationally. In 1890, it was moved to 5324 Northrup Ave., 63110, and renamed Vashon High School. It was relocated to 3026 Laclede, 63103, in 1925. In 1963, it was moved again to Hadley Technical School at 3405 Bell, 63106 (533-9487). A PARENT-INFANT INTERACTION PROGRAM (531-9028) is also located at 3405 Bell, 63106.

VASQUEZ - Was at Glasgow and Cass Avenues, 63106, in a rented building.

VISUAL AND PERFORMING ARTS - 3616 N. Garrison, (371-1045). *See Central School.*

VISUAL AND PERFORMING ARTS - 2900 Hadley, 63107. *See Ames School.*

VISUAL AND PERFORMING ARTS CENTER - 5329 Columbia, 63139 (776-5091). *See Shaw School.*

VOCATIONAL-TECHNICAL EDUCATION - 3815 McCausland, 63109 (781-6615). *See Lindenwood School.*

VOLUNTEER SERVICES - 1110 Victor, 63104 (771-1485).

*WADE ELEMENTARY SCHOOL - 2030 S. Vandeventer, 63110 (771-6649). It was opened in 1930 and named for Festus Wade, president of Mercantile Trust Company and a St. Louis real estate company. It is now called Meda Washington Education Center in honor of its founding supervising teacher, who died in 1982.

*WALBRIDGE ELEMENTARY SCHOOL - 5000 Davison Ave., 63120. It was opened in 1922, and is now a pre-school (383-1829). There also is a:

*WALBRIDGE COMMUNITY SCHOOL - 5019 Alcott, 63120 (261-8282). Both schools were named for Cyrus P. Walbridge, the president of a St. Louis drug company and a mayor of St. Louis.

WALNUT PARK ELEMENTARY SCHOOL - 5814 Thekla, 63120. It was opened in 1908. It was named for the subdivision in which the school is located. It is now a pre-school (383-0088).

WARING ELEMENTARY SCHOOL - 25 S. Compton Ave., 63103. It was opened in 1940. It was at 2841 Laclede, 63103, in 1872. It was named for Oscar Minor Waring, a Greek and Latin scholar. He served as the first black principal of Sumner High School in 1879. It is now the ACADEMIC BASIC INSTITUTION (533-1944).

*WASHINGTON ELEMENTARY SCHOOL - 1130 N. Euclid, 63113. It was opened in 1956. Washington School was named for George Washington, the first president of the United States (1789-1797). It is now WASHINGTON MONTESSORI (361-0432). In 1859 the first Washington School was at 11th and Spruce, 63103. It was renamed Sumner High School in 1875.

WASHINGTON - 814 N. Ninth St., 63101. It was named for Booker T. Washington. *See Franklin School.*

WAYMAN CROW - 3325 Bell St., 63106. *See Carver School.*

*WEBSTER ELEMENTARY SCHOOL - 2127 North 11th Street, 63106. It was opened in 1906. It was at 12th and Jefferson (Clinton), 63106, in 1866. It was named for Daniel Webster, a statesman and orator. It is now a MIDDLE SCHOOL (231-9196). It also was at 11th and Jefferson (Clinton), 63106 (231-9196). Webster Avenue in 63106 was changed to Tyler after Mary Lawrence Tyler, the daughter of a landowner.

*WELLS ELEMENTARY SCHOOL - 5234 Wells Ave., 63113. It was built in 1928, and was named for the street, which had been named for Erastus Wells, the first president of the Street Railway Co. in St.

Louis. He also served in Congress.

*WEST BELLE - It was at 3963 W. Belle Place, 63108, in 1920. West Belle Place was named for the subdivision.

WHEATLEY ELEMENTARY SCHOOL - It opened as Colored School #7 at 4239 Papin Street, 63110. It also opened in 1880 in the Rock Springs area, which was also known as McRee City, and is now the Tower Grove area, 63110. It was named for Phyllis Wheatley (1753-1784) in 1890. A former slave and poet, Wheatley was the second woman in the United States to have her works published. The school closed in 1973, and was sold in 1974.

WHEELER SCHOOL FOR SEVERLY HANDICAPPED - 5707 Wilson Ave., 63110. It was named for Hubert Wheeler.

WILKINSON ELEMENTARY SCHOOL - 7212 Arsenal St., 63143. It was opened in 1927. It was named for Melville Wilkinson, a St. Louis merchant and the president of Scruggs-Vandervoort-Barney department store. It is now the EARLY CHILDHOOD CENTER, (645-1202).

WILLIAMS ELEMENTARY SCHOOL - 3955 St. Ferdinand, 63113. It was opened in 1964. It was named for Frank L. Williams, the black principal of Sumner High School from 1908-1928. He also served as curator of Lincoln University and was active in YMCA work. It is now a MIDDLE SCHOOL, (652-4545). In 1953 Branch #2 was at 4146 Garfield, 63113; it was closed in 1977. In 1957 Branch #1 was at 2611 Warne, 63113. William Place, 63120, was named after President William McKinley.

*WINDSOR ELEMENTARY SCHOOL - 4092 Robert Ave., 63116. It was opened in 1952. It was named for Adelaide M. Windsor, a founder of the Child Conservation Conference of St. Louis. It was closed in 1982. It is now being used as a COMMUNITY SCHOOL (352-5949).

WOERNER ELEMENTARY SCHOOL - 6131 Leona St., 63116. It was opened in 1931. It was named for J. Gabriel Woerner, a newspaperman, lawyer, judge and Missouri senator. It is now used as the GUIDED EDUCATION & INVESTMENT LEARNING CENTER (481-8585).

WOODWARD ELEMENTARY SCHOOL - 725 Bellerive Blvd., 63111. It was opened in 1921. It was named for Calvin Milton Woodward, who developed a system of manual training used all over the United States. He was also a dean at Washington University and served on the Board of Education. It is now a pre-school (353-1346).

WORK PERMITS - 1517 Theresa, 63104 (865-4550).

WORK STUDY CITY HALL PROGRAM - 1300 Convention Plaza, 63103 (621-0535).

WYMAN ELEMENTARY SCHOOL - 1547 S. Theresa, 63104. It

was opened in 1901. It was named for Edward Wyman, educator and founder of several schools. He was also the director of St. Louis Public Schools and curator of the University of Missouri. It is now a pre-school (772-9328).

YEATMAN SCHOOL - (MIDDLE SCHOOL) - 4265 Athlone, 63115 (261-8132). It was opened in 1967. It was named for James E. Yeatman, a businessman who organized the Western Sanitary Commission. The bulding also houses a COMMUNITY SCHOOL (261-8133). *See Central School.*

Appendix IV
Streets and Zip Codes

LOCATION OF ZIP CODES

63101, 63102, 63103	Downtown St. Louis
63104	Near South Side St. Louis
63105	Clayton
63106	Near North Side St. Louis
63107, 63113, 63115	North St. Louis
63108, 63110, 63112	West/Central St. Louis
63109, 63139	Southwest St. Louis
63111	Carondelet
63114	Overland
63116, 63118	Southwest St. Louis
63117	Richmond Heights
63119	Webster Groves
63120	Pine Lawn
63121	Normandy
63122	Kirkwood
63123	Affton
63124	Ladue
63125	Lemay
63126	Crestwood
63127	Sunset Hills
63128	Sappington
63129	Oakville
63130	University City
63131	Des Peres
63132	Olivette
63133	Wellston
63134	Berkeley

63135	Ferguson
63137, 63138	Bellefontaine Neighbors
63140	Kinloch
63141	Creve Coeur
63143	Maplewood
63144	Brentwood
63145	Lambert Field
63147	Baden
63005, 63006, 63017	Chesterfield
63010	Arnold
63011, 63021	Ballwin
63016	Cedar Hill
63019	Crystal City
63025	Eureka
63026	Fenton
63031, 63032, 63034	Florissant
63033	Blackjack
63039	Gray Summit
63042	Hazelwood
63044	Bridgeton
63043	Maryland Heights
63045	Earth City
63049	High Ridge
63051	House Springs
63052	Imperial
63074	St. Ann
63088	Valley Park
63069	Pacific
63301, 63302, 63303, 63304	St. Charles
63366	O'Fallon
63367	Lake Saint Louis
63376	St. Peters
63385	Wentzville

APPENDIX V
Miscellaneous Vignettes

"A"
The four murals at the Old Courthouse
The four murals on the dome of the Old Courthouse are: The discovery of the Mississippi by De Soto in 1641; the founding of St. Louis in 1764 by Laclede; the Indian attack on St. Louis in 1780; and a Western scene of a buffalo hunt. They were all painted by artist Carl Wimar (1829-1863).

"B"
Thomas Jefferson's epitaph
Twenty-three years after the Louisiana Purchase, shortly before he died, Thomas Jefferson wrote his own epitaph. In it, he identified himself as the father of the University of Virginia and as the author of both the Declaration of Independence and the Statute for Religious Freedom in Virginia. He did not mention the Louisiana Purchase.

"C"
"The Great Gatsby" setting
After the Revolutionary War, Bristol, Rhode Island, was one of the biggest slave trading towns in our country. Bristol became a very wealthy town by running slaves, rum and molasses between Africa, the Caribbean, and New England. The legacy of this wealth lives on in the large, palatial 18th- and 19th-century homes that attract tourists to this town. One of these homes was used as the setting for the movie "The Great Gatsby."

"D"
Smart thinking or exploitation?
William Penn in 1696 purchased a tract of land from the Indians. The size agreed upon was to be "as far as a man can go in a day and a half." He had a trail cleared and hired the three best runners he could find. This strategy gave the Penn family a half million acres. Smart thinking or exploitation?

"E"
President for a day

In 1849, the official inauguration day for the president of the United States fell on Sunday, March 4. Zachary Taylor, the president-elect, refused to be sworn in on the Sabbath; he waited until Monday noon, March 5, 1849. President James K. Polk's official term of office ended at noon March 4, 1849. George M. Dallas, the vice-president under Polk, had already resigned. The presiding officer of the Senate was next in line for the presidency, after the president and vice-president. Missouri's senator, David Rice Atchison, was the presiding officer of the Senate. He technically became president from noon on Sunday March 4, 1849, until noon on Monday March 5, 1849, when Zachary Taylor was sworn into office. No official action was needed during this time, so Atchison is known as the only United States president who slept through his entire term in office. Atchison served in the U.S. Senate from 1843-1855; he died in 1866. Atchison County, Missouri, and Atchison, Kansas, are named for him.

"F"
Round-trip to New Orleans

In 1819, traveling round-trip from St. Louis to New Orleans by steamboat took four to six months. This time improved, as shown by the results of the race in 1870 of the Natchez and the Robert E. Lee. Lee won, taking only three days, 18 hours and 14 minutes. The Natchez used three days, 23 hours, and 58 minutes. The Mississippi River is a 7,000-mile system; it has 86 river terminals and handles 24 million tons of freight a year, twice as much as the next river port in the United States. St. Louis is still a river city, extending for 19 miles along the Mississippi River.

"G"
Getting rid of "Bloody Island"

The Mississippi River once started to flow away from Missouri and closer to Illinois because of a sandbar called Bloody Island. St. Louis residents believed that St. Louis would eventually be some distance from the river. Since the vitality and commerce of St. Louis depended on the river, it was extremely important that the river be returned to its original channel. Henry Shreve, an experienced river man and steamboat captain, was selected to do this job. He was ably assisted on the project by Lt. Robert E. Lee, a young Army engineer recently graduated from West Point. They used the currents of the river to eliminate the sand island and return the river to its former bed. We have a street named Shreve; Shreveport, Louisiana is also named for him. Henry Shreve is remembered for another reason. He named the cabins on his steamboats for states. Since then, the cabins of all ships have been called "staterooms."

"H"
Hospitality for $37

Lafayette visited St. Louis in 1824, when William Carr Lane was mayor. Mayor Lane wanted to entertain Lafayette, but the city had no funds. He approached Governor Frederick Bates for help; Bates informed him the state had no funds either. Pierre Chouteau offered his home, Thomas Biddle offered his carriage and two white horses, James Peck offered two more white horses, and Mr. Bennetts offered the use of the grand ballroom at Bennetts Mansion House Hotel. When Lafayette left the next day, Mayor Lane totaled the expenditures that Lafayette's visit cost St. Louis. It came to the staggering sum of $37. John James Audubon stayed at the Glasgow Hotel in 1843 and wrote friends how expensive it was. His room cost nine dollars a week, chickens sold three for 25 cents, potatoes cost 10 cents a bushel and beef was 3 cents a pound. When the emperor and empress of Japan visited St. Louis in May 1994, the cost of their visit was in excess of $90,000.

"I"
"Frankie and Johnnie" were in St. Louis

Josephine Baker, a famous singer, grew up on the corner of Targee and Gratiot; "Chestnut Valley" is what this area of the city was called at that time.

There is another story about Targee Street. On October 15, 1899, St. Louis police arrested a different Miss Baker, age 22, for the fatal shooting of a man named Albert Britt, age 17. She was a regular in the "tenderloin," or "red light" district of the city, where fancy sporting houses occupied the once-elegant mansions on Lucas Place. Years later, Republic Pictures made a movie based on a song about this incident, starring Helen Morgan and Chester Morris; Miss Baker sued the studio, claiming it was her story. During the trial, testimony showed that this story had been told in song and more than 300 known verses existed; it was considered a folk song. Miss Baker, whose first name was Frankie, lost her case. The song was first called "Frankie and Albert." It was later changed to "Frankie and Johnny"; the title of the movie was also "Frankie and Johnny." Frankie Baker lived at 212 Targee Street. She died in Portland, Oregon, in a mental institution, in 1950.

"J"
Into the arms of President Tyler

President John Tyler and his wife of 29 years, Letitia Christian, had seven children; she died in 1842 while he was president. President Tyler, Secretary of State Abel P. Upshur, Navy Secretary Gilmer, New York

State Senator Gardiner, Missouri Senator Thomas H. Benton, and various other officials and numerous ladies were guests on the "U.S.S. Princeton," the Navy's new 905-ton frigate for the "maiden voyage" on February 28, 1844. The ship carried two smooth-bore 12-inch wrought iron guns, one called "Dragon," the other "Peacemaker." When "Peacemaker" was fired it blew up, killing Upshur, Gilmer and Gardiner. Gardiner's daughter Julia was actually blown into the arms of President Tyler. He and Julia were married almost four months later on June 26, 1844, when he was 54 and she was 24; they also had seven children. John Tyler's first child, born in 1815, was five years older than Tyler's second wife and 45 years older than Tyler's last child, born in 1860, two years before Tyler himself died January 18, 1862, at the age of 71. Because his sympathies were with the Confederates and he served in the Confederate legislature, he is the only president whose death was not recognized by the United States government.

John Tyler was the president who asked Texas to join the Union. The street in St. Louis named for President Tyler was changed to Branch Street, after the Rocky Branch creek.

"K"

Where was Wherry Creek?

In the Southhampton area, the land sloped down from Brannon to west of Macklind; it also sloped east from Hampton to Macklind. Storm water collected into a ditch called Wherry Creek that flowed from Sutherland and Macklind into open lands west of Hampton, and drained into the River Des Peres. This drainage ditch was eventually paved over, and is now known as Wherry Avenue.

"L"

"Frost Campus" at St. Louis University

Major Richard Graham married Catherine Mullanphy. Their home, Hazelwood, was one of the first brick houses west of the Mississippi and was said to have been built in 1807. It was purchased in 1875 by Gen. Daniel M. Frost, who married a daughter of the Grahams.

General Frost was in charge of the state troops at Camp Jackson, located in Lindell's Grove, at the start of the Civil War. He surrendered to Capt. Nathaniel Lyon. Later, at the battle of Wilson's Creek near Springfield, Missouri, Lyon was killed. A statue of him was erected in Lindell's Grove.

After Frost's first wife died, he married Harriet M. Chenier, a descendant of Madame Chouteau; they had two daughters, Harriet and Emily.

When General Frost died in 1900, he left Hazelwood to his daughter Harriet and her husband, Samuel Wesley Fordyce, who was a lawyer.

Samuel Fordyce died in 1948. In 1952 Harriet Fordyce gave the 25-room mansion, Hazelwood, to St. Louis University to be used as a retreat house.

When St. Louis University wanted to expand its campus east of Grand Boulevard — which would include the site of Camp Jackson in Lindell's Grove — Harriet Graham Fordyce, daughter of General Frost, said she would give a large sum of money to St. Louis University if the statue of General Lyon was removed from that area. The statue is now in Lyon Park on South Broadway across from Busch's Brewery. That part of St. Louis University is now known as the Frost Campus. After the death of Mrs. Fordyce in 1964, the mansion Hazelwood was sold and demolished.

"M"

Three out of 10 isn't bad

Of the 10 best architectural structures in the United States, St. Louis can claim three: the Eads Bridge, the Wainwright Building and the Arch. (Certain cities of the world are instantly recognized by landmarks or symbols, such as the Eiffel Tower in Paris, the Statue of Liberty in New York and the Gateway Arch in St. Louis.)

"N"

Three wives for Mr. Geyer

A street is named for Henry Sheffie Geyer, the lawyer who replaced Thomas Hart Benton in the U.S. Senate. Geyer was born December 9, 1790, and married Clarissa B. Starr on January 1, 1818; she later died. On April 25, 1831, Geyer married Mrs. Joanna Quarles, the daughter of Rufus Easton; she later died. On February 12, 1850, Geyer married Mrs. Jane Charless. Henry Sheffie Geyer died March 5, 1859. Geyer Avenue is in ZIP code 63104. Geyer Road is in 63122, 63127 and 63131.

"O"

Wild Bill and the "dead man's hand"

James Butler Hickok ("Wild Bill"), born in 1837, served as a Union scout at Springfield, Missouri, during the Civil War. He remained in Springfield after the war and became friends with Dave Tutt, a former Confederate soldier. They quarreled after drinking together on July 21, 1865, and met in the Springfield town square; "Wild Bill" killed Tutt. Hickok was arrested, tried, and acquitted, largely through the efforts of his lawyer, John Smith Phelps. "Wild Bill" was later appointed deputy marshall of Fort Riley, Kansas, and left there in 1876 for Deadwood, South Dakota. He was killed on August 2, 1876, at the age of 39, while playing poker. He was shot in the back by Jack McCall, who was later hanged. Hickok was holding a pair of aces and a pair of eights in his hand when he was shot. This has been known as the "dead man's hand" ever since. That same year (1876), Phelps, the lawyer who won acquittal for

Hickok in Springfield, Missouri, in 1865, was elected the 24th governor of Missouri.

"P"
Campbell House history

Robert Campbell was 20 when he was told by his doctor, Bernard Farrar, to go west for his health and live outdoors. Campbell joined William Sublette in the fur trade; they founded Fort Laramie in Wyoming. They were attacked by Indians on one of their ventures and had little hope of survival, so they made oral wills to each other. Sublette was wounded but both men managed to escape. They later decided that at age 31, they were getting too old for this type of work, so they returned to St. Louis.

In 1837 Campbell met Virginia Kyle of North Carolina. Her parents were horrified when they learned he was from St. Louis; to them St. Louis represented the wilderness. Campbell had to wait four years before he received their permission to marry her in 1841; she was 19, he was 37. They first lived at Fifth and Elm, and then moved to 20 Lucas Place, which is now 1508 Locust. They had 13 children, but only three lived past childhood.

In 1851 when Father De Smet was asked by the U.S. government to help bring about peace with the Indians, Robert Campbell went with him. Both of them were well-respected by the Indian tribes.

Campbell was born in 1804, died in 1879; his wife lived until 1882. The surviving sons, James, Hugh, and Hazlett, continued to live in their home on Locust. When the last one died in 1938, the house was easy to restore because the brothers had taken very good care of it and threw little away. It remains today as one of the most complete museums depicting early St. Louis.

"Q"
Eads Bridge claimed lives

James Buchanan Eads was a cousin of President James Buchanan. He arrived in St. Louis in 1832. Eads Bridge took seven years to build. During construction, 13 men died, 91 were seriously afflicted and 100 others afflicted in a lesser degree due to the "bends."

"R"
A fountain in the Merchant's Exchange

The Merchant's Exchange Building was built in 1875. In 1880, a huge fountain, gift of John A. Scudder, was placed in the middle of the trading floor. In 1903 the fountain was removed and rebuilt in what is now called Fountain Park. The Merchants Exchange Building was razed in 1958.

"S"
Neighbors of President Grant

Dr. Antoine Francois Saugrain was born in 1763 near Paris, France. He married Genevieve Rosalie Michan in 1790. He received a 17,000-acre Spanish land grant and arrived in St. Louis in 1797. He was one of St. Louis' early doctors. Marie Elise Provenchere (1806-1868), married Frederick Saugrain, son of Dr. Antoine Saugrain; the couple were neighbors of Ulysses S. Grant. One daughter of Dr. Saugrain married Henry Von Phul, a merchant and boat owner. His daughter Eliza, married James Kennerly, whose brother-in-law was William Clark. Their home, "Persimmon Hill," was located at Taylor and Kennerly.

"T"
Sullivan: first U.S. Congresswoman from Missouri

Leonor K. Sullivan was born August 21, 1902 and is honored by having part of Wharf Street named after her. Her husband, John Sullivan, died January 30, 1951, at the age of 52, while serving as congressman from Missouri. Claude Bakewell was appointed to fill his unexpired term. At the next election, Mrs. Sullivan defeated Bakewell to become the first woman from Missouri to serve in the U.S. House of Representatives. She served until her retirement in 1976. She was known as a "tough battler" who refused to compromise when the people's interest was at stake.

In 1954, she originated the federal food stamp program with the intention of feeding 6 million hungry people; 5 million more were added to the rolls between November 1974, and June 1975. She was exceedingly upset that employed, or employable, recipients outnumbered welfare recipients. Regulations had to be bypassed to open the program unreservedly, losing sight of who it was originally designed to help. "It was never intended to be a welfare program," she said. "Stringent restrictions were put in place, to be sure it would provide nutritional supplements only for hungry people."

She also worked for the Truth in Lending Act and Fair Credit Reporting Act in 1968. She was responsible for legislation to bar sex descrimination in credit, and to tighten regulations on meat and poultry inspection. She served as House Subcommittee chairman on Consumer Affairs for 12 years and also as Merchant Marine and Fisheries Committee chairman.

In 1981, she married Russell L. Archibald. He died March 19, 1987; Congresswoman Sullivan died September 1, 1988.

"U"
It Cuts Both Ways

Benjamin Lincoln was a general on the staff of George Washington during the Revolutionary War. When the Americans defeated Cornwallis at Yorktown, the British commander was so humiliated for having to surrender to this "rag-tag" army, he sent his aide to surrender his sword. The aide first offered the sword to the French officer, who directed him to Washington. Washington also refused to accept Cornwallis' sword and directed him to his aide, Gen. Benjamin Lincoln, who accepted the sword of surrender.

"V"

Farewell to Arms

On September 30, 1884, Frank James surrendered to Governor Crittenden saying, "I want to hand over to you what no other living man has been permitted to touch since 1861." He then handed the governor his pistol and cartridge belt. Frank James died in 1915 at the age of 72.

Appendix VI
Bibliography and Sources

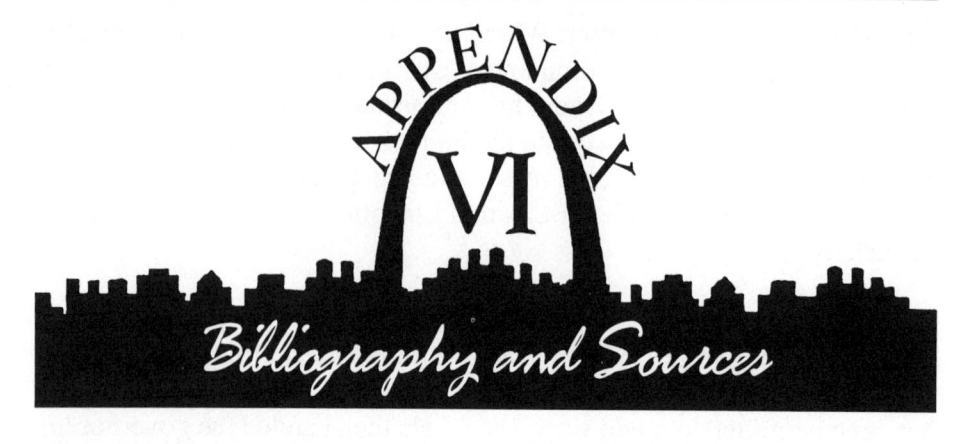

AAA Tour Book, Illinois, Indiana, and Ohio Automobile Association of America. 1965.

Berhman, Rev. E. H., M.A. *Story of the Old Cathedral.* St. Louis. Wiese-Barnes Printing Co., 1949.

Billon, Frederic L. *Annals of St. Louis in Its Early Days Under the French and Spanish, 1764-1804.* 1886.

Billon, Frederic L. *Annals of St. Louis in its Territorial Days 1804-1821.* 1886.

Blue Book. Official Manual State of Missouri, 1963.

Board of Education, St. Louis. *One Hundred Years of Teacher Education in the St. Louis Public School System.* St. Louis. Board of Education, St. Louis, 1958.

Boxwell, Harry James. *St. Louisians with Records, City Builders; Representative Missourians.* 1911.

Boyer, Mary Jane. *Old Gravois Coal Diggings.* Festus, MO; Tri-City Independent, 1952.

Cornwell, Charles H. *St. Louis Mayors Brief Biographies: short sketches from 1823-1965.* St. Louis. St. Louis Public Library, 1965.

Darby, John F. *Personal Recollections of Many Prominent People Whom I Have Known.* St. Louis, 1880.

Davis Realty Co. *St. Louis, the Coming Giant of America.* St. Louis. Davis Realty Co., 1909.

Dry, Camile N. *Pictorial St. Louis. The great metropolis of the Mississippi Valley; a topographical survey drawn in perspective.* Rich J. Compton ed., 1875.

Edwards, Edward. *History of the Volunteer Fire Department of St. Louis.* Published under auspices of the Veteran Volunteer Firemen's Historical Society, 1906.

Faherty, Wm. B., S.J. *Better the Dream.* St. Louis. St. Louis University,

1968.

First National Bank of St. Louis. *St. Louis, the First Two Hundred Years:. The story of the beginning and growth of a settlement on the Mississippi River which has become one of the great cities of the world.* St. Louis First National Bank, 1964.

Funk & Wagnalls Standard Reference Encyclopedia Standard Reference Works Publication. (25 Volumes). 1956.

Gill, McCune B. *The St. Louis Story; Library of American Lives.* Hopkinsville, KY & St. Louis. Historical Records Association, 1952.

Gill, McCune B. *St. Louis in 1821.* The Title Insurance Corporation of St. Louis, 1947.

Hill, Walter Henry. *Historical Sketch of St. Louis University. The celebration of its 50th anniversary.* 1909.

Hyde, William & Howard L. Conrad, 3rd. *Encylopedia of the History of St. Louis* (four volumes). Southern History Company, 1899.

Mills, William W. *St. Louis; the Central Great City of the Union.* New York, NY, SN.,1909.

Mulligan, James. *The St. Louis Post Office/Post Office Department, United States of America.* St. Louis. United States Post Office Department, 1937.

Robbins, Leroy K. *St. Louis in the War for American Independence*, 1940.

Sharf, J. Thomas. *History of St. Louis City and County* (two volumes), 1883.

St. Louis Plat and Record Co. *Atlas of the City of St. Louis.* 1905.

St. Louis, the Center of America. Economic facts concerning the commerce, industry, finance, and trade of St. Louis. Board of Public Service, 1945.

St. Louisan, The. *St. Louis: St. Louis Convention, Publicity and Tourist Bureau*, 1926-1933.

Stevens, Walter B. *St. Louis, The Fourth City, 1764-1909.* St. Louis. S. J. Clarke Pub. Col., 1909.

Stevens, Walter B. *St. Louis: One Hundred Years in a Week, Celebration of the Centennial of Incorporation,* 1909.

Stevens, Walter B. and William Vincent Byers. *St. Louis in the Twentieth Century: A Hundred Years of Progress.* Woodward & Tiernan Printing Co., cir. 1909.

Van Loon, Hendrick. *Story of America.* New York. Dell Publishing, 1928.

Water Division. *The St. Louis Waterworks System.* St. Louis. City of St. Louis, 1930.

Whittemore, Katheryne and Thomas Svec. *United States, Canada & Latin America*, 2nd ed. Melvin Ginn and Company. 1966.

Wilder, Ludlum and Brown. *This is America's Story*. New York. Houghton-Mifflin Co., 1963.

Rodabough, John. *Frenchtown*. Sunrise Publications, St. Louis, 1980.

Wayman, Norbury L. *Kingshighway Hills Neighborhood Assn., A Brief History*.

U.S. Census Bureau. *1990 Census records*.

Eckert, Gayle and Clara Pixley. *Lindenwood Area - 6900 Arthur Block Party* (unpublished manuscript), 1990.

Goodbrake, John E. *Southhampton* (unpublished manuscript), 1973.

    Reference books in libraries in:
- Honolulu, Hawaii
- Avila College, Kansas City, Missouri
- Madison College, Oshkosh, Wisconsin
- Alderson-Broddus College, Philippi, West Virginia
- Santa Rosa Beach, Florida
- Montreal, Canada
- Marshall, Texas
- Missouri Historical Society
- Carondelet Historical Society
- Jennings Historical Society
- Southern Illinois University, Edwardsville, Illinois
- Fontbonne College Library
- Pius XII Library, St. Louis University

Part III

Index of Street Names

Streets with an asterisk (*) are located in St. Louis County. All others are in the City of St. Louis. Key for abbreviations: Avenue-Ave., Boulevard-Blvd., Center-Ctr., Heights-Hgts., Lane-Ln., Place-Pl., Road-Rd., Street-St., Square-Sq., Terrace-Tr.

The index below also includes page numbers in boldface which refer to other pages in the book where that street name is mentioned.

Abner Pl. A brother of President William McKinley - 63102

Accomac. An Algonquin Indian village where Chief Powhatan lived - 63104; **55**

Acme. Named for subdivision - 63136

***Adams Ave.** U.S. President John Adams - 63122, **100**

Adelaide Ave. Relative of John O'Fallon; some was O'Fallon - 63107, 63105, 63147; **31**

Adele. In South St. Louis, changed to Indiana - 63111

Adkins. Henry Adkins, a steamboat captain - 63116

***Air Cargo Rd.** For the location - 63134

Agnes. Named for a daughter of Dr. Farrar - 63107; **91**

Alabama. Named for the state - 63111; **112**

Alaska. Named for the territory/state - 63111; **112**

Albion Pl. A place in England - 63104; **37**

Alcott. For Louisa May Alcott, an author; named by Clara Bircher - 63120; **52**

Aldine Ave. It was once Lucky; also Victoria - 63113

Alexander St. For Alexander Lacey Lyle, Carondelet Park was his estate; or, for B. W. Alexander, a St. Louis banker. Some was called Lily - 63116; **62, 100**

Alfred Ave. A relative of Thomas Payne - 63110, 63116; **69,** 72

Algernon St. Was named by John O'Fallon - 63107; **31**

Alhambra Ct. Named for Alhambra Grotto - 63118; **100**

Alice Ave. A relative of John O'Fallon - 63107, 63115; **31**

Allemania St. Named by Trampitsch; in Austria Heights - 63116; **63**

Allen Ave./Allen Market Ln. Thomas Allen, a railroad man and son-in-law of William Russell - 63104; **57**

Allen. Was changed to Fassen - 63111; **100**

Almond. A tree street; changed to Valentine - 63104; **35**

Amelia. A relative of Jennings - 63120.

Amherst Place. For the subdivision - 63112,

Anderson Ave. John J. Anderson, merchant, railroad man and banker. Could also be for Dr. Thomas Anderson, one of the founders of the St. Vincent de Paul Society in the United States. The other founders were: Dr. Moses Linton, John Everhart and Bryan Mullanphy - 63115

Angelica St. For the wife of James E. Yeatman - 63107, 63147

Angelrodt St. E.C. Angelrodt was one of the founders of Bremen - 63107

Ann Ave. The daughter of William Russell, and wife of Thomas Allen - 63104; **57**

Anna. The daughter of Willam Carr Lane; changed to St. George - 63104; **58**

Annie Malone Dr. A businesswoman; was Goode Street - 63113; **32-33, 145**

Antelope St. An animal trail - 63147

Arcade Avenue. For the subdivision - 63112

*****Archie Moore Dr.** For a famous black boxer - 63121; **32**

Arendes Dr. Gus Arendes was a developer - 63116, **62**

Arkansas Ave. For the state - 63104, 63118; **61, 66, 112**

Arlington Ave. Named for home of Robert E. Lee; or, it could have been named for the Arlington Grove subdivision - 63112, 63120; **52**

Armand Pl. Named in honor of Charles Armand, French officer in the American Revolution - 63104

Armstrong. David H. Armstrong was a land owner - 63104

Arrow. Changed to Shenandoah - 63104; **57**

Arsenal St. For the Arsenal, built on land formerly owned by Arend Rutgers; some was Susquehanna - 63116, 63118, 63139; **35, 66, 71, 72, 75, 100**

Art Hill Pl. Named for location - 63139; **100**

Arthur Ave. U.S. President Chester Arthur - 63139; **79, 89**

*****Arv-Ellen.** Named by builder for his son, Harvey, and daughter, Ellen - 63123

Ashland Ave. City in Kentucky, named by Henry Clay - 63107, 63115, 63120; **39, 145**

Ashley St. William Ashley, a trader, explorer and congressman, married Elizabeth, a daughter of William Christy - 63102; **27**

Athlone Ave. Named by John O'Fallon - 63115, 63147; **31**

Atlantic. The start of Atlantic & Pacific Railroad (MOPAC) - 63103; **84, 98**

Aubert Ave. For the subdivision - 63108, 63113, 63115

Audubon Ave. John James Audubon, naturalist and artist; was Cass - 63110; **178**

Augusta. Was changed to Farragut after Admiral Daniel G. Farragut. Some is now Penrose - 63107

Austin Ave. For Moses Austin, father of Stephen - 63104

Austria Ave. Named by developer Trampitsch after subdivision - 63116; **63**

Autumn. Was changed to Rutger Street - 63104

Bacon St. Henry D. Bacon married Julia, daughter of Daniel Page -

63106; **25**

Baden Ave. The city of Baden was first called Germantown. It was changed to Baden by Frederick Kraft, the first postmaster of Baden, who came from Baden-Baden, Germany. He owned a saloon at Broadway and Bittner - 63147; **52, 146**

Baker. For Esther Baker, sister of Peter Lindell; is now West Pine - 63108; **30**

Bailey Ave. A relative of John O'Fallon - 63107; **31**

Baldwin St. For Richard Baldwin, president of MOPAC Railroad - 63106

Baltimore. Changed to Vandeventer - 63107

Bamberger Ave. Named for amusement park; was Hunt - 63116; **73, 100**

Bancroft Ave. For George Bancroft, a historian - 63109; **75**

*****Baptist Church Rd.** Led to Concord Baptist Church, founded by Rev. Eli Musick - 63123, 63128

Barat Hall Ct. Named for location - 63108

*****Barlow Ln.** A relative of the Chouteau family - 63123; **28**

Barn. Was Rue de Granges, Second Street - 63101; **35**

Barnes Hospital. Named for location, Hospital Plaza, named for Robert Barnes - 63110

*****Barnes Rd.** A relative of the Chouteau family - 63124; **28**

Barrett St. John Richard Barrett, lawyer and relative of John O'Fallon; now Carter - 63107; **31**

Bartmer Ave. Henry W. Bartmer, landowner - 63112

*****Bartold Ave.** Henry and Fredrick Bartold had a tavern on Manchester Road - 63143

Barton St. David Barton, lawyer and first senator of Missouri - 63104; **21**

Bates St. Frederick Bates, governor of Missouri; was Pennsylvania - 63111, 63116; **51, 96, 100, 116, 117, 146**

Bates. Changed to Davis, then Dickson - 63107; **51**

Bates. Changed to Duncan - 63110 (Some Bates' were relatives of the Chouteaus); **28**

*****Baumgartner Rd.** George and Michael Baumgartner, landowners - 63129

*****Baxter Rd.** Baxters were landowners in Manchester - 63011

*****Bayless.** Samuel Mead Bayless, school teacher and owner of a nursery - 63123, 63125

Beacon Ave. Named for Beacon Masonic Lodge - 63120; **100**

Beaumont St. For Dr. William Beaumont; was 28th St. - 63103, 63106; **36, 146**

Beck Ave. John Beck, a landowner - 63116; **72**

Becket Hgts./Ct. Was named for the area - 63115

Beckwith. Relative of the Chouteaus; became 11th St. - 63104; **28**

Beethoven Ave. Ludwig Beethoven, a German composer; named for

subdivision - 63116; **72**
Bell Ave. Daniel W. Bell, merchant - 63106, 63108; **146-147**
Bell. Changed to Calvary - 63147
Bell. Changed to Penrose - 63106
Bell Ctr. Named for location - 63101
Belle Pl. Named for subdivision - 63108; **86**
Bellgrade. Changed to Clay - 63115
*****Bellefontaine Rd.** Road to large spring on Missouri River - 63137, 63138; **80, 87**
Bellefontaine. Changed to Calvary - 63147
Bellefontaine. Changed to Union - 63115
Bellerive Blvd. Named for Louis St. Ange de Bellerive, commandant from Illinois. Was Berthold, Kingshighway SW, also Cedar - 63111, 63116; **12, 55, 63, 67, 87, 100**
Belleview. Changed to Von Phul - 63107
Belt Ave. For Henry Belt, a developer - 63112, 63120
*****Bender Ln.** Road to farm of Ferdinand Bender - 63128
Benedict Ave. Changed from Short Street - 63147
Benjamin St. Benjamin Gratz Brown, governor of Missouri - 63107; **121**
Bent Ave. For Lucy Bent, wife of James Russell - 63116; **58, 71, 99**
Bent. For Silas Bent, father of Lucy; changed to Dorcas - 63118; **58**
Benton Pl./Tr. Sen. Thomas Hart Benton - 63102, 63104, 63139; **100**
Benton St. Thomas Hart Benton; was Green - named by Christy - 63102, 63106; **21, 37, 50, 74, 91, 143**
Berlin. Changed to Pershing for Gen. John J. Pershing during World War I - 63108, 63112; **28**
Bernard St. Was Pacific; some was Clark - 63103
Berra Ct. Named for Midge Berra, politician; was Shaw - 63110
*****Berry Rd.** Road to Joseph S. Berry property - 63119, 63122
Berthold Ave. Bartholomew Berthold, fur trader, married Pelagie, daughter of Pierre Chouteau. He spoke French, Spanish, Italian and German - 63110, 63139; **28, 82**
Berthold. Changed to Bellerive - 63111; **100**
Bessie. Bessie Place Addition - 63115
Beverly. Beverly Place Addition - 63112
Biddle St. Changed from Willow for Thomas Biddle, husband of Ann Mullanphy - 63101, 63102, 63106; **27, 34, 35, 46, 47, 151, 178**
*****Big Bend Blvd.** Originally ran from Sutton's blacksmith shop (Manchester & Sutton) to the "Big Bend" on the Meramec River - 63105, 63117, 63119, 63122, 63143; **82**
Billon Ave. Frederick L. Billon, secretary to MOPAC Railroad; some of street changed to Hampton - 63139; **75, 77**
Billups Ave. Kenneth B. Billups, an African-American teacher; was

Pendleton - 63113; **32**
Bingham Ave. John Bingham, land and mine owner - 63111, 63116; **72**
Bircher Blvd./St. For Dr. Rudolph Bircher, known as the "Leech Doctor" - 63115, 63120; **52, 67**
Bischoff Ave. For Ferdinand Bischoff, an engineer - 63110
Bishop Scott Lane. Was part of Warne; named for Bishop Phillip Lee Scott, pastor of the Lively Stone Church of God - 63113
Bissell St. Louis Bissell, riverboat captain and merchant - owned Bissell's Ferry - 63107; **63**
Bittner St. For Arnold Bittner, a German gardener - 63147
Blaine Ave. James G. Blaine ran against Cleveland; was Carolina - 63110; **71**
Blair Ave. Frank P. Blair, lawyer and Union general; was Guy, after son of John Gano Bryan - 63106, 63107; **96, 31, 45, 147**
Blase Ave. John Blase, a merchant - 63147
*****Bleeck Ave.** A real estate developer - 63143
Block. Changed to Keokuk - 63116; **100**
Blow St. Henry Blow, a paint manufacturer, married Minerva, daughter of Thornton Grimsley. Susan Blow was their daughter - 63109, 63111, 63116; **37, 40, 62, 101, 147**
Blue Ridge. Changed to Sublette - 63139; **77**
Bogy. For Lewis V. Bogy, a lawyer. It was changed to Brooklyn. Some Bogys were relatives of the Chouteaus - 63106; **28**
*****Bompart.** Henrietta, Louis and Mary Bompart, landowners - 63119
*****Bonhomme.** French for "good man." Usually used to describe a farmer - 63105
Bonita Ave. Formerly Wiesenhan; was changed during World War I - 63109, 63116
Botanical Ave. For Missouri Botanical Garden. It was first named Tyler, for Mary Lawrence Tyler - 63110; **69**
Bowen St. John Bowen, a Confederate general - 63111, 63116; **61, 100**
Bowman Ave. Thomas Bowman, minister - 63139
*****Boyce Pl.** Relative of Mullanphy - 63136; **27**
Boyle Ave. For Rev. Joseph Boyle, a friend of Peter Lindell; was Virginia - 63108, 63110; **30, 61**
Bradley Ave. For an early developer - 63139; **79**
Branch St. Northern boundary of North St. Louis, named for the Rocky Branch Creek - 63107, 63147; **30, 51, 100, 179**
Brannon Ave. For Thomas M. and Louisa J. Brannon, landowners; or, for John B. Brannon, a St. Louis deputy sheriff - 63109, 63139
Bremen Ave. After a city in Germany - 63107, 63147; **13**
Broadway. A street in New York City - 63102, 63104; **13, 50, 60, 80**
Broadway, North. Was Bellefontaine - 63137; **80**

Broadway, South. Was Carondelet - 63111, 63118; **80**
Brooklyn St. For an area of New York City - 63102
Brown Ave. For Benjamin Gratz Brown, a Missouri governor - 63115; **92, 121**
*****Brown Rd.** For relatives of Mullanphy - 63134; **27**
Bruno Ave. For Jean Baptiste Bruno, a farmer - 63139; **84**
Brunswick. Changed to January during World War I - 63116; **28**
Bryan. Changed to Prairie - 63107; **31**
Bryan. In South St. Louis; changed to Zepp - 63111; **31**
*****Bryon.** For Bryon Cates - 63143
Buchanan St. George Buchanan, a founder of Bremen - 63107, 63147
Buckingham Ct. From England - 63108
Buel. Part became 10th St.; part became Lemp, part became Menard - 63104
Burd Ave. John W. Burd, landowner - 63112, 63120
Burgen. Burgen Place Addition - 63116
Busch Pl. Named for location - 63118; **61, 100**
*****Bussen Rd.** Led to quarry established by John William Bussen - 63129

Cabanne Ave. Dr. John S. Cabanne, married a Chouteau - 63112, 63113; **28, 81, 82, 94**
Cabanne. Became Cushing - 63104
Cadet Ave. Nickname of Pierre Chouteau - 63110
Cahokia St. Named for the Cahokia Indians - 63118; **55**
California Ave. Named for the state - 63104, 63111, 63118; **112**
California. Changed to Cote Brilliante - 63112; **112**
Calvary Ave. Named for location by cemetery; was Goethe, also Bellefontaine - 63147; **51, 100**
Cambridge Ln. In England - 63147; **85**
Campbell Ave. For Robert Campbell, a fur trader - 63147 (see Appendix V "P"); **31, 181**
Canaan Ave. Named by early Jewish settlers - 63147; **52**
*****Canterbury.** In England - 63143, **85**
*****Canton.** After the home of President William McKinley - 63130
Capitol. Changed to Salena - 63118
Cardinal Ave. John Cardinal, killed in 1780 Indian attack; some was once Julia - 63103, 63104, 63106; **13, 99**
Carlsbad Ave. City in Europe - 63116
Carolina. Changed to Blaine - 63110
Caroline St. Changed to Fair - 63107
Caroline. Changed to Upton - 63111
*****Carondelet Blvd.** After the city - 63125
Carondelet. In the city, became South Broadway - 63104, 63111; **24, 60,**

80

Carrie Ave. Daughter of John O'Fallon - married Dr. Charles Pope - 63115; **31**

Carr St. For William C. Carr, lawyer. A public school is named for him - 63101, 63102, 63106; **46, 47, 50, 143, 148**

Carr Lane Ave. Dr. William Carr Lane, for the first mayor of St. Louis. A public school is named for Mayor Carr Lane - 63104; **58, 133, 149**

Carroll St. C. C. Carroll, an early landowner - 63104; **149**

Carson. Changed to Garfield - 63113

Carter Ave. Daughter of John O'Fallon, married Walker R. Carter; some was Barrett - 63107, 63115; **31**

*****Case.** Calvin Case, a streetcar line owner - 63134, 63140

Cass. Changed to Audubon - 63110

Cass. Cass Gilbert, architect of the St. Louis Public Library and Art Museum - 63102, 63106, 63113; **50, 100**

Castleman Ave. George A. Castleman, a lawyer - 63110

Catalan St. Louis Catalan, an early landowner in Carondelet. The Carondelet common field was once called Catalan Prairie - 63111; **80**

Catalpa St. Named for tree on Hodiamont farm - 63112

Cates Ave. Catherine Cates, daughter of Elizabeth Mullanphy Clemens - 63108, 63112; **27**

Cave. Named for street leading to the Cherokee cave - 63118; **98, 100**

Cecil Pl. Named for Viscount Cecil of Chelwood, a British statesman. Was changed from Hasburger in World War I - 63116; **28**

Cedar St. Named for tree - 63102; **35**

Cedar. Changed to Bellerive - 63111

Center Ct. Named for location - 63116; **99**

Center. Changed to Graham - 63139

Centerre Plaza. Named for location - 63101; **100**

Central Industrial Ave. Named for location - 63110

*****Central Plank Rd.** Was the extension of Olive Street in St. Louis County - now Olive Street Road - 63130, 63017

Cerre St. For Gabriel Cerré. His daughter, Marie Theresa, married Auguste Chouteau. His other daughter, Julia Cerré, married Antoine Soulard - 63102; **12, 13, 35, 39, 55, 57, 75**

Chamberlain Ave. Named for Chamberlain Park subdivision - 63112

Chambers St. Capt. William Chambers, one of the founders of North St. Louis in 1816 and father of Mary Lawrence Tyler. Some Chambers were relatives of the Chouteaus, also the Mullanphys - 63102, 63106; **27, 28, 50, 69**

Channing Ave. For a minister, named by William G. Eliot - 63103, 63106

Chariton St. A river in Missouri - 63111; **55, 56**

Charless St. Joseph Charless, a printer, banker and manufacturer - 63104; **149**

Cheltenham. After a city in England; was the name of a railroad station. Some parts of Hampton, West Park and Sublette streets also had this name - 63110, 63139; **77, 149**

Cherokee St. Named for Indians; was Harney - 63118; **55, 56**

Cherry. Named for the tree; changed to Franklin - 63106; **35**

Chestnut St. Named for tree - 63102, 63103; **35**

Chestnut Valley. Named for location - Chestnut to Market, 18th to 20th - 63104.

Chevrolet Ave. Named for location - 63120; **100**

Childress Ave. Levi Wade Childress, businessman - 63109, 63139

Chippewa St. Named for Indians; some called "Mine Road"- 63109, 63116, 63118; **10, 55, 56, 72, 75, 104**

Chouteau Ave. For Auguste Chouteau, co-founder of St. Louis - 63102, 63103, 63110; **12, 28, 59, 82, 94, 100, 143, 150**

Christian Ave. For Christian Oberbeck, a landowner - 63147

*****Christopher Dr.** Led to estate of Jacob Arthur Christopher, it is now the Jesuit White House Retreat Center. White House took its name from the train station once located near the Christopher estate, called "White House Station" - 63129; **37**

Christy Ave./Blvd. For William Tandy Christy who came to St. Louis from Tennessee in 1837. He established a clay plant in 1857 - 63116; **67, 72**

Christy. For Maj. William Christy, one of the founders of North St. Louis in 1816. He died in 1837. Became Lucas after J.B.C. Lucas - 63102; **50, 69**

Church Rd. Named for Holy Cross Catholic Church, which was built for Irish and German Catholics in 1863 on land purchased from Frederic Kraft. The Irish built Our Lady of Mount Carmel in 1872 - 63147; **99**

Church. Was Rue de Eglise; became Second Street - 63102; **35**

Claggett. For Dr. Hezekial Claggett; now St. Louis Avenue - 63102, 63106

Claxton. An author; named by Clara Bircher - 63120

Clamorgan Alley. For Pauline Clamorgan, daughter of Jacques Clamorgan - 63102; **31-32**

Clara Ave. Daughter of John Burd - 63112, 63120

Clara. Clara Bircher - 63115

Clara. Changed to Texas - 63111

Clarence Ave. For Clarence, son of John O'Fallon - 63115; **31**

Clark. Now Eichelberger - 63109, 63111, 63116

Clark. Some Clarks were relatives of the Chouteaus; changed to Bernard - 63103; **28**

Clark Ave. William Clark, explorer and Indian agent; was Myrtle - 63102, 63103, 63110; **15, 30, 35, 53, 100, 116, 143, 150**
Clarkson Pl. For Robert Clarkson, an early landowner - 63108
Clay Ave. For Henry Clay, a senator from Kentucky - 63115; **39, 150**
Clay. Became Leffingwell - 63106
Clayton Ave. Ralph Clayton, a landowner - 63110, 63139; **82**
Clemens Ave. For Elizabeth Mullanphy Clemens - 63112; **27, 150**
Clemens. Became Potomac - 63118
Cleveland Ave. U.S. President Grover Cleveland - 63110. A public school is named for him. **71, 150**
Clifton Ave. Named after area - 63109, 63139; **74, 79, 104**
Clinton St. George Clinton, vice president of United States. Was Jefferson Street and Exchange Street - 63102, 63106. There is also a public school named for him; **50,150-151**
*Clymer Dr. Relative of Mullanphy - 63123; **27**
Cochran Pl. For John Cochran - 63106
Cole St. For Nathan Cole; was Wash, also Hickory - 63101, 63106. A public school also is named for him; **46, 136, 151**
Coleman St. An early landowner - 63106
College Ave. John O'Fallon gave land to St. Louis University when it was still a college. The area became known as "College Hill"; the street took its name from the area. Some of College Avenue was changed to Fair - 63107; **30, 99**
Collins Ct. For Thomas Collins, developer; some was Jefferson - 63102, 63116
Cologne Ave. A city in Germany - 63116; **61**
Colorado Ave. Named for state - 63111; **112**
Columbia Ave. For Christopher Columbus; some of it was Old Manchester Road - 63139; **51, 69, 79, 151**
Columbia. Became Cass - 63102; **51**
Columbia Bottoms Rd. Changed to Riverview Drive - 63137, 63138
Columbus. Some became Second; some became Third - 63102; **11**
Columbus Sq. Dr. Named for the area - 63101; **100**
Compton Ave. Named after Compton Hill for the wife of Mayor John S. Thomas (1854); some was Kansas - 63103, 63104, 63106, 63111, 63118; **63, 64, 66, 74, 100, 113, 151**
Concord. For vineyards in the area - 63147
Concordia Ave. Named for the area - 63116
Conde. Changed to Montgomery in 63106; **30**
Conde St. Dr. Andre August Conde was one of the first doctors, if not the first, in St. Louis. He arrived in St. Louis in 1765 - 63107; **29, 30**
Congress St. For the U.S. Congress - 63118; **60, 98**
*Conn. For Luther Conn, a real estate man. He purchased property from

Ulysses Grant, and later sold it to Busch (Grants Farm) - 63125; **29**
Connecticut St. Connecticut Mutual Life Insurance Co., financed housing in area - 63116, 63118, 63139; **61, 112**
Convent St. For the home of the Sisters of Charity. They moved in 1874. The street is still there - 63104; **25-26, 99**
Convention Plaza. Named for area - 63101, 63102, 63103; **100**
*****Conway Road.** Capt. Joseph Conway, a friend of Daniel Boone, arrived in St. Louis County in 1798. He was held prisoner by Indians for four years; tomahawked, scalped three times and shot, yet survived - 63124, 63131, 63141; **82**
Cook Ave. John E. Cook, landowner - 63106, 63113; **151-152**
Cooper. James F. Cooper, now Marconi - 63110; **75, 77**
Cooper. Became Gratiot - 63110; **57**
*****Coppinger Dr.** A relative of Mullanphy - 63135; **27**
Cornelia. For the daughter of Wayman Crow; was changed to Newstead, the name of poet Lord Byron's home. He was the favorite poet of Nathaniel Pendleton Taylor. There are streets for Pendelton and Taylor - 63113, 63115
Coronado Ave. Named after the hotel by the developers - 63116; **62**
Costa Pl. For Felix Coste - 63111
Cote Brilliante Ave. Named after Indian mound in area; means "shining hill." The mound was destroyed in 1877 - 63112, 63113; **81, 152**
Cottage Ave. Named for the subdivision - 63113
Council Grove. Where William Clark met with the Indians - 63120; **53**
County Rd. Changed to Kingshighway - 63115
County Rd. Changed to Fyler - 63139
Courtois St. An early landowner; changed from Franklin - 63111; **59, 100**
Cozens Ave. For William Cozens, a surveyor - 63106, 63113
Cozens. Became Papin - 63110
Cozens. Became Lilly for Lilly Graham, wife of Gen. Daniel M. Frost - 63110
Cozens. Changed to January - 63139
Crane Circle. Named for Cyrus Crane Willmore, a real estate developer - 63109; **77**
Crittenden St. Named for Thomas Theodore Crittenden, Missouri governor from 1881-1885. Some had been Rappahanak - 63118; **123, 183**
Cupples Pl. For Samuel Cupples, a manufacturer - 63113; **152**
Curtis. For Samuel Curtis, a Union officer - 63121

Daggett Ave. For John D. Daggett, steamboat owner and mayor - 63110; **75, 134**
Dakota St. Named for the Dakota Indians - 63111; **55, 112**

N. Dakota St. 63111; **114**
Dale Ave. Descriptive name in Gratiot tract - 63110, 63139; **98**
*****Dale.** Was Valley Road - 63117
Dalton Ave. For John Dalton, an early landowner - 63139; **75**
Darby Ave. For John F. Darby, lawyer who served as mayor of St. Louis - 63120; **36, 41, 133**
Daren. Changed to President - 63118
Davison. For an author; named by Clara Bircher - 63120; **52**
Davis St. In North St. Louis; became Palm - 63107
Davis St. For Samuel C. Davis, an early banker; was Mallett; was also Guion after Vincent, father-in-law of Wilson Primm - 63111; **62**
Davis St. In North St. Louis; became Bates, then changed to Dickson - 63102
Dayton St. For B. B. Dayton, a developer - 63106
*****Deaver Ln.** A relative of the Chouteaus - 63141; **28**
De Baliviere Ave. Named for a nun who taught Kingsbury children - 63112; **81, 82**
Decatur. Named for Commodore Stephen Decatur. Changed to Ninth St. - 63104 (See Chapter 12); **92**
Deer St. An early animal trail - 63113
De Giverville Ave. For husband of Sarah Mary Virginia Kingsbury, Armand Francois Robert Count De Giverville - 63112; **28, 81, 82**
De Kalb St. Baron Johann De Kalb, a foreign officer who helped the Colonists in the Revolutionary War- 63104, 63118; **38**
Delaware. For an Indian tribe; was changed to Geyer - 63104; **55, 112**
Delmar Blvd. Named for first three letters of Delaware and Maryland; some was Oak, then Morgan - 63103, 63108, 63112; **13, 35, 79, 103, 152**
Delor St. For Clement Delor, founder of Carondelet. Some of Delor was named Termination; some of Delor was changed to Hill - 63109, 63111, 63116; **59, 72, 81, 100**
DeMenil Pl. For Dr. Nicholas DeMenil, married a Chouteau - 63118; **28, 59, 60**
Dempsey Ave. For Timothy Dempsey, a priest (Charities) - 63110
*****DeMun.** For Jules DeMun, an early settler who married Isabelle, daughter of Charles Gratiot - 63105. Related to the Chouteaus; **28, 82**
*****Denny Rd.** For Samuel Denny, a farmer and landowner. Lindbergh Road was once Denny Road - 63126. Related to the Chouteaus.
De Soto Ave. For Hernando De Soto, an early Spanish explorer; was Hall - 63107; **11, 121**
Des Peres Ave/Blvd. "River of the Fathers" - 63112, 63123; **11, 15, 152-153**
Des Peres. Changed to Hancock - 63109

Destrehan St. For N. N. Destrehan, one of the founders of Bremen - 63107, 63147
De Tonty St. For Henri De Tonty, an early explorer - 63110; **11, 70**
Devolsey. Changed to Victor - 63104
Devonshire Ave. For an area in England - 63109; **10, 75**
Dewey Ave. For Admiral George Dewey - 63116; **153**
Diana. Changed to Lancaster, then Dorcas, for the wife of William C. Carr - 63104
Dick Gregory Pl. For the comedian; was Wagoner Place - 63113; **32**
Dickson St. For Charles K. Dickson, a real estate developer; was Bates - 63102, 63106; **32, 51**
Dickson. Between Jefferson and Webster; renamed James "Cool Papa" Bell in the 1980s for the black baseball player - 63106
Dillon Ct./Dr. For a granddaughter of Chouteau - 63104; **28**
Dock St. Named for location - 63147; **99, 100**
Doddridge St. Member of Hornsby family, early settlers - 63147
Dodier St. For Gabriel Dodier, an early St. Louisan - 63107; **29, 153**
Donnell Ave. For Gov. Forrest C. Donnell - 63137; **128,** 129
Donovan Ave./Pl. For Daniel H. and Joseph T. Donovan, real estate developers - 63109, 63110; **77**
Dorcas St. For wife of William C. Carr; was Diana, also Lancaster - 63118; **58, 148-149**
Douglass St. Frederick Douglass, abolitionist; or for Maj. Thompson Douglas, who married Cornelia, a daughter of Daniel Bissell - 63147; **153**
Dover Pl./St. For a city in Delaware - 63111, 63116; **62, 100**
*****Dowler.** For Theodore Dowler, a landowner - 63121; **53**
Dr. Martin Luther King Dr. Was Easton - 63101, 63102, 63106, 63112, 63113; **32, 54**
Dresden Ave. For a city in Germany - 63116; **61**
Drury Ln. Street in London - 63147, **85**
Duke St. For Basil Wilson Duke, a lawyer and Confederate officer with Morgan's Raiders; or, for Mrs. Sarah Christy Duke - 63116; **99**
Duncan Ave. For Thomas O. Duncan, a banker - 63110
*****Dunklin Dr.** For Missouri Gov. Daniel Dunklin - 63138; **117**
Dunnica Ave. For James Dunnica, a steamboat captain - 63116, 63118. A public school is named for him; **73, 154**
*****Dupree Ave.** Relative of the Chouteaus - 63135; **28**
Durant. Named for the subdivision; also for an author, named by Clara Bircher - 63115; **52**
*****Dyer Ave.** Relative of the Chouteaus - 63114; **28**

Eads Ave. Named for James Buchanan Eads; it was Susan, for Susan

Compton - 63104. (See Appendix V "Q"); **42, 57, 95**
Eads Bridge. Named for location - 63102; **100, 154, 181**
Eager Rd. Changed to McRee - 63110
East Ct. Named for location - 63116; 99
***Eastgate Ave.** Location of a gate for the Delmar Racetrack - 63130; **79**
Easton Ave. For Rufus Easton, a lawyer, and first St. Louis postmaster. Mary Easton, daughter of Rufus, married Major Sibley, the founder of Lindenwood College. Alton, Illinois, was named for Rufus' son, Alton. Easton was changed to Martin Luther King Drive in 1972 - 63112, 63113; **50, 54**
East Rd. On the east side of Forest Park - changed to Kingshighway - 63110
***Easy St.** Named by first resident of the street - 63074; **86**
***Ecoff.** Asa B. Ecoff, early landowner - 63143
***Eddie & Park Rd.** Led to the estates of the Thomas Eddie and Jonah Parke families - 63123, 63126, 63127
***Edgar Rd.** For T. P. Edgar, a landowner - 63119
Edward. Changed to Maury - 63110
Edwards St. For Richard Edwards, publisher; some Edwards' were relatives of the Chouteaus - 63110; **28**
Eichelberger St. A surveyor; was Clark - 63109, 63111, 63116; **72, 74, 100**
Eighth St. 63102, 63104; **46**
Eighteenth St. 63103, 63104, 63106, 63118; **36, 97, 98, 100**
Eiler St. Laurentius M. Eiler platted Carondelet - 63111, 63116; **100**
Elias Ave. Named by early Jewish settlers - 63147; **52**
Elizabeth Ave. Wife of a Methodist minister, Thomas Bowman; was Johnson - 63110, 63139; **57**
Elizabeth. In South St. Louis; changed to Hickory - 63104; **57**
***Ellendale.** Granddaughter of James Sutton - 63143; **84**
Ellenwood Ave. Named for Ellen Christy; also after subdivision - 63116; **72**
Elliott Ave. Richard Elliott, real estate developer - 63106, 63107; **83, 154**
Elm. One of the tree streets; no longer exists - 63102; **35**
Emma. For relative of Jennings; or, for the sister of Clara Bircher - 63136; **52**
Emerson Ave. For Ralph Waldo Emerson; named by Clara Bircher - 63120; **52, 154**
Emily St. For a daughter of Dr. John Gano Bryan - 63107; **31**
Emily. Changed to Ohio - 63104
Endora. Now Gustine - 63116; **100**
Enright Ave. For one of the first soldiers killed in World War I; was von Versen - 63108, 63112; **154**

Espenschied St. For Louis Espenschied, a landowner. Some was Hill - 63111. His daughter, Philippine, married Henry Overstolz, mayor of St. Louis from 1876 to 1881 - 63111; **59, 137**
Essex Pl. James C. Essex, a printer, related to Finney - 63115
Estelle. In South St. Louis; changed to Hickory - 63104
Etzel Ave. For Susan R. Etzel - 63112
Euclid Ave. Named for street in Cleveland, Ohio. Some was Snead. Euclid was named for the Greek mathematician, the "father of geometry" - 63108, 63113, 63115; **155**
Eugene Ave. For Eugene Field, a poet - 63116; **62, 155**
Evaline. For wife of John Gano Bryan; changed to 20th - 63107; **31**
Evans Ave. For the A. H. Evans family - 63106, 63113
Evergreen. Changed to Gratiot - 63110
Ewing Ave. Between Olive and Martin Luther King; Ewing was changed to Huntley - 63103; **32**
Ewing. William L. Ewing, a grocer, married Clara Berthold, granddaughter of Pierre Chouteau - 63103, 63104; **28, 47, 137**
Exchange. First changed to Jefferson, then changed to Clinton after George Clinton, vice president under Madison - 63106

Fair Ave. After the Fairgrounds; some was Caroline, some was College - 63107, 63115
Fairfax Ave. Part of it was changed to Banks in 1981 for Cornelius David Banks - 63113
Fairgrounds Pl. After the Fairgrounds - 63107; **100**
Fairmont Ave. Named for subdivision - 63139; **155**
Fairview Ave. Named for subdivision - 63116, 63139
Farlin Ave. An early family - 63115
Farragut St. For Admiral Daniel Glasgow Farragut. When he captured Mobile Bay during the Civil War, he said, "Damn the torpedoes! Full speed ahead!" Some was Augusta - 63107; **155**
Farrar St. Dr. Bernard S. Farrar married Sarah, daughter of William Christy. He died in the cholera epidemic in 1849 - 63107; **91, 104**
Fassen St. For Louis Fassenor, a landowner - 63111; **100**
Federer Pl. William Federer, a real estate developer - 63116; **62**
*****Fee Fee Rd.** English phonetic spelling for French "Fi Fi" - 63141
Federal. Was changed to North Broadway - 63102
Fendler. Fendler Addition - 63116
Ferry St. Led to Bissell Ferry - 63107; **63, 99**
Field Ave. Roswell Field, a lawyer and father of poet Eugene Field - 63116; **40, 62, 155**
Fifteenth St. 63103, 63106
Fifth St. Was changed to Broadway in 1866 - 63102; **46, 75**

Fifty-Ninth St. 63110, 63139; **99**
Fillmore St. For U.S. President Millard Fillmore; was Grundy - 63116; **101**
Fillmore. In North St. Louis; changed to Garrison - 63107
Fine Arts Dr. Named for location - 63110; **100**
*****Fine Rd.** For Phillip and David Fine, early settlers - 63129
Finkman St. Louis Finkman, a landowner - 63109; **77**
Finney Ave. William and John Finney, early landowners and real estate developers - 63113
First St. Was Grand Rue, then Main - 63102, 63104, 63118, 63147
*****Fletcher St.** Missouri Gov. Thomas Clement Fletcher - 63121; **121**
Flad Ave. Henry Flad, an engineer who helped James Eads - 63110
Flora Ave./Blvd./Ct. Named by Henry Shaw - 63104, 63110; **69, 70, 74**
Floral. Changed to Flora - 63104, 63110; **69**
Florence. Named for daughter of John W. Burd. Changed to Belt for a real estate developer - 63112
Florida. 63102; **113**
Florence. Changed to Newstead - 63115
Florissant Ave. The road to Florissant - 63106, 63107, 63115, 63120; **52**
*****Folk.** For Joseph Folk, Missouri governor - 63143; **125**
Folsom Ave. Frances Folsom, wife of President Grover Cleveland - 63110
Foot of Arsenal St. Named for location - 63118; **100**
Foot of Haven St. Named for location - 63111; **100**
Foot of Iron St. Named for location - 63111; **100**
*****Forder Rd.** Samuel W. Forder - 63129
*****Fordyce Ln.** Relative of Mullanphy - 63124; **27**
Forest Park Ave. Named for location - 63108, 63112
Fountain Ave. Named for location near Fountain Park - 63113 (See Page 181 "R"); **99, 100, 181**
Fourth St. 63102, 63104, 63118; **13, 34, 36, 50**
Fourteenth St. 63103, 63104, 63106, 63107; **46**
Francis St. David Rowland Francis, mayor of St. Louis, Missouri governor and promoter of 1904 World's Fair - 63106; **54, 96, 124, 137**
*****Francisca Dr.** Relative of Mullanphy - 63031 (Florissant)
Franke Ct. Charles H. Franke, real estate developer - 63139
Franklin Ave. For Benjamin Franklin, statesman - 63106. Originally was Cherry, a tree street; **35, 156**
Franklin. In South St. Louis; changed to Courtois - 63111; **100**
Frederick St. Frederic Kraft, first postmaster of Baden; he came from Baden-Baden, Germany - 63147
Fremont Ave. Union Gen. John C. Fremont - 63147; **156**
French Ave./Ct. Named for Mary Field French, a cousin of Eugene Field

- 63116; **62**
Frieda Ave. Named for a nursemaid/housekeeper of Busch - 63116; **61**
*****Friendly Dr.** Was named First Street. The neighbors changed the name because everyone was so friendly - 63126
*****Frisco.** After the railroad - 63119, 63122
*****Frost Ave.** Relative of Mullanphy - 63134; **27**
Fulsom. Named for Frances Fulsom, wife of Grover Cleveland - 63110; **71**
Fulton. Changed to Eighth Street - 63102
Fyler Ave. James D. Fyler, landowner; part was County Road - 63116, 63139; **75, 99**

Gamache. In Carondelet; was changed to Loughborough - 63111
Gamble St. Hamilton Rowan Gamble, lawyer, provisional governor of Missouri during Civil War - 63106; **52, 95-96, 120, 156**
Gamble. Changed to Scott - 63103
Gannett St. George Alfred Gannett, a landowner - 63116
Gano Ave. For Dr. John Gano Bryan; was Wilkinson - 63107, 63147; **31, 148**
Gardenville Ave. Named for area - 63116; **99, 156**
Gardner Dr. Gov. Frederick Dozier Gardner - 63136; **126-127**
Gardner Ln. Gov. Frederick Dozier Gardner - 63134; **126-127**
Garesche Ave. Alex J. P. Garesche, landowner and lawyer - 63120; **86**
Garfield Ave. U.S. President James Garfield; was Boston - 63113. A public school is named for him; **156**
Garibaldi. Changed to Newhouse - 63107
Garnier St. Joseph V. Garnier, married Marie, daughter of Charles Sanguinette. The Garniers' only daughter, Harriet, married John Hogan, a postmaster - 63116; **29, 79**
Garrison Ave. Oliver L. Garrison, a real estate developer. Some was Fillmore, some was Lindell - 63103, 63106, 63107; **47, 103**
Gasconade St. Named for the river - 63116, 63118; **55, 56**
Gast Pl. For August and Leopold Gast - 63147
Gate St. Changed to Withnell, a brewery owner - 63118; **35**
Genevieve Ave. For wife of George W. Strodtman - 63120. Some was Bellefontaine - 63115
Germania St. Named by Sturmfels; in Austria Heights - 63111, 63116; **63**
Gertrude Ave. A nursemaid/housekeeper for Busch - 63116; **61**
Gettysburg Ct. After the city in Pennsylvania where the famous Civil War battle was fought - 63120
Geyer Ave. Henry Sheffie Geyer, a lawyer who replaced Thomas H. Benton in the Senate; was Delaware - 63104; **91, 96, 180**

Gibson Ave. Charles A. Gibson, a lawyer and nephew of Governor Gamble - 63110; **37, 96**
Giles Ave. John Giles, early landowner who worked in the Gravois Coal Diggins - 63116; **73**
Gilmore. An author; named by Clara Bircher - 63120, 63147; **52**
Gilson Ave. George W. Gilson, Union captain - 63116
Gimblins. Gimblins Estate Addition - 63147
Glades. Descriptive name; Gratiot tract - 63139
Glasby. Changed to Parkview - 63109
Glasgow Ave. William Glasgow, wine merchant; some was Thompson - 63106; **36, 54, 157**
Glendale. Changed to Warne - 63107
Goethe Ave. Johann Wolfgang von Goethe, considered one of the greatest of all German writers (1749 -1832) – 63109, 63116
Goethe. In North St. Louis; changed to Calvary after the cemetery - 63107; **51**
Goode Ave. G. W. Goode, landowner; was changed to Annie Malone Drive - 63113; **32**
Goodfellow Blvd. David W. Goodfellow, a landowner who purchased 1,500 acres from William Clark - 63112, 63120, 63147; **52, 53, 54, 157**
Government Dr. Street in Forest Park from World's Fair - 63110; **100**
Government. Changed to Utah - 63118; **35**
Grace Ave. Thomas Grace, an early landowner who worked in the Gravois Coal Diggins - 63116; **73, 99**
Graham St. David W. Graham, operated Sulphur Springs; was named Center - 63139; **75**
*****Graham Rd.** For Maj. Richard Graham who married Catherine Mullanphy - 63034; **27, 86-87**
Grand Ave./Blvd./Dr. Named by Hiram Leffingwell, a developer - 63103, 63104, 63106, 63107, 63108, 63111, 63118; **30, 67-69, 98, 100, 103**
Grande. Named after Grande Prairie Common Field; changed to Spring, Claggett, St. Louis - 63107
Grand, N. Was Lindell's Lane - 63107
Grand Rue. Became Main, or First Street - 63102; **35**
*****Grant Rd.** For Ulysses S. Grant, a Union general and U.S. president - 63119, 63123, 63125; **29, 45, 157**
Grant Pl./St. For Ulysses S. Grant- 63107, 63116; **29**
Grape. For vineyards located there - 63147
Gratiot St. For Charles Gratiot, husband of Victoire Chouteau; was changed to Mulberry, Sherman, Cooper, then Evergreen - 63102, 63103, 63110. A public school is named for Gratiot; **12, 28, 55, 69, 82, 83, 157**
Gravois Ave. Means "rubble," "rubbish," "gravel," "garbage" - 63104,

Streets of St. Louis ~ 205

63116, 63118. A public school is named Gravois; **61, 100, 157**

Green/Greene. In North St. Louis; changed to Benton Street - 63106

Green. James S. Green, lawyer; was first Prune, then Christy, now Lucas - 63101, 63102, 63103; **35, 46**

Green Lea Pl. Greanlea Place Addition; some was Shreve - 63107, 63115

*****Green Park Rd.** Road to Greene Parke's farm; he was the son of Jonah Parke (both spelled "Parke" with an "e"). See Eddie & Park Road - 63123, 63125

Greer Ave. Early landowner; some was Lucas - 63107, 63115, 63120. Some Greers were relatives of the Chouteaus; **28**

Gregg Ave. Morris B. Gregg, paint manufacturer - 63139

Gresham Ave. Was Kaiser; the name changed to Gresham for a military man during World War I - 63109; **28**

Grundy. Changed to Fillmore - 63111

Gurney Ave./Ct. For the family whose members were superintendents of Tower Grove Park for over 100 years - 63110, 63116; **70, 100**

Gustine Ave./Tr. Relative of James Russell - 63116; **72, 100**

Guy. Son of John Gano Bryan; changed to Blair after Frank Blair - 63107; **31**

Hadley St. Herbert Spencer Hadley, a Missouri governor - 63101, 63106, 63107. A public school was named for him; **125-126, 157**

Half St. Descriptive name - 63139; **99**

Hall St. For Dr. John Hall - 63147; **80**

Hall St. Named for Willard Preble Hall; changed to De Soto for Hernando De Soto, an early Spanish explorer - 63107; **120-121**

Halliday. Named for Ellen M. Halliday, land owner - 63118

Halls Ferry Rd. Road to ferry over Missouri River operated by Edward Hall - 63147; **62**

Ham. In Soulard, a relative of the Chouteaus; became Ninth Street - 63104; **28**

*****Hamburg.** Named by Trampitsch; in Austria Heights - 63123; **63, 99**

Hamilton Ave. Hamilton Rowan Gamble, provincial Missouri governor - 63112, 63120; **52, 120, 156**

Hammett Pl. Real estate developer - 63113

Hampton Ave. Southhampton western border street; parts were once Billon, West Park, Sulphur and Cheltenham - 63109, 63139; **77, 79**

Hampton Village/Plaza. Named for location - 63109; **100**

Hamtranck. Changed to 13th Street - 63104

Hancock Ave. Union Gen. Winfield Scott Hancock - 63139

*****Hanley Rd.** C. Hanley, landowner - 63105, 63114, 63121, 63130, 63134; **82, 86**

Happy Hollow. For the area between Gratiot, Sixth, Papin, Seventh - 63102

Haren. Changed to President - 63118

Harlem. Changed to Taylor after Nathaniel Pendleton Taylor - 63115

Harney Ave. Union Gen. William S. Harney; his wife was a Mullanphy - 63115, 63120

Harney. In South St. Louis; changed to Cherokee - 63118

Harper St. A real estate developer - 63107

Harper. In South St. Louis; was Lane, then changed to Lynch - 63118

Harris Ave. Dr. John W. Harris, married daughter of John O'Fallon; some was Sophia - 63107, 63115, 63147; **31, 158**

Harrison. For James Harrison, a wealthy merchant; changed to Tyler, then changed to Branch - 63107; **41, 51**

*Hart. E. S. Hart was an early mayor of Webster - 63119

Hartford St. Named for the location of the Connecticut Mutual Life Insurance Co. - 63116, 63118; **61**

Haven St. Should be HAREN after landowner and banker Edward Haren. The street sign was printed wrong and never corrected - 63111, 63116; **101, 104**

*Hawkins Rd. C. M. Hawkins (Hawkins' Rifle) - 63129

Hawthorne Blvd. Nathaniel Hawthorne, novelist - 63104; **66**

Hawthorne. Changed to Red Bud - 63147

Hayes Lane. Was changed from Greer to Tyrus Court (was East Norwood Drive); named for Robert Hayes, Olympic gold medalist in 1964 - 63115

Hazel. Changed to Papin - 63102; **35**

Heaven. Changed to Steins - 63111; **59**

Hebert St. Francis Hebert, who was killed in the Indian attack of 1780. His daughter, Helene, was one of the first children baptized in St. Louis in 1767. She married Paschall Hyacinthe St. Cyr in 1782 - 63107, 63120; **13**

Heger Ct. Frederic Heger, real estate developer; was Maury - 63110; **70, 100**

*Heidelburg. Named by Trampitsch; in Austria Heights - 63123; **63**

Helm Dr. Keith Helmkamp, real estate developer and surveyor - 63109

*Heman Ave. Named for August Heman, mayor of University City from 1913 to 1920. Heman Park also is named for him - 63130

Hemp Ave. This is the shortest street in the city - 63110

Hempstead St. Charles Hempstead, lawyer, banker and member of Board of Education. His daughter, Susan, married a Chouteau. Another daughter, Mary, married fur trader Manuel Lisa - 63102; **28, 31, 82, 158**

Henrietta Pl./St. It is said that one of the men who built nine of the houses on this street named it after the wife he had abandoned in

Canada; or, for Henrietta Thomas, the daughter of the developer of Compton Hill subdivision - 63104; **57**

Henry Ave. For Patrick Henry, governor of Virginia, who is remembered for saying "Give me liberty or give me death!" - 63116; **158**

Hereford St. Frances Hereford married into the Sublette family - 63109, 63110, 63139; **76**

Hiawatha. Named for the Indian chief; changed to Pulaski - 63111; **55, 56, 100**

High St. Changed to 23rd - 63107

High St. In South St. Louis; was changed to Indiana - 63104, 63118; **98**

Hickory. Changed to Wash, then Cole - 63106; **35, 57**

Hickory Ln./Pl./St. Named for the tree - 63104, 63110; **47**

High Circle. Named for location - 63109

Highfield Rd. Named for location - 63109

Highland Park Dr. Named for location of amusement park - 63110

Hilgard Pl. For H. C. Hilgard, a surveyor - 63109; **77**

Hill St. Hill was an early landowner, doctor and alderman; it once was Delor. Some of it was changed to Espenschied - 63111; **98**

Hi View Ave. Named for location - 63109

Hodiamont Ave. Emanuel de Hodiamont, land owner - 63112; **52**

Hoffman. For H. L. Hoffman, a member of first School Board - 63139; **143**

Hogan St. John Hogan, a Methodist minister, was appointed postmaster in 1858 by President Buchanan - 63106; **29**

Holly Ave. Named by O'Fallon; some was Moore - 63115, 63147; **31**

Holly Hills Ave./Blvd. Named for subdivision; once was Kansas, also Kingshighway, Southwest - 63109, 63111, 63116; **67, 101**

Holt Ave. Joseph Holt, attorney general of Missouri; or, for John Holt, a coal miner - 63116

***Honey Ln.** Possibly a relative of the Chouteaus - 63129; **28**

Hoover Way. For President Herbert Hoover. It is only a walkway, there are no houses facing it - 63116; **63**

Horatio. Changed to Lawrence, for Mary Lawrence Tyler - 63110

Hornsby Ave. Early family in area - 63147

Hortense Pl. A private place, named for Hortense Goldman whose family lived at No. 9. Jacob Goldman built his own private street after he was denied admittance to other private places because he was Jewish - 63108

Horton Pl. Early family in area - 63112

Hortus Ct. No street, just a sidewalk between 10 houses - 63110; **100**

Howard St. After Benjamin Franklin Howard, the territorial governor (1810-1812) - 63102, 63106; **67, 116, 159**

***Hudson Rd.** Relative of Mullanphy - 63135; **27**

Hull St. Named for landowner, Elizabeth Hull - 63107

Humbolt Ave. Baron Alexander von Humbolt, German scientist - 63147; **53, 159**

Hummel. Named for the Hummelsheim family - 63116

*****Hummelsheim.** In Austria Heights. Named by Trampitsch for the Hummelsheim family - 63123; **63**

Humphrey St. Humphrey Green, president of the Connecticut Mutual Life Insurance Co. - 63116, 63118; **61, 72**

Hunt. For an early landowner; changed to Bamberger - 63116; **73**

Hunt Ave. Was first called Ridge; changed to Hunt for Charles L. Hunt, secretary to McRee Racetrack - 63110; **70**

*****Huntleigh Dr.** Named for a riding club - 63122

Hurck St. Peter J. Hurck, early landowner and real estate developer - 63116

Hydraulic Ave. After a nearby brick yard - 63116

Idaho Ave. Named for the state - 63111; **113**

Illinois Ave. Named for the state - 63118; **61, 113**

Illinois Ave. Changed to Iron - 63111; **101**

Indiana Ave. Named for the state - 63104, 63118; **113**

Iowa Ave. For the state - 63104, 63111, 63118; **113**

Iron St. After the Iron Mountain Railroad - 63111, 63116; **99, 101**

Irving Ave. For Washington Irving, an author - 63120; **159**

Itaska St. Lake Itaska in Minnesota - 63109, 63111, 63116; **55, 56**

Ivanhoe Ave. Named for subdivision; some say also for *Wilfred of Ivanhoe*, a novel by Sir Walter Scott, published in 1819. It was Lake Street, as it led to the Lake family farm - 63109, 63139; **79**

Ivory Ave. John C. Ivory, landowner and real estate developer - 63111

Jackson St. U.S. President Andrew Jackson - 63147; **15, 159**

Jackson St. In South St. Louis; changed to Third Street - 63118

Jackson St. In Carondelet area; changed to Vulcan for the Vulcan Iron Works - 63111; **120**

James St. For James W. Kingsbury; was called Second Carondelet. It is now 18th St. - 63104

James St. Changed to Salena - 63118

James "Cool Papa" Bell. Named for the baseball player; was Dickson - 63106; **32**

Jamieson Ave. For Will and James Jamieson, land and mine owners - 63109, 63139; **77, 79,** 104

January Ave. For Derrick A. January, a real estate developer; some was McNair, some was Cozens - 63109, 63110, 63139; **100**

Jefferson Ave. President Thomas Jefferson; was Pratte - 63103, 63104, 63106, 63107, 63118; **14, 34, 36, 50, 98, 100, 159, 176**

Jefferson Ave. North St. Louis; changed to Clinton - 63106, 63107
***Jefferson Barrracks Rd.** Was changed to Reavis Barracks Road - 63123, 63125
Jennings Rd. Dr. James Jennings, a landowner - 63136 ; **86**
***Jerome Ave.** Lawyer who worked for the state of Missouri - 63143
***Jesse Jackson.** Runs from Lucas and Hunt to Cherry; was Curtis, changed in 1983 - 63121
Jessica Ave. Daughter of John Bingham - 63116; **72**
Joab. Changed to Ewing - 63103
John Ave. Dr. John Gano Bryan - 63107, 63147; **31**
John. In South St. Louis, some changed to Wisconsin, some to Lemp - 63118; **59**
Johnson. Changed to Elizabeth; some Johnsons are related to the Chouteaus - 63139; **28**
Joliet Ave. Louis Jolliet (He spelled it with two l's), early French explorer with Jacques Marquette - 63120; **11**
Jones St. Jonathan Jones, storekeeper - 63113
Jordan Ave. Named by Jewish settlers - 63147; **52**
Jules St. Named for Jules Cabanne Kingsbury - 63104
Julia St. Julia Soulard - 63104; **58**
Julia. Changed to Cardinal - 63106
***Julia Dent Dr.** Daughter of Frederick Dent and wife of Ulysses S. Grant - 63123; **29**
Juniata St. Named for the river in Pennsylvania - 63116, 63118, 63139; **55, 56**

Kaiser. Changed to Gresham - 63109; **28**
Kansas. Changed to Holly Hills - 63116; **55, 56, 57, 113**
Kansas. Changed to Compton - 63111, 63118; **113**
***Kassabaum Ln.** August Kassabaum, county collector of revenue - 63129
Keber. An agent of John O'Fallon - 63107; **31**
Keith Pl. For Keith Helmkamp, a real estate developer and surveyor - 63109;
Kemper Ave. After Kemper College - 63139; **75, 100**
Kennerly Ave. James Kennerly, merchant who married Eliza, granddaughter of Dr. Antoine Francois Saugrain - 63112, 63113 (see Appendix V "S"); **91, 182**
Kennett Pl. After Mayor Luther Kennett; changed to Hall Street - 63115; **37, 135**
Kennett Pl. After Mayor Luther Kennett - 63104; **37, 135**
Kensington Ave./Pl. Named after Kensington Garden amusement park - 63108

Kentucky Ave. Named for the state - 63110; **113**
***Kenwood.** Named for the home of Theodore Dowler - 63121; **53**
Keokuk St. Named for Indian chief; some was Block - 63116, 63118; **55, 56, 100, 133**
***Kerth Rd.** George, Rosina and Peter Kerth, landowners - 63128
***Ketmore.** Kettler and Morganford combined - 63123
Kienlen. 63121, 63133; **52**
Kimberly Ave. For early landowners - 63120
Kingsbury Ave./Blvd./Pl./Sq. Julia Antoinette Cabanne, great-granddaughter of Madame Chouteau; married Capt. James Wilkinson Kingsbury - 63112; **28, 74, 81, 82**
Kingsbury. Changed to Shenandoah - 63104; **57**
Kingshighway Blvd. Name for roads separating the common fields from the King's land; some was a county road - 63108, 63109, 63110, 63113, 63115, 63139; **10, 17, 52, 67, 69, 72, 75, 82, 100**
Kingsland Ct. The developer of Matt Brick's last name was German for king, or "Koenig." He named the street he lived on Kingsland - 63111, 63116; **63**
Kinsey Pl. Edmund Kinsey, surveyor - 63109; **77**
Kirk. Changed to Koeln - 63111
Klemm St. Richard Klemm, surveyor - 63110; **69**
Klocke. Klocke Addition - 63118
Knachstedt St. Named after a family who owned a dairy farm in the area - 63116; **62, 100**
Knapp St. George Knapp, an editor - 63106, 63107
Knox Ave./Ct. Sam Knox, real estate developer and congressman - 63139
Koeln Ave. For Christian Koeln, an early German family - 63111, 63116; **59, 101**
***Kohrs Ln.** Adam Kohr, a wagon maker - 63123
Kosciusko St. Foreign officer who helped colonists during the Revolutionay War - 63104, 63118; **38**
Kossuth Ave. For Lajos Kossuth, a famous Hungarian lawyer and newspaper editor - 63107
Kossuth. Changed to 25th Street - 63107
Krauss St. John Krauss, blacksmith; was Olive - 63111; **59, 101**
Krum Ave. John M. Krum, a lawyer and mayor; one son was a Union general, another was a Confederate general in the Civil War - 63113; **135**

LaBarge. Changed to Maple - 63112
La Beaume St. Louis A. La Beaume, an early landowner - 63102
Labadie Ave. Sylvester Labaddie (He spelled it with two d's) married

Adele, daughter of John P. Cabanne, also Martha, daughter of James Russell, a relative of the Chouteaus - 63107, 63115, 63120; **28, 82**

Labadie. Changed to La Salle - 63104; **35**

Lackland Ave. Rufus J. Lackland arrived in St. Louis in 1835 when he was 16 years old. He became a banker and worked for the gas company - 63116

*Lackland Rd. Named for country home of Rufus J. Lackland - 63114, 63146; **88**

Laclede Ave./Ct. Pierre Laclede, co-founder of St. Louis - 63103, 63108; **12, 15**

*Laclede Station Rd. Led to station on MOPAC Railroad - 63117, 63119, 63143; **83**

Lafayette Ave. French officer who fought for the Colonies in America during the Revolutionary War; some was Soulard Street - 63104, 63110; **36, 37, 38-39, 68**

Lafayette. Changed to Soper - 63111; **101**

Laflin St. Sylvester Laflin, landowner - 63106

Lake Ave. It led to lake on the Cabanne farm; some changed to Euclid - 63108

Lake Ave. Led to Lake farm; changed to Ivanhoe - 63139; **79**

Lami St. For Michael Lami, an early settler who died in 1784. Some was Ohio, some Lauri - 63104; **57, 114**

*LaMotte Ln. Relative of Mullanphy - 63135; **27**

Lancaster. Changed to Dorcas - 63118

Lane. William Carr Lane, first mayor of St. Louis. It was changed to Harper, then Lynch - 63118; **57-58**

Lansdowne Ave. In England - 63109, 63116

*Larimore Rd. For Newell G. Larimore, a pioneer - 63138

*Larkin Ave. A relative of Mullanphy - 63135

La Salle Ln./St./Park/Ct. An early French explorer, named the Louisiana Territory. Some was Sycamore, from 800-999 is now Lebanon, some was Virginia - 63104, 63110; **11, 35**

Laura. A relative of Dr. James Jennings - 63136; **85**

Laurel St. For a tree on Hodiamont farm - 63112

Laurel. Changed to Washington - 63102; **35**

Lauren. Changed to Rowan - 63112

Lauri. Changed to Lami - 63118

Lavernell Ct. For a daughter of developer August Sturmfels - 63116; **63**

Lawn. Named for the Forest Lawn subdivision - 63109, 63139

Lawrence St. Named for Mary Lawrence Tyler; some was Horatio - 63110; **69**

Lawton Pl./Promenade/Walk. Named after Henry Ware Lawton, a military man - 63103

Lea Pl. Was Pamela - 63115

Lebanon Dr. Named for ethnic church in area; was La Salle - 63104

Leduc St. For Marie Philip Leduc, a judge - 63113

Lee Ave. Patrick Lee married Dr. Conde's daughter, Constance - 63107, 63115; **52**

Leffingwell Ave. Hiram Wheeler Leffingwell helped develop Grand Boulevard, Forest Park and Kirkwood. Some was Clay - 63103, 63106; **67, 83, 94**

*****Lemay Ferry Rd.** The road to the ferry operated by Francois LeMais - 63125, 63129; **62, 85**

Lemp Ave. For Adam Lemp, a brewer - 63104, 63118; **59-60**

Leona. For the Leona Park Addition - 63116

Leonard Ave. For a minister; named by W. G. Elliot, founder of Washington University. Some was once Valley - 63103, 63106

Leonor K. Sullivan. For Congresswoman Leonor K. Sullivan; was Wharf - 63102, 63104 (See Appendix V "T"); **182**

Lewis St. For Meriwether Lewis, of Lewis and Clark expedition; was Madison - 63102; **15, 116**

Lewis Pl. For Turner and Benjamin W. Lewis, real estate developers - 63113; **74**

Lexington Ave. For a city in Kentucky, named by Henry Clay - 63107, 63115; **39**

Liberty. Changed to Wisconsin - 63118

Liberty. A patriotic name - 63111; **98**

Lierman Ave. For an early landowner; was Rebecca - 63116; **73**

Lilburn Ave. For Lilburn W. Boggs, the sixth governor of Missouri. He married Silas Bent's daughter - 63115; **117**

Lillian. Named by Clara Bircher for her mother - 63136; **52**

Lilly Ave. Named for James Lilly, a landowner - 63110

Lily. Changed to Alexander for Alexander Lacy Lyle - 63116; **100**

Lincoln Ave./Way. For President Abraham Lincoln - 63113, 63120; **25, 51**

*****Lindbergh.** For aviator Charles A. Lindbergh - 63114, 63122, 63123,

Lindeel. Changed to Garrison - 63107

Lindell Blvd. For Peter Lindell, merchant - 63103, 63108, 63112; **30,** 67

Lindell Ln. Changed to North Grand - 63107; **30**

Linden. Changed to Gamble - 63106

Lindenwood Ave./Ct./Pl. For Lindenwood College; or, some say, for the linden tree - 63109; **79**

*****Lindsay Ln.** For a relative of Mullanphy - 63031 (Florissant); **27**

Linton Ave. Dr. Moses L. Linton was one of the founders of the St. Vincent de Paul Society in the United States - 63107

Lisa. Manuel Lisa, a fur trader, married Mary Hempstead; was changed to

O'Fallon - 63102, 63106; **31**

Lisette Ave. For a relative of Finkman - 63109; **77**

*****Litzinger Rd./Ln./Dr.** William and John Litzinger, landowners - 63124, 63144, **85**

*****Little Ln.** Possibly a relative of the Chouteaus - 63124; **28**

Livingston Dr. For Donald Livingston, a real estate developer - 63116; **62**

Locust St. Named for the tree - 63101, 63102, 63103; **35, 50, 103**

Lombard St. Named for the tree - 63102; **13, 35**

*****Long.** Nicholas Long settled in Gumbo/Chesterfield area in 1797. The flood of 1844 influenced him to move to Bridgeton, then called Marais des Laird - 63017

Longfellow Blvd. For poet Henry Wadsworth Longfellow - 63104; **66**

Loran. Named for Thomas V. Loran, secretary of Hamilton Finance - 63109

*****Lorraine.** For Alsace-Lorraine, a region in France - 63121

Loughborough Ave. For John M. Loughborough, a surveyor; was Gamache and Pine - 63109, 63111, 63116; **101**

Louisa. For a daughter of William Carr Lane - 63104; **58**

Louisa. Changed to Red Bud - 63107

Louisiana Ave. For the state - 63104, 63111, 63118; **63, 66, 72, 113**

Louis St. Named for Louis St. Ange de Bellerive - 63116

Louisville Ave. City in Kentucky - 63139

Love Joy Ln. Rev. E. P. Lovejoy, radical abolitionist publisher (killed in Alton, Illinois, just before the Civil War) - 63106

Lowell Ln./St. For James R. Lowell, a poet - 63147

Lucas Ave. For Jean Baptiste Charles Lucas, a lawyer; was Prune, then Christy, then Green. The 2600-3599 blocks were changed to Samuel Shepard, for an educator - 63101, 63102, 63103; **29, 35, 46, 47, 74, 91, 103**

Lucas. Changed to Greer - 63107; **32**

Lucille. Named for a daughter of the Jennings family - 63136; **86**

Lucky St. Changed to Aldine - 63113

Lucy St. For Lucy Bent Russell - 63116; **71**

Luther. Honors Luther Kennett, a mayor of St. Louis - 63115; **135**

Lynch St. Bernard M. Lynch was a slave trader; some changed to Magnolia - 63118; **58**

Mackay Pl. Named for James Mackay, an early fur trader (1799), surveyor and explorer. Lewis and Clark used his maps as far as South Dakota. He owned 225 acres by what is now Lafayette Park - 63104

*****Mackenzie Rd./Ct.** Kenneth Mackenzie, a fur trader and landowner - 63123; **83**

Mackenzie. In South St. Louis; was changed to Virginia - 63111

Macklind Ave. For James Macklind, a surveyor; or, for Thomas H. Macklind, a city engineer. Was St. Louis Avenue - 63109, 63110, 63139; **69, 72, 75, 77, 78, 100**

Madison St. For President James Madison. Named by William Christy. A public school also is named for Madison - 63102, 63106; **50, 67**

Maffitt Ave. Dr. William Maffitt, who married Julia Chouteau - 63113; **28**

Magazine. In South St. Louis; changed to Winnebago - 63118; **100**

Magazine St. For powder works in area - 63106; **99**

Magnolia Ave. Named by Henry Shaw. Was named Payne, between Alfred and Kingshighway, for Thomas Jefferson Payne. Some was Powhattan, some Lynch - 63110, 63118, 63139; **68, 70, 71**

Main St. Was Grand Rue, then First, now Leonor K. Sullivan Boulevard - 63102

Mallett. Changed to Davis - 63111

Mallinckrodt St. Emil Mallinckrodt was one of the founders of Bremen. The public school is named for Edward Mallinckrodt - 63107

Manchester Ave. The road to Manchester, which is named after the city of Manchester, England, was first called Hoardstown. Some was changed to Southwest Avenue, some was changed to Columbia - 63110, 63139; **62, 76, 81, 84**

Mansion House Ctr. Named for location - 63102; **100**

Maple Ave./Pl. Named for tree on Hodiamont farm - 63112, 63113; **82**

Marceau St. For early settler; was "Marsot" - 63111; **59**

Marceline T. Named by Vera Sturmfels, wife of developer August Sturmfels - 63116; **63**

Marconi Ave. For the inventor; was Cooper - 63110; **77**

Marcus Ave. Marcus A. Wolff was a railroad man; some was Papin - 63108, 63113, 63115

Mardel Ave. Delmar reversed; named after Maryland and Delaware - 63109; **79, 113**

Margaret. Changed to Charless - 63104

Maria. Daughter of John Gano Bryan; changed to Carter - 63107; **31**

Marine Ave. For hospital located there - 63118

Marion St. For Francis Marion, the "Swamp Fox" of the Revolutionary War. There are more streets, cities and counties in the United States named for this man than any other person, except George Washington - 63104

Market St. Named for the location of the market on what was Rue de La Place - 63101, 63103, 63110; **17-18, 34, 35, 36, 81, 97**

Market St. In north St, Louis; was changed to North Market - 63102, 63106, 63113; **50**

Streets of St. Louis ~ 215

Market St. Changed to Bowen - 63111; **100**
Marmaduke Ave. John S. Marmaduke, governor of Missouri - 63139; **93, 123**
Marnice Pl. An early landowner - 63115
Marquette Ave. After Marquette School, which was named for Father Jacques Marquette, a Jesuit priest and explorer - 63139; **11, 79**
*****Marshall Ave./Pl.** Daughter of James C. Sutton, sold her lands for subdivision and called it Sutton City. The name was later changed to Maplewood - 63119, 63143; **84**
Martha. Changed to Lami - 63104
Marwinette Ave. After MARie Federer, WINifred Livingston and JeanETTE Arendes - 63116; **62**
Mary Ave. Relative of John O'Fallon - 63107; **31**
Mary Ann. For Mary Ann Thomas; changed to St. Vincent - 63104; **57**
Maryland Ave. Named by Peter Lindell for the state - 63108; **30, 113**
Maryville Ave. Named for subdivision - 63112
Maurice Ave. For J. B. Maurice, a landowner - 63139
Maury Ave. William L. Maury, a friend of Thomas Payne. Some was Edward, some was changed to Heger Court - 63110, 63116; **69**
May. Changed to East Grand - 63107
May. Changed to Arkansas - 63118
Mayfair Plaza. Named for location - 63101
McCausland Ave. For James McCausland, a landowner. His daughter, Rosanna, married Ralph Clayton - 63109, 63139; **77, 82**
McCombs. For Elizabeth McCombs, sister of Peter Lindell; was changed to Theresa - 63103; **30**
McCullagh Pl. After Confederate Gen. Benjamin McCullagh - 63116
McCune Ave. John S. McCune was a boat captain - 63139
McCune. Changed to Red Bud - 63107
McDonald Ave. For James McDonald, an early landowner - 63116; **72, 73**
McGirk St. Matthias McGirk, a lawyer; arrived in St. Louis in 1814, died in 1841 - 63118
McKean Ave. One of the workers building the houses had a girlfriend named Molly McKean, the street is supposedly named for her; or, for Reginald McKean of the Frisco Railroad - 63118; **73**
McKenzie. Changed to Virginia - 63111
McKinley Ave. President William McKinley. A public school is named for him. Or, for Andrew McKinley, a real estate developer - 63110
McKissock Ave. T.M. McKissock, a railroad man - 63147
*****McKnight Rd.** Residents John and William McKnight - 63117, 63119, 63124, 63132; **85**
McLaran Ave. Charles McLaran, son-in-law of Dr. Jennings - 63147; **86**

McNair Ave. Alexander McNair, governor of Missouri; was Sophia. A public school also is named for him - 63104, 63118; **53, 116, 143**
McNair. Changed to Nicholson - 63104
McNair. Changed to January - 63139
McPherson Ave./Ct. William M. McPherson - 63108, 63112
McRee Ave. Mary McRee was the owner of a race track - 63110; **41, 70**
***Meckelsburg.** Named by Trampitsch; in Austria Heights - 63123; **63**
Melrose Ave. After a place in England - 63147
Memorial Dr. After location - 63102
Menard St. Pierre Menard, from an early French family, was the first lietuenant governor of Illinois. Was Buel - 63104; **59**
Menkins. Changed to Schirmer - 63111
Meramec St. Named for the river; some was Pritchard. A public school is named Meramec - 63116, 63118; **55, 63, 100**
Meramec. Changed to McNair - 63118
Mercantile Ctr. Named for location - 63101; **100**
Mercer. Changed to 22nd Street - 63106
***Meyer Ave.** Roman Meyer was a German-born farmer - 63130
Miami St. For the Indian tribe - 63116, 63118, 63139; **55, 57**
Michigan Ave. For the state - 63104, 63111, 63118; **113**
Milentz Ave. For an early German family - 63109, 63116
Miller St. Peter Miller was an early landowner; some was changed to Mott - 63104; **101, 117**
Miller. Changed to Haven - 63111; **139**
Mills St. For Adam M. Mills, a landowner - 63106
Milton Blvd. For English poet John Milton - 63104; **66**
Mimika. Named for a member of the Jennings family - 63136, 63147
Mine Rd. Changed to Chippewa - 63116; **72**
Minnesota Ave. For the state - 63104, 63111, 63118; **66, 114**
***Minoma Ln.** Named for the home of Jefferson Clark, son of William Clark, which was called "Minoma Mansion" - 63121; **53**
Mississippi Ave./Alley. Named for the state - 63104; **61, 114**
Missouri Ave. Named for the state - 63104, 63118; **37, 61, 114**
Mitchell Ave./Pl./Tr. For John F. and Robert S. Mitchell, architects - 63139
Mobile Ct. Site of mobile home parking - 63139
Moellenhoff St. For Herman Moellenhoff, a farmer and land developer - 63109; **77**
Monroe St. Named by Christy for U.S. President James Monroe. Was once called Washington. A public school is named Monroe - 63102, 63106; **14, 50, 164**
Montana. Named for the territory of Montana - 63116, 63118; **114**
Montgomery St. Named by Christy for Montgomery Blair, a lawyer,

who served as Lincoln's postmaster general. Or, for Revolutionary general, Richard Montgomery - 63102, 63106; **30, 37, 50**
Montrose Ave. Named for subdivision - 63104
*****Moody.** August Moody ran a general store in Webster - 63119
Moore. Changed to Penrose - 63115
Moore. Changed to Holly - 63147
Morgan St. An American officer and Revolutionary War hero; was Oak, some now Delmar - 63102; **13, 35, 80**
Morganford Rd. The road to Morgan's Ford on the River Des Peres from Arsenal to Beck; was Russell Lane - 63116; **61, 71, 72, 74, 100, 104**
Morrison Ave./Ln. J.L.D. Morrison, a lawyer, married a Sarpy (Chouteau) - 63104
Morrow. Changed to Spring - 63116
Morter. Changed to Tesson - 63111
Morton. Became 13th Street - 63118
Motard Ave. Joseph Motard, Frenchman, fur trader, merchant and farmer who owned 228 acres near what is now Lafayette Park - 63104
Mott St. For Frederick W. Mott, the first pupil enrolled at Blow School. He organized the Southern Railroad, was also in real estate. Some was Miller - 63111; **60**
Mound St. Site of large Indian mound - 63102, 63106; **52, 98**
Mount Vernon. Changed to Newstead - 63108
Mount Pleasant St. Named for area - 63111; **99**
Mulberry. Changed to Gratiot - 63102; **35**
Mullanphy St. For John Mullanphy, a business man. He was the first millionaire of the city - 63102, 63106; **25-27, 46, 50;** Son Bryan **100, 134-135, 164**
Murdoch Ave. John J. Murdoch, a farmer - 63109; **83, 104**
*****Murdoch Cut Off.** People used to take a "short cut" through the Murdoch farm - 63119; **83**
Muriel. For the daughter of Edward L. Kuhs, a real estate man - 63147
*****Murphy.** For T. D. Murphy, an early landowner - 63117
*****Murray St.** A relative of the Mullanphys - 63121; **27**
*****Musick Rd.** The road to the farm of Eli and Nancy Musick. The first Baptist minister permanently established in Missouri; he founded Concord Baptist Church - 63123
Myrlette Ct. For the daughter of developer August Sturmfels - 63116; **63**
Myrtle. Changed to Clark - 63102; **35**

Nagel Ave. For Charles Nagel, lawyer and congressman; or, for Herman Nagel, a Carondelet merchant. Was St. Louis - 63109, 63111; **101**
Nashville Ave. For a city in Tennessee - 63110, 63139
Nassau Dr. Named for the island - 63147

Natural Bridge. The road over a natural limestone bridge. At one time it was known in the county as "Natural Bridge Plank Road." During the 1930s, an attempt was made to change the name from Natural Bridge to Airport Road but it was unsuccessful - 63107, 63115, 63120; **30, 52, 53**
Nebraska Ave. For the territory - 63104, 63111, 63118; **114**
Nebraska. Changed to Krauss - 63111
Neosho St. River in Kansas; some was once O'Meara - 63109, 63116; **55, 56**
Newcomb Pl. For an early family - 63113
Newport Ave. Named for the subdivision - 63116; **72**
Newstead Ave. Home of Lord Byron, the favorite poet of Nathaniel Pendleton Taylor who named the street. Was Cornelia, White, and Mount Vernon - 63108, 63113, 63115
Nicholson Pl. For David Nicholson, a liquor dealer - 63104; **37, 100**
Nineteenth St. 63103, 63106, 63107
Ninth St. 63101, 63102, 63104, 63106, 63118, 63147; **75**
Norfolk Ave. Named for a city in Virginia - 63110
North Market St. Was Market in North St. Louis; also Parsons after Gen. Lewis B. Parsons - 63102, 63106, 63113
Northrup Ave. Ashley K. Northrup owned the land from Kingshighway to Macklind, Northrup to Pattison - 63110
North St. On north side of Forest Park; changed to Lindell Boulevard - 63112
Norwood Ave./Ct./Dr. Named for Norwood Park Addition - 63115
Nottingham Ave. For a county in England - 63109; **10, 75**

Oak. Changed to Morgan, then Delmar, then three blocks were changed back to Morgan - 63102; **35**
Oak Hill Ave. After James Russell's home - 63116; **71**
Oakland Ave. Named after oak trees in area - 63110, 63139
Obear Ave. E. G. Obear, a real estate man, married Maria, daughter of Dr. John Gano Bryan - 63107; **31**
Odell St. For Capt. H. W. Odell (War of 1812) - 63139
O'Fallon St. John O'Fallon; was Lisa - 63102, 63106; **30-31, 47, 67, 100**
O'Fallon St. For O'Fallon Park; now Warne - 63107
Ohio Ave. Named after state - 63103, 63104, 63111, 63118; **57, 114**
Ohio. Named after river; changed to Lami - 63104; **114**
*****Oldenburg.** Named by Trampitsch; in Austria Heights - 63123; **63**
Oleatha Ave. Named for wife of Sam Rathell - 63116, 63139; **69, 79**
Olive St. Named for tree - 63101, 63102, 63103, 63108; **35, 50, 81**
Olive. Changed to Krauss - 63111; **101**
*****Oliver Ave.** Relative of Mullanphy - 63135; **27**
O'Meara. Changed to Neosho - 63116

Streets of St. Louis ~ 219

Oregon Ave. Named for territory - 63104, 63111, 63118; **114**
Oriole Ave. One of the "bird" streets - 63147; **52**
Osage St. Named for the Indian tribe - 63118; **53, 55, 56**
Osceola St. For an Indian chief - 63111, 63116; **55, 56, 72**
Oxford Ln. For city in England - 63147

Pacific. Changed to Grove - 63107
Pacific. Changed to Scott - 63103
Page Blvd. Daniel Page was a baker, banker and St. Louis mayor - 63106, 63112, 63113; **24-25, 82, 133**
Palm St. William Palm was a member of the City Council (1849-51). He left a large legacy to Washington University. Some of Palm was Sullivan, some Davis, some Soft - 63107, 63115, 63120, 63147
Pamela. Changed to Lea - 63115; **31**
Papin St. Joseph Papin married Marie Louise Chouteau, a sister of Auguste and daughter of Madame Marie Therese Bourgeoise; was Hazel, some was Steward - 63102, 63103, 63110
Papin. Changed to Shreve; some to Marcus - 63115; **28, 35, 81, 82**
*****Pardee Rd./Ln.** For I. G. Pardee, a landowner - 63123, 63126
Paris Ave. For a city in France; or, for Julius B. Paris, a real estate developer - 63115
Park Ave./Ln. Named for street bordering Lafayette Park - 63104, 63110, 63139; **36-37, 99, 100**
Park Pl. Changed to Mississippi - 63104
Parker Ave. George Ward Parker, who married Rusella Lucy Russell, daughter of James Russell - 63116, 63139; **71**
Parkview Dr./Pl. Was Glasby - 63109
Parnell St. John O'Fallon named this street for Charles Stewart Parnell, an Irish nationalist leader - 63106, 63107
Parsons. For Gen. Lewis B. Parsons; now North Market - 63102, 63106, 63113
Partridge Ave. George Partridge was a grocer - 63120, 63147; **52**
Pattison Ave. For Everett W. Pattison, a lawyer - 63110; **78**
Patton Ave. An early landowner - 63112
Paul. Rene Paul, married Marie Therese, oldest daughter of Auguste Chouteau; some changed to Ninth Street - 63104; **28**
Pauline. Between Tholozan and Oleatha; changed to Alfred - 63116; **69**
*****Payne.** Elbridge Gerry Payne was an early settler in the Gumbo/Chesterfield area. After the flood in 1844, he moved to Bridgeton, then known as Marias des Laird - 63017
Payne. Changed to Magnolia; some changed to Tower Grove Place - 63110; **67, 69**
Peabody Ct. Named for area - 63104

Pear. Changed to Carr - 63102; **35**
Peck St. O'Fallon named the street for James H. Peck, a lawyer - 63107; **31**
Pendleton Ave. To honor Nathaniel Pendleton Taylor - 63108, 63113; **32**
Pennsylvania Ave. For the state - 63104, 63111, 63118; **66, 114**
Pennsylvania Ave. Changed to Bates - 63111; **100**
Penrose St. For Clement B. Penrose. He arrived in St. Louis in 1805, having been sent by President Thomas Jefferson to be land commissioner. Some was Augusta, some was Bell, some was Moore - 63107, 63115, 63147. A public school is named Penrose.
Penrose. Changed to Senate - 63118
Penrose. Changed to Madison - 63106
Pernod. Aime R. Pernod, an early landowner - 63139; **82, 104**
Pershing Ave. Gen. John J. Pershing, was Berlin; changed during World War I - 63108, 63112
Pestalozzi. For Johann Heinrich Pestalozzi, Swiss educational reformer - 63118; **58, 66**
Phare. Changed to Shaw - 63139
Phillips Ave./Pl. R. F. Phillips, landowner, worked in the Gravois "Coal Diggins." Adelle Phillips was a niece of Mrs. Adele Tholozan - 63116; **73**
*****Piccadilly.** A street in London - 63143, **85**
Pierce Ave. For President Franklin Pierce - 63110
Pine. Changed to Loughborough - 63111; **101**
Pine Blvd./Mall/Pl./St. Named after the tree; was Rue Quicapou (Kickapoo) - 63101, 63103, 63108; **35**
Pittsfield. Changed to Ohio - 63118
Pitzman. Named for Louis Pitzman, a real estate developer - 63115
Plainview Ave. Named for location - 63109
Plateau Ave. Descriptive name - 63139; **98**
Plaza Sq. Named for location - 63103
Plover Ave. One of "bird" streets - 63120; **52**
Plum St. Named for tree; some changed to Cerre - 63102; **35**
Plymouth Ave. Named for subdivision - 63112
Poepping St. Bernard Poepping, an early Carondelet family - 63111; **59**
Point Blvd. Named for area - 63147
Polk St. Trusten Polk, a lawyer, Missouri governor and U. S. senator. He served 53 days as governor when he was appointed to the U. S. Senate - 63111; **119**
Pontiac. For an Indian chief; was changed to Russell - 63104; **12, 55**
Pope Ave. For Dr. Charles A. Pope, son-in-law of John O'Fallon - 63115, 63147; **30-31,** 99
Poplar. One of the tree streets - 63102; **13, 35**

Portis Ave. Thomas J. Portis married Sue Russell, granddaughter of James Russell - 63110, 63116; **71**
Portland Terrace. A city in Oregon - 63147
*****Post.** Justice Post purchased 21,204 acres in the Gumbo Chesterfield area when he arrived in 1815 from Vermont. After the flood of 1844, he moved to Illinois - 63141
Potomac St. For the river - 63116, 63118, 63139; **55, 56**
Powder. Changed to Madison - 63106
Powhatan. Changed to Magnolia - 63118; **55, 57, 58**
Prague Ave. For a city in Czechoslovakia - 63109; **77**
Prairie Ave. Named for the Grande Prairie common fields; some was Bryan - 63107, 63113, 63147; **31**
Prairie. Changed to Texas - 63118; **98**
Prange. Frederick W. Prange was an author. The street was named by Clara Bircher - 63120; **52**
Prather Ave. For James V. Prather, a landowner - 63109, 63139; **77**
Pratte. Bernard Pratte, first St. Louis-born mayor and a fur trader, married a Chouteau. The name was changed to Jefferson - 63104; **28, 134**
President St. Was Guthrie; also Haren - 63118; **60, 98**
Preston. Named for Francis Preston Blair Jr. - 63104
*****Priest Dr.** Possibly a relative of the Chouteaus - 63021; **28**
Primm St. For Wilson Primm, a lawyer; some was St. Dennis - 63111, 63116; **59**
Pritchard. Changed to Meramec - 63116; **100**
Produce Row. Named for location - 63102; **100**
Prospect Ave. Street in Cleveland, Ohio - 63110
Provenchere Pl. Jean Louis Provenchere was an early settler. His daughter, Mary Amelia, married George Maguire, mayor of St. Louis (1842-1843) - 63118
Provenchere. Changed to 10th Street - 63106; **134**
Providence. Was Knapstein; changed during World War I - 63111
Pruitt Pl. For Rev. George H. Pruitt, between Newberry Terrace and Page. He was the pastor of the Pleasant Green Baptist Church - 63113
Prune St. Changed to Christy, Green, then Lucas - 63102; **35**
Pulaski St. Casimir Pulaski was a Polish officer who helped the Colonists during the Revolutionary War. It was Hiawatha - 63111; **38, 100**

Quincy St. After a city in Massachusetts or Illinois - 63109, 63111, 63116; **101**

Race Course Ave. Named for McRee Racetrack; part was once Eager Road - 63110; **70, 100**
Railroad Ave. Named for location - 63147

Rainor Ct. It has been said that this should be Trainor Court. The sign was printed without the "T," so they left it Rainor - 63116

Randolph. Some Randolphs are relatives of the Chouteaus. It was changed to Blow - 63111; **28, 101**

*****Rankin.** James Rankin was the first sheriff of St. Louis - 63117, 63144

*****Rannells.** For Charles S. Rannells, a lawyer - 63143; **41**

Rappahanock. Changed to Crittenden - 63118; **55, 56**

Rauschenbach Ave. For a surveyor - 63106, 63107

Ray Ave. Named for the developer of the area, Frederick Ray - 63116

Raymond Ave. An early landowner - 63113

*****Reavis Barracks Rd.** Was Jefferson Barracks Road - 63123, 63125

Rebecca. Changed to Lierman - 63116

Reber Pl. Sam Reber was a lawyer - 63139

Red Bud Ave. Named by John O'Fallon. Was Hawthorne; some was Louisa, some was McCune - 63115, 63147; **31**

Redd Foxx Ln. Part of Spring Avenue - 63113; **32**

Regal. Named after the subdivision - 63109, 63139; **99**

Renard. Changed to Caroline - 63104

Rev. T.E. Huntley Ave. Was Ewing Avenue. Changed in 1984 for the Rev. Thomas Elliot Huntley, who was pastor of the Central Baptist Church from 1942 to 1983 - 63103; **32**

Rhodes. Named for Cecil John Rhodes, a British statesman who founded the Rhodes Scholarship program - 63109, 63116

Richard Pl. Named for a member of the John G. Bryan family - 63115

Ridge Ave. Changed to Hunt - 63110

Ridge Ave. Named for a road along a ridge - 63112, 63113, 63133

Ridgewood. Named for the ridge along the woods in the Christy property - 63116

Ripple. Was Spring; changed to simplify the street name - 63139; **99**

River Bluff Pl. For location; was Delor - 63111; **99, 100**

Riverview Blvd. Some was Tracy - 63120, 63147

Riverview Dr. Was Columbia Bottoms Road - 63137, 63138

Robert Ave. Was Taylor - 63109, 63111, 63116; **59, 101**

Robin Ave. A "bird" street - 63120, 63147; **52**

*****Robyn Rd.** Led to the country home of musician Henry Robyn - 63126, 63127

*****Rock Hill Rd.** Named for the rocky hill on the road to Manchester. This is where James C. Marshall and others built a church. - 63119, 63123, 63124

Roger Pl. Was Russell Place - 63116; **71, 100**

Rolla. Named for Rolla Wells, mayor of St. Louis - 63115

Roosevelt Pl. Named for President Theodore Roosevelt - 63120. A public school also is named for him.

Streets of St. Louis ~ 223

Rosa Ave. Named for the subdivision; or, it could be named for Rosa Weil - 63109, 63116
Rosalie. Named for Rosalie Saugrain, wife of Henry Von Phul - 63115
Rosati. In Soulard, for a Catholic bishop of St. Louis; became 12th Street - 63104
Rosedale Ave. Named after the subdivision - 63112
Roswell Ave. For Roswell Field, father of poet Eugene Field - 63116; **40, 62**
Rowan Ave. For Hamilton Rowan Gamble, a provincial governor of Missouri during the Civil War - 63112; **52, 120**
*****Roy Ave.** Possibly a relative of the Chouteaus - 63114; **28**
Rue Missouri. Became Chestnut - 63102; **35**
Rue de Eglise. Became Church, or Second Street - 63102; **35**
Rue de Grange. Became Barn, or Third Street - 63102; **35**
Rue de la Tour. Became Walnut Street - 63102; **35**
Rue de la Place. Became Market Street - 63102; **17, 35**
Rue de Quicapou. Became Pine Street - 63102; **35**
Ruskin. For John Ruskin, an English author; named by Clara Bircher - 63115; **52**
Russell Ave./Blvd. Named for William Russell, an early landowner - 63104, 63110; **57, 66, 72**
Russell Ln. Changed to Morganford Road - 63116; **71, 104**
Russell Pl. Changed to Roger Place - 63116; **71**
Rutger Ln./St. Arend Rutgers, a landowner - 63104, 63110; **32, 35, 58**
Ruth Dr. Daughter of developer August Sturmfels - 63116; **63**
Ruth. Changed to Fair - 63115; **31**

Sacramento Ave. City in California - 63115
Salena St. Was Capitol, James and Iroquois - 63104, 63118
Salisbury St. For Mary Salisbury, an early school teacher; or, for Philander, a riverboat captain - 63107, 63147; **41**
Salzburger Ave. Named by Trampitsch; in Austria Heights - 63116; **63**
Samuel Shepard Ave. An educator; was Lucas Avenue - 63103; **32**
Sanford Ave. Possibly a relative of the Chouteaus - 63139; **28**
San Francisco Ave. A city in California - 63115
*****Sappington Barracks Road.** The road from Dr. John Sappington's house to Jefferson Barracks - 63125, 63127
*****Sappington Rd.** Led to home of Dr. John B. Sappington - 63122, 63126, 63128; **85**
Sarah St. For Sarah Coleman, niece of Peter Lindell - 63108, 63110, 63113, 63115; **30, 32**
Sarah St. Named for a daughter of William Carr Lane; became Rutger Street - 63104; **58**

*Sarah St. For a daughter of James Sutton - 63143; **84**
Sarpy Ave. Gregoire Sarpy married Pelagie Labaddie, a granddaughter of Chouteau - 63110; **28, 31, 82**
Scanlan Ave. Phillip Scanlan was a land developer and parks director (1906). He married a Christy - 63139; **77, 79, 95**
Schiller Ave. For Johann Christoph Friederich von Schiller, a German writer - 63147; **51**
Schiller Pl. Christopher Schiller, a land owner - 63116; **51, 74**
Schirmer St. Was named for Charles Schirmer, a politician in Carondelet. Was Menkins - 63111, 63116; **59**
*Schofield Pl. Possibly a relative of the Chouteaus - 63133; **28**
Schroeder Pl. John H. Schroeder, a manufacturer - 63116
Scott Ave. John Scott, first congressman; was Pacific, also Gamble - 63103; **21**
Scott Ave. Union Gen. Winfield Scott - 63110; **21**
Scudder. John A Scudder, a riverboat captain; became Potomac - 63118
Second Carondelet. Became 18th Street - 63118
Second St. Was Church - Rue de Eglise - 63102, 63104, 63118, 63147
Sells Ave. For Miles Sells, an early landowner - 63147
Semple Ave. Charles Semple was an early landowner - 63112, 63120; **54**
Senate St. For the U.S. Senate - 63118; **60, 98**
Serbian Dr. After a church in the area; was McNair Avenue - 63104
Seventeenth St. 63103, 63106; **46**
Seventh St. 63101, 63102, 63104, 63106, 63118; **34, 36, 46**
Sharp Ave. For Fidelio C. Sharp, a landowner - 63116; **99**
Shaw Blvd./Ave./Pl. For Henry Shaw, a businessman, landowner; part was Phare. A public school is named for Shaw - 63110; **16, 31, 32, 36, 45, 67, 69, 70, 71, 74, 94**
Shenandoah Ave. Named for the river in Virginia; some was Arrow - 63104, 63110. A public school also is named for this river; **55, 56**
Sheridan Ave. Union Gen. Phil Sheridan - 63106
Sherman Pl. Union Gen. William T. Sherman. A public school also is named for him - 63107
Sherman. Changed to Gratiot - 63110
Short St. Changed to Benedict - 63147
Shreve Ave. For Henry Miller Shreve, a riverboat pilot; was Papin - 63115; **177-178**
Shreve. Changed to Greenlea - 63107
Shreve. Changed to Calvin - 63115
Sidney St. Nickname for William Carr Lane's daughter, Sarah - 63104; **58**
Sigel Ave. Union Gen. Franz Sigel - 63116; **62, 94**
Simpson Ave./Terrace. For Matthew Simpson, a Methodist minister in

Philadelphia - 63139
Simpson Pl. For William Simpson, an iron manufacturer - 63104; **37**
Sixteenth St. 63103, 63106
Sixth St. 63101, 63102, 63104
Skinker Blvd./Parkway. For Thomas Skinker, a landowner - 63112; **82, 94**
Slattery St. For Dennis P. Slattery, a landowner - 63106
Smiley Ave. For Charles D. Smiley, a land developer - 63139
Smith. For William Smith, a mill operator. Was changed to Columbia, then to Cass - 63102. Some Smiths are relatives of the Chouteaus; **28, 51**
*****Smith Ave.** Relative of Mullanphy - 63135; **28**
Soft St. Changed to Palm - 63107
Soper St. A. W. Soper, railroad man; was Lafayette - 63111; **59, 101**
Sophia. Became Missouri; some became McNair - 63118
Sophia. Changed to Harris - 63107; **31**
Soulard St. For Antoine Soulard who married Julia Cerré; was Lafayette - 63104; **38-39,** 58
South. Became 10th Street - 63104
Southwest Ave. Was Old Manchester Road - 63110, 63139; **76**
Spring Ave. Named by Peter Lindell. A spring on his land formed the Rocky Branch Creek. Some of Spring was called Morisse, Mercy, Cabanne, Gregor, Olivia, Tiffany and Morrow - 63107, 63108, 63110, 63113, 63116; **30, 70,** 99, 100
Spring. Became St. Louis Avenue - 63106
Spring Ave. Changed to Ripple - 63139
Spring Ave. Part of it was named Redd Foxx Lane in 1973 - 63113
Spruce St. Named for the tree - 63102, 63103; **35**
St. Ange Ave./Ct. For Louis St. Ange de Bellerive - 63104
*****St. Charles Rock Rd.** Early road to state Capitol - 63114, 63133; **81, 88**
St. Charles St. Start of road to St. Charles; was Vine - 63101, 63103, 63031
*****St. Cyr Rd.** Paschall Hyacinthe St. Cyr married Helene Hebert - 63136, 63137
St. Dennis. Changed to Primm - 63111
St. Elizabeth Ave. Named for St. Elizabeth Academy; was Tennessee - 63118; **66, 100**
St. George. Was Anna - 63104; **58**
St. Louis Ave. Named for city - 63102, 63106, 63107, 63115, 63120; **32**
St. Louis Ave. Changed to Macklind Avenue - 63110
St. Louis Union Station. Named for location - 63103; **100**
St. Mary's Dr. Named after St. Mary's High School; was Itaska - 63116; **100**

St. Vincent Ct./Ave. After a cemetery once located there - 63104
Stadium Plaza. Named for location - 63102; **100**
Stansbury St. For Ira Stansbury, a landowner - 63118
State St. Became 13th Street - 63104
Steffens Ave. Named for Edward Steffens, a local farmer - 63116
Steinlage Dr. Named for Adolph A. Steinlage, a German dairy farmer - 63115
Steins St. Jacob Steins, glazier and innkeeper; was Heaven - 63111, 63116; **59**
Stephen. Named for David Stephen, an architect with the William B. Ittner firm - 63110
*****Stephens Pl.** Missouri Gov. Lon Vest Stephens - 63074; **124**
*****Stephens Rd.** Missouri Gov. Lon Vest Stephens - 63017; **124**
Sterling. Became Missouri - 63118
Steward. Became Papin - 63110
Stewart. For the Stewart Addition - 63112; **119, 120**
Stoddard St. For Amos Stoddard, first American governor of the Missouri Territory; or, for Henry Stoddard, a real estate developer - 63106; **15, 116, 169**
Stoddard. Became 10th Street - 63118
Stoddard. Changed to 11th Street - 63104
Stolle St. Was Helvetia - 63116; **28**
Stringtown Rd. Changed to Virginia - 63111
Strodtman Pl. For George W. Strodtman, a railroad man - 63107
Sublette Ave. William and Solomon Sublette were fur traders. Part of Sublette was named Blue Ridge - 63110, 63139; **75, 76-77**
Suburban Tracks. Named for location - 63108
Sullivan. Changed to Palm - 63107
Sulphur Ave. Road to Sulphur Springs; was Cheltenham - 63109, 63110, 63139; **77**
Summer. Changed to 13th Street; some was Lemp, some Wisconsin - 63118
Summitt. Changed to California - 63118
Superior. Changed to Missouri - 63118
Susan. Named for Susan Thomas; changed to Eads - 63104; **57**
Susquehanna. For the river; changed to Arsenal - 63118; **55, 57**
Sutherland Ave. Place in England - 63109; **10, 75**
*****Sutter Ave.** German-born dairy farmers - 63130
*****Sutton.** James C. and John L. Sutton, operated a blacksmith shop at what is now Sutton and Manchester - 63117, 63143, 63144; **82, 84**
Sweringen Ave. George Sweringen, an early landowner - 63147
Switzer Ave. For Mary J. Jennings, a daughter of Dr. Jennings - 63147; **86**

Sycamore. In the West End; changed to Hamilton - 63112
Sycamore. Changed to La Salle - 63102; **35, 57**

Taft Ave. U.S. President William Howard Taft - 63111, 63116
Talmage Ave. For A. R. Talmage, a railroad man - 63110; **61, 72**
Tamm Ave. Jacob Tamm, farmer, landowner, woodenware - 63109, 63139; **77-78**
Targee. Thomas B. Targee was a volunteer fireman killed in 1849 fire. This street was located at Kiel Auditorium site - 63103; **42**
Taylor Ave. Nathaniel Pendleton Taylor. Some Taylors are related to Chouteaus. - 63108, 63110, 63113, 63115, 63147; **28, 32**
Taylor. Changed to Robert - 63109, 63111, 63116
Tayon. Changed to 18th Street - 63106
Tedmar Ave./Ct. For Theodore and Marvin, sons of Volo Voester. Some say it was named for Theodore Vollmar, another developer - 63139
Tennessee Ave. Named for state - 63104, 63111, 63118; **66, 114**
*****Tennyson.** Named for Alfred Lord Tennyson, the English poet - 63143
Terminal Row. Named for the location - 63147
Termination. Changed to Delor - 63111; **100**
*****Tesson Ferry Rd.** Road leading to the Tesson ferry - 63123, 63128
Tesson St. Michael and Francis Tesson, merchants and ferry owners; some was Motier - 63111, 63116; **59, 62**
Texas Ave. Named for state; some was Prairie, some Clara - 63104, 63118; **115**
Thatcher Ave. For George Thatcher, a landowner - 63147; **52**
*****Thatcher Ave.** Relative of Mullanphy - 63135; **27**
Thekla. For a relative of Harney; or, for an author, named by Clara Bircher - 63115, 63120, 63136; **52**
Theodore Ave. Theodore Dowler a landowner; or, for Theodore Chambers, a landowner - 63115, 63120; **53**
Theodosia Ave. For Theodosia Hunt Patterson - 63112, 63113
Theresa Ave. For Theresa Paul Taylor (Chouteau); was Wear - 63103, 63104; **30**
Third St. Was Rue de Granges, Broadway and Barn - 63102, 63104, 63118, 63147; **13, 35, 36, 80, 98**
Thirteenth St. 63103, 63104, 63106, 63107, 63118
Thirty Eighth St. 63116; **99**
Thirty Ninth St. 63110, 63116; **71, 99**
Thirty Seventh St. 63116
Tholozan Ave. Named by Adele Sanguinette Tholozan, wife of John Eli Tholozan, a storekeeper - 63109, 63116; **30, 69, 71, 72, 104**
Thomas St. Mayor James S. Thomas - 63106; **37, 136**
Thomas St. Changed to Rankin - 63104

Thomas St. In South St. Louis; changed to Virginia - 63104
***Thomas Ave.** Related to Mullanphy - 63135; **27**
Thompson. Changed to Glasgow - 63107
Thrush Ave. A "bird" street - 63120, 63147; **52**
Thurman Ave. Allen G. Thurman, vice president during President Cleveland's administration - 63110; **71**
Tiffany. For Louis Tiffany, a landowner; changed to 39th Street - 63110; **71**
Tillie. Member of Kraft family - 63147
Toenges Ave. Real estate developer - 63116; **63**
Toney. Changed to California - 63118
Tower Grove Ave./Pl. After Shaw's country home - 63110; **68, 70**
Tracy. Some Tracys are relatives of the Chouteaus; changed to Riverview - 63120; **28**
Trainor. An English name - 63116
Tubman Ln. For Harriet Tubman, a poet - 63106; **32**
Tucker Blvd. For Mayor Raymond Tucker; was 12th Street - 63101, 63102, 63104; **140**
Turner Ave. Maj. Henry S. Turner married Julia M. Hunt, daughter of Theodore and Ann Lucas Hunt - 63115
Twelfth St. 63104, 63118
Twentieth St. Was Evaline - 63103, 63106, 63107; **31, 46, 100**
Twenty Fifth St. 63106, 63107
Twenty First St. 63103, 63106, 63107
Twenty Second St. 63103, 63106, 63107
Twenty Third St. 63103, 63106, 63107; **47, 68**
Tyler St. For Mary Lawrence Tyler, daughter of William Chambers; was Webster - 63102, 63106; **51**
Tyler St. For Mary Lawrence Tyler; changed to Botanical - 63110; **51, 69**
Tyler St. U.S. President John Tyler (1840-1844); was changed to Branch - 63107; **178-179**
Tyrolean Ave. Named by Trampitsch; in Austria Heights - 63109, 63116; **63**
Tyus Ct. From Norwood to Kingshighway, was named for Leroy Tyus, a Missouri state representative - 63115

Ulena. Named for a female relative of the developer of Wanda Place - 63116; **74**
Ulrick. Changed to 20th Street - 63107
Union Blvd. Named by Governor Gamble; was Bellefontaine, also Second Kingshighway - 63108, 63113; **53, 67, 82, 120**
Union. Changed to Salena - 63118
Union. Changed to Upton - 63111

Union. Named by Clara Bircher, wife of William John Bircher - 63115

University Ct./St. Named for land given to Washington University by John O'Fallon - 63103, 63107; **30, 99**

Upton Court/St. Was named for Emory Upton, a Union officer. Was previously Caroline and Union - 63111, 63116; **101**

Utah Place/St. Named for Ute Indians; was Wall and Government - 63116, 63118; **35, 55, 115**

Valle. Became 10th Street - 63104

Van Buren St. U.S. President Martin Van Buren (1838-1842) - 63111

Valentine. Named for a Capuchin friar who was the first Roman Catholic priest in St. Louis. Was Almond - 63102

Valley. Changed to Leonard - 63106

*****Valley Rd.** Changed to Dale - 63117

Vanderberg. Named after a land owner; originally named Milburn, some of it was renamed Alhambra Court - 63104

Vandeventer Ave. For Peter Vandeventer, a landowner. Was Old Manchester Road; some was Baltimore - 63107, 63108, 63113; **41, 69, 100**

Vandeventer. Changed to 39th Street - 63110

Varrelmann. Named for Charles Varrelmann, street commissioner for Mayor Rolla Wells - 63116

Vermont Ave. Named for the state - 63111; **115**

Vernon Ave. Named for Maris Vernon, real estate agent. Related to Mullanphy - 63112-63113

Vest Ave. George Graham Vest, U.S. and Confederate congressman - 63107; **124**

Victor St. For Victor Ralph Carr Lane, only son of William Carr Lane. Victor died at the age of 15 - 63104; **58**

Victoria. Changed to Lucky; then Aldine - 63113

Victoria. Named for the queen of England - 63110, 63139

Vienna Ave. City in Austria - 63109; **77**

Vine. Changed to St. Charles - 63102; **13, 35, 80**

Vine. Changed to Koeln - 63111

Vinegar Hill. 14th and Gay - 63106

Vine Grove. Vine Grove Addition - 63115

Vineyard. Changed to Howard - 63106

Virginia Ave. Named for the state; was McKenzie, also Stringtown Road - 63103, 63104, 63111, 63118; **66, 104, 115**

Virginia. Changed to La Salle - 63104; **57**

Virginia. Changed to Boyle - 63110; **61**

Vivian. Named for Vivian Switzer - 63136, 63147

Voerster Ave. For Volo Voerster, a developer - 63139

230 ~ *Streets of St. Louis*

Volo Ave. For Volo Voerster, a developer - 63139
Von Phul St. Henry Von Phul, merchant, boat owner; married daughter of Dr. Antoine Francois Saugrain - 63107; **182**
***Vontalge Rd.** Von Talge family owned a farm in area - 63128
Von Versen. Named after Alice (Clemens) Von Versen, the granddaughter of John Mullanphy. Von Versen was changed to Enright for one of the first soldiers killed during World War I - 63112; **27, 28**
Vulcan St. After Vulcan Iron Works; was Jackson - 63111

Wabash Ave. Named for the railroad - 63109
Wacousta. Indian name; was changed to Pestalozzi - 63118; **55**
Wade Ave. Festus J. Wade, a banker and railroad man - 63139
Wagner Ave. Named for Wagner Electric Co. -63133
Wagoner St. Changed to Dick Gregory in 1977 - 63113; **32**
Walbridge Pl. Cyrus P. Walbridge, mayor of St. Louis - 63115; **138**
Wall St. Changed to Utah - 63118; **35**
Wallace St. John A. Wallace, a landowner - 63116
Walnut St./Pl. Named for tree - 63102, 63103; **13, 34, 35**
Walsh St. John B. Walsh, the first mayor of Carondelet. Some Walshes were relatives of the Chouteaus - 63109, 63111, 63116; **28**
Walter. Named for John T. Walter, developer of the Walter Place Addition - 63147
Walton. Named for Izaak Walton, a British author - 63108, 63113, 63115
Wanda. Named after the subdivision - 63116, 63123
Ward. Changed to Theresa - 63104
Warne Ave. For Marinus W. Warne, a banker; was O'Fallon - 63107, 63113
Warne. Some changed to Bishop Scott Lane; named for Bishop Phillip Lee Scott, pastor of the Lively Stone Church of God - 63113; **31**
Warren St. For Gen. Joseph Warren, a Revolutionary War hero at Bunker Hill; named by William Christy - 63102, 63106; **50, 90**
Wash. Judge Robert Wash, lawyer, married Frances Christy, daughter of Maj. William Christy. It was changed to Cole, some to Sarah - 63102; **46**
Washington Ave./Blvd. For President George Washington - 63101, 63102, 63103, 63108, 63112; **18, 37, 38, 50, 68, 100, 103, 115**
Washington Terrace. Private place - 63108; **74**
Washington. In North St. Louis; changed to Monroe - 63102
Water. Named for location - 63111; **99**
Waterman Ave./Blvd./Pl. Alfred M. Waterman married Adele Louise Kingsbury, a relative of the Chouteaus - 63108, 63112; **28, 81, 82**
Watson Rd. Wesley Watson, a landowner; some Watsons are relatives of the Chouteaus - 63109, 63139; **28, 62, 75, 100**

Waverly Pl. Named by the Archibald Gamble family, originally McNair; later became Easton Place after Gamble's widow, Louisa Easton Gamble - 63104; **100**
Wear. Minister, named by William G. Eliot; now Theresa - 63103, 63104
*****Weaver Ave.** A lawyer, worked for the state of Missouri - 63143
*****Weber Rd.** John Weber, a landowner - 63123, 63125
*****Webmore.** Combination of Weber and Morganford - 63123
Webster Ave. Daniel Webster, U.S. senator; changed to Tyler - 63106; **51**
Webster. Daniel Webster, U.S. senator - 63106; **51**
*****Weil.** Joseph Weil, a landowner - 63119; **77**
Wells Ave. Erastus Wells, a railroad man - 63112, 63113; **37, 52, 138**
Wenona. Changed to Texas - 63118
Wenzlick Ave. Albert Wenzlick, a real estate developer - 63109; **29, 77**
West Ave./Ct. Named for location - 63116; **99**
West. West side of Forest Park; changed to Skinker - 63112
West. Named for Allen T. West, an investment broker - 63116
*****Westgate.** Location of a gate to the Delmar race track - 63130; **79**
Westminster Pl. From England - 63108, 63112; **74**
Westmoreland Pl. From England - 63108; **74, 79**
West Park. Continuation of Park Avenue by Lafayette Park - 63110, 63139; **77**
West Pine Blvd. Was Baker, for a sister of Peter Lindell - 63108; **30**
Wharf. Named for location; was Main, also First and Grand Rue, some now named for Congresswoman Leonor K. Sullivan - 63102, 63104, 63111, 63147; **99, 100, 182**
Wherry Ave. Named for Mackey Wherry, a surveyor and engineer. Wherry was a creek that was paved over - 63109; **179**
White Rd. Named for landowner Capt. J. M. White; changed to Newstead - 63115
Whitman. Thomas J. Whitman, brother of poet Walt Whitman - 63107
Whittemore. For Henry Whittemore, a real estate developer; or, for Robert B. Whittemore, a hat merchant - 63104; **27**
Wichita Ave. For the Indians who traded with Pierre Chouteau - 63110
Wicklow Pl. In England - 63111
Wiesehan. Changed to Bonita during World War I - 63109; **28**
Wilcox Ave. Leonard Wilcox, a lawyer. Some Wilcoxes are related to the Chouteaus - 63116; **28**
Wilkerson. In South St. Louis; changed to Arkansas - 63104
Wilkinson. Some Wilkinsons are related to the Chouteaus; changed to Theresa - 63104; **28**
Wilkinson. Changed to Gano - 63107
*****Wilshusen.** John and Claus Wilshusen, landowners - 63119

William Pl. For President William McKinley - 63120
Williams Ave. 63143; **117**
Willmore Rd. Cyrus Crane Willmore, a real estate developer - 63109; **77, 96**
Wilmington Ave. For a city in Delaware - 63111, 63116; **62**
Willow. A tree street; is now Biddle - 63101, 63102, 63106; **35**
Wilson Ave. For J. C. Wilson, an early water commissioner; or, for George W. Wilson, a hardware dealer. Some Wilsons were related to the Chouteaus - 63110, 63139; **28**
Windermere Pl. In England - 63112; **74**
Windsor Pl./Prkwy. In England - 63113, 63116
Winnebago St. Named for Indians; was Magazine - 63109, 63116, 63118; **55**
Winona Ave. Daughter of Carl Wimar, the artist who painted the dome of the Old Courthouse - 63109; **72, 75**
Winter. Changed to Rutger - 63104; **58**
*****Winthrop Ct.** Possibly relatives of the Chouteaus - 63123; **28**
Wisconsin Ave. Named for the state - 63118; **115**
Wise Ave. Henry J. Wise, an early landowner; or, for William Wise, sewer commissioner of St. Louis. Some of Wise was known as Plateau, some Berthold - 63110, 63139
Withers Ave. Named for George Withers, an English poet - 63147
Withnell Ave. John Withnell, a brewery owner; was Gate - 63118; **35**
Wood St. Eliminated - 63118
Woods Rd. Changed to 59th Street - 63139
*****Woodson Rd.** Missouri Gov. Silas Woodson - 63114, 63132, 63134; **122**
Wren Ave. A "bird" street - 63120; **52**
Wright St. For Major Thomas Wright, one of the founders of North St. Louis in 1816. He married a daughter of William Christy - 63107, 63147; **50**
Wyoming Pl./St. Wyoming Valley in Pennsylvania - 63116, 63118, 63139; **55, 56, 115**

*****Yeager Rd.** Road to the Johann Yeager farm - 63129

Zealand. Father Zealand, S.J., president of St. Louis University in 1870 - 63107
Zepp St. Jacob Zepp, an early settler, arrived in 1834 - 63118